THE HISTORY OF
Remington Firearms

E. Remington & Sons
Remington Arms Company
Remington Arms—Union Metallic Cartridge Company
Remington Arms Company, Inc.

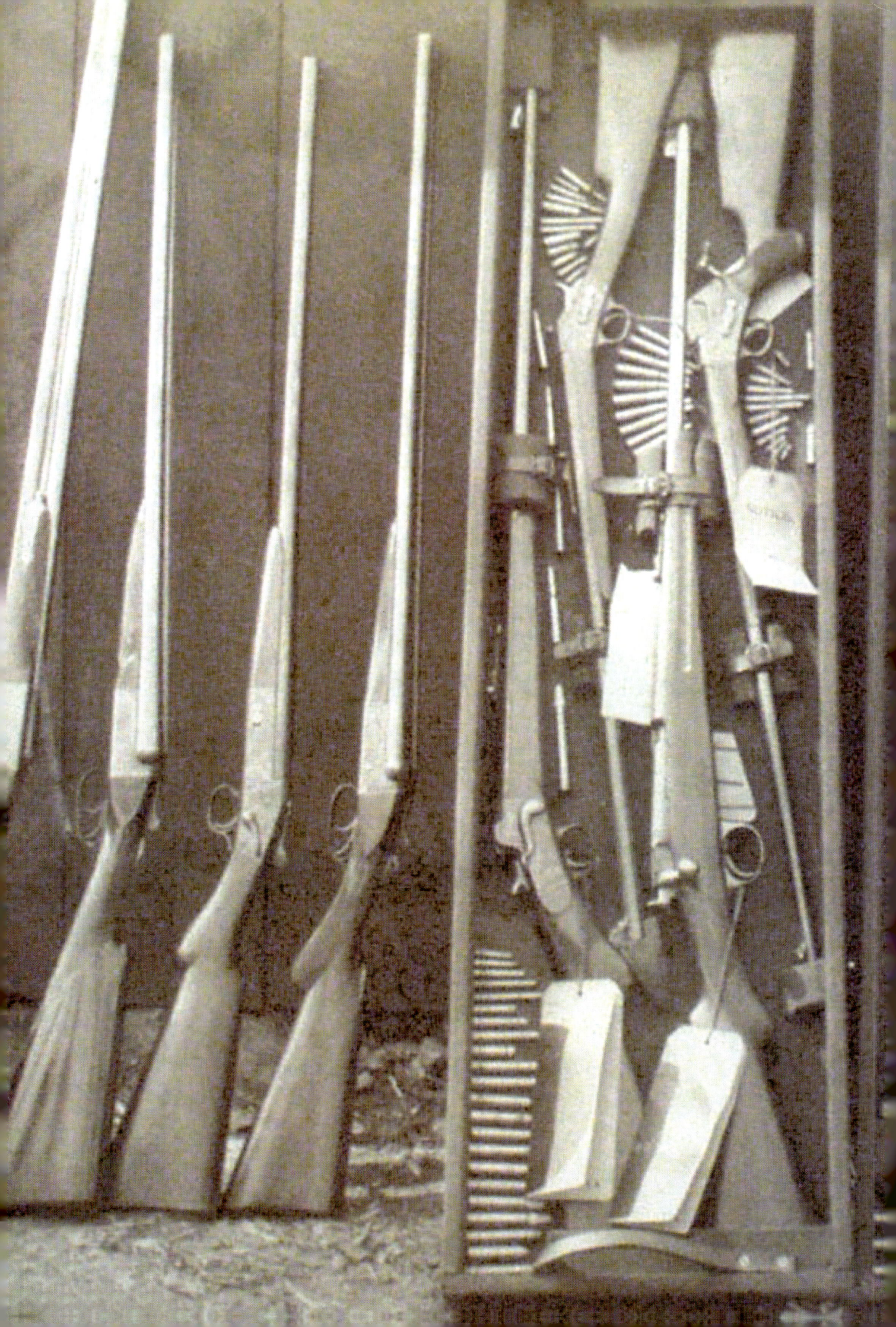

The History of
Remington Firearms

Roy Marcot

CHARTWELL
BOOKS, INC.

"Protecting The Nest" original painting by unknown artist—circa early 1900s.

Copyright © 2010 Pepperbox Press Ltd.

This edition published in 2011 by CHARTWELL BOOKS, INC.
A division of BOOK SALES, INC.
276 Fifth Avenue Suite 206
New York, New York 10001
USA

All rights reserved. No part of this publication may be reproduced, stored in a retreival system or transmitted by any other means, electronic, mechanical, photocopying or otherwise, without the prior written consent of the publisher and copyright holder.

ISBN 978-0-7858-2855-6

Printed in Indonesia

CONTENTS

Introduction 7

CHAPTER ONE
Remington Company History 8

CHAPTER TWO
Remington Pistols and Revolvers 22

CHAPTER THREE
Remington Rifles and Carbines 42

CHAPTER FOUR
Remington Shotguns 100

Index 126

Barrel straightener at Remington's Ilion factory - circa 1900.

Introduction

The history of Remington firearms mirrors that of the history of the United States. From its inception in 1816, Remington has embraced both industrial innovation and entrepreneurship. Encouraging product design, inventing innovative machine tools, incorporating the concept of interchangeable parts, and offering diversified product lines to the consumer have been hallmarks of Remington's continuing commitment to excellence, since the days of its founder–Eliphalet Remington.

The name *"Remington"* is synonymous with quality and innovation because of the vision that Eliphalet inspired. Few recognize that Remington is one of the oldest companies in America still making its original product! This company is now nearly 190 years old, having started making gun barrels in upstate New York in frontier America.

The Remington Arms Company has always encouraged innovation, but the company's proud history shows that it has continually offered products that have helped American Enterprise. Not the least of which have been sporting firearms, ammunition, military weaponry, typewriters, sewing machines, bridges, agricultural tools, and powdered metal products. And, through this commitment to quality and innovation the company has produced many breakthroughs that profoundly influenced America's industrial development, including the production of the world's first effective typewriter, innovations in smokeless powder ballistics, powdered metal technology and fine products for sportsmen, target shooters and hunters for nearly two hundred years.

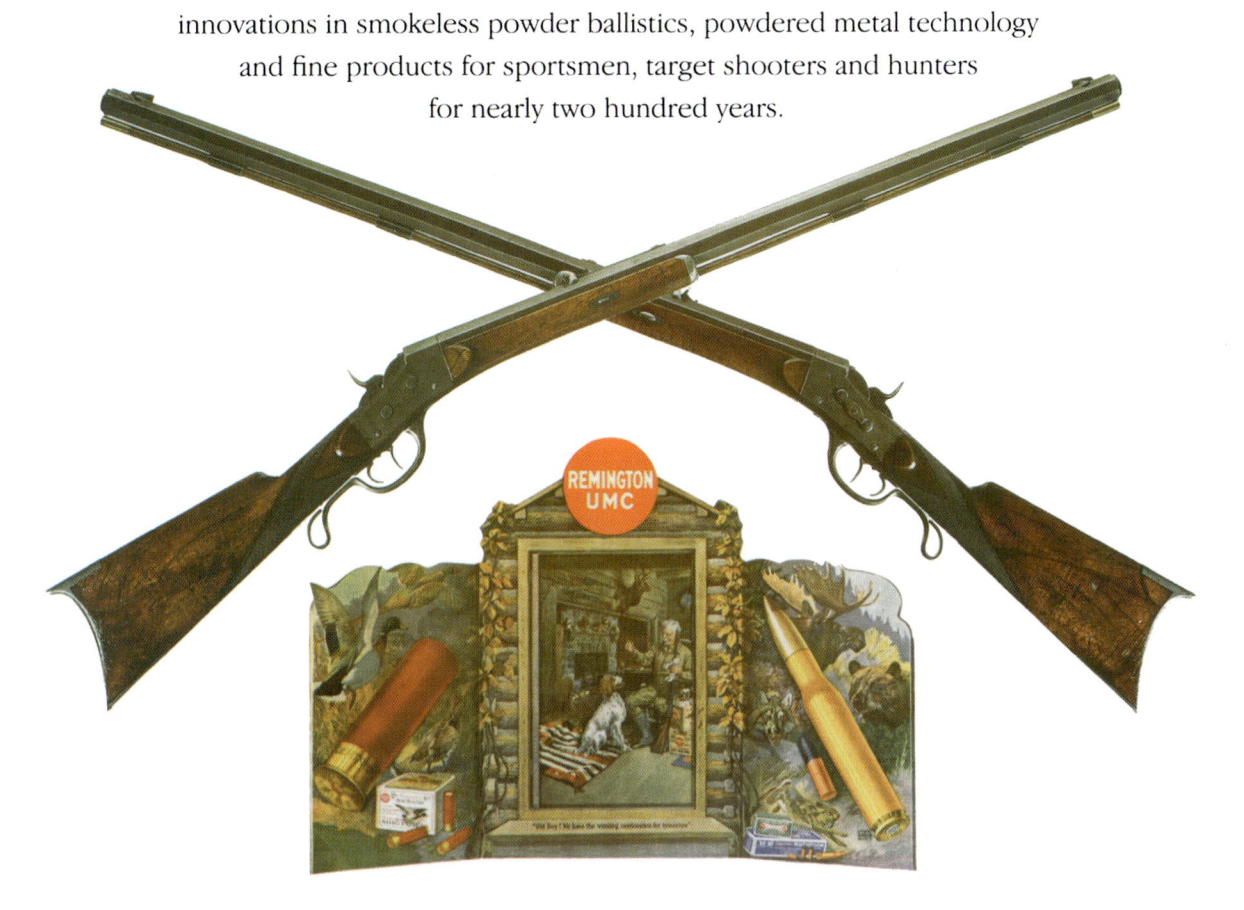

CHAPTER 1

Remington Company History

Eliphalet Remington, Sr. (Father of the founder of Remington Arms) settled in the Mohawk River Valley in 1799 to establish his business as one of the finest forging operations in the frontier. Remington fashioned quality iron implements sought by settlers—agricultural tools, hardware, sleigh runners and other rudimentary products. As it turned out, Eliphalet's choice of locating his business paid handsome dividends, because just a few years later, in 1824, the Erie Canal was constructed only a few miles to the north. The waterway provided a direct link to Albany and New York City (to the East) and to Buffalo and the frontier (to the West).

The legend states that in 1816, young Eliphalet asked his father for money for a rifle and was refused. Thereupon—so goes the tale—"*the young man went out to the smithy and forged and welded a rifle barrel of his own.*" Then putting it on his shoulder, he walked to Utica to have a gunsmith ream and rifle the barrel. The gunsmith is reported to have praised Eliphalet's work, and the lad hiked home, finished the rifle—and he was in the gun business! This story has been retold countless times since, but is not reality.

It is unlikely that a country boy would have possessed the skills to make up an entire flintlock rifle in 1816. There is little doubt that young Eliphalet forged his first rifle barrel in that year, after all, he was the son of a commercial iron forger with the facilities of an ironworks at his disposal. The reality is that to make his barrel, young Eliphalet would have started with a flat iron bar (possibly three quarters of an inch thick, about five inches wide, and as long as the finished barrel was to be—36 or 39 inches). Heating a short stretch of the bar, young Remington would have forged it lengthwise around a mandrel—a rod used to form and maintain the hollow bore. Bringing the iron to a welding heat he would have hammered the joint under a triphammer until it was securely welded together. He would have proceeded, inch by inch, until the whole barrel was done. Then he would have ground the exterior to an octagon form, and the barrel would have been ready for reaming and rifling. This would have been the customary way to make an iron rifle barrel in the early 19th century.

Whether Eliphalet *"finished up the rifle after the Utica gunsmith had reamed and rifled the rough barrel"* is much more questionable. To

Above center: The earliest known likeness of the founder—Eliphalet Remington II.
Right: One of the original Remington forge buildings, dating from the early 19th Century.

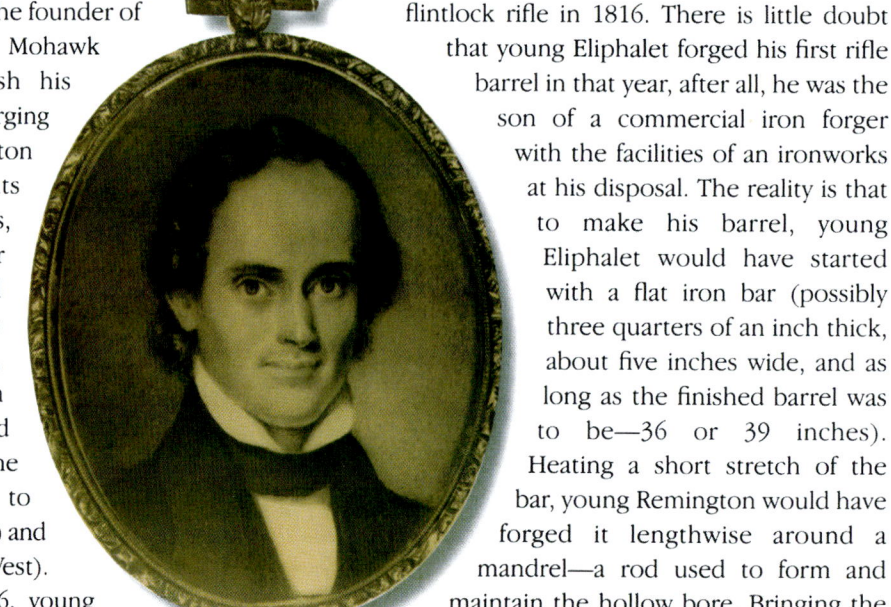

Right, above: The original Remington Homestead, built circa 1809 by Eliphalet Remington I.
Right, below: One of the first factory buildings to be constructed after the move from the gorge in 1828.

REMINGTON COMPANY HISTORY • 9

Above: Another of the original armory buildings built in what would become Ilion, New York, circa 1854. Right: Aerial view of E. Remington & Son's Armory—circa 1875.

make a full length stock for a muzzle–loading rifle was a job for an experienced gunsmith who has specialized tools. Eliphalet's skill was not advanced enough to undertake such a task successfully. Proper functioning of the rifle depended on precisely inletting these components into the wood of the stock, and a single small error would have yielded a non–functioning firearm. It seems very likely that young Eliphalet would have left completion of the rifle to the Utica gunsmith who finished the bore.

It has also been said that *"Eliphalet's finished rifle was so successful that neighbors wanted one for themselves, and he found himself in the gunsmith business."* But this is also not true. No evidence has turned up to indicate that Eliphalet made complete flintlock or percussion sporting or hunting rifles for others until much later. The 1820 Census of Manufactures report shows no gun materials at all among the products of the Remington forge. J. Leander Bishop published his *History of Manufactures in the United States* which stated: *"for many years the business was restricted to the manufacture of rifle barrels."* By the middle 1820s, Remington's forge was making rifle barrels, as well as numerous agricultural tools.

Long before industrial processes as we know them today were in use, and even before the concept of a factory was fully developed, Eliphalet Remington utilized a system to organize groups of journeymen into what became known as the *"inside contracting system."*

While these teams of workers had the financial and mechanized support of Remington, they were inspired to innovate and succeed on their own. Eliphalet Remington's organizational principles anticipated by more than 100 years the "quality team" concepts so familiar to us today.

Word of the success of Remington's Armory spread and the town of Ilion (incorporated in 1852) became a magnet for skilled craftsmen, inventors, and industrial entrepreneurs. As the years followed, individuals with a new process or product who joined Remington knew they could use manufacturing facilities to turn their dreams into reality. As the markets in the frontier West (at that time, Northern Ohio, Indiana, Illinois, and the Great Lakes) began to open, the demand for firearms grew rapidly.

Left: The old armory buildings constructed in the 1830s, and still in use in 1875
Below: Winter view of the Armory—circa 1880s. Note the Remington family mansion seen in the center rear of this photograph.

To satisfy the need for quality and quantity of gun barrels (and later complete firearms), the elementary science of metallurgy and of machine tool technology had to be improved and extended. New alloys were needed and new heat treatment processes were devised to improve machining characteristics, strength, and durability. At this time, Remington introduced the use of *"cast steel"* barrels. The Jenks carbines supplied by Remington to the U.S. Navy under contract in 1848 and 1849 were the first unwelded steel barrels ever used by the armed forces. New materials dictated new technologies, and Remington designed and built machine tools to drill, ream, rifle, and finish these new solid steel barrels. Remington was also one of the first to utilize a deep–hole barrel–drilling machine to drill up to five barrel blanks simultaneously.

Following the Mexican War in the late 1840s, Remington took a commanding lead in fabricating interchangeable parts, the forerunner of modern industrial

Below: 1847 Remington Jenks Navy Rifle.

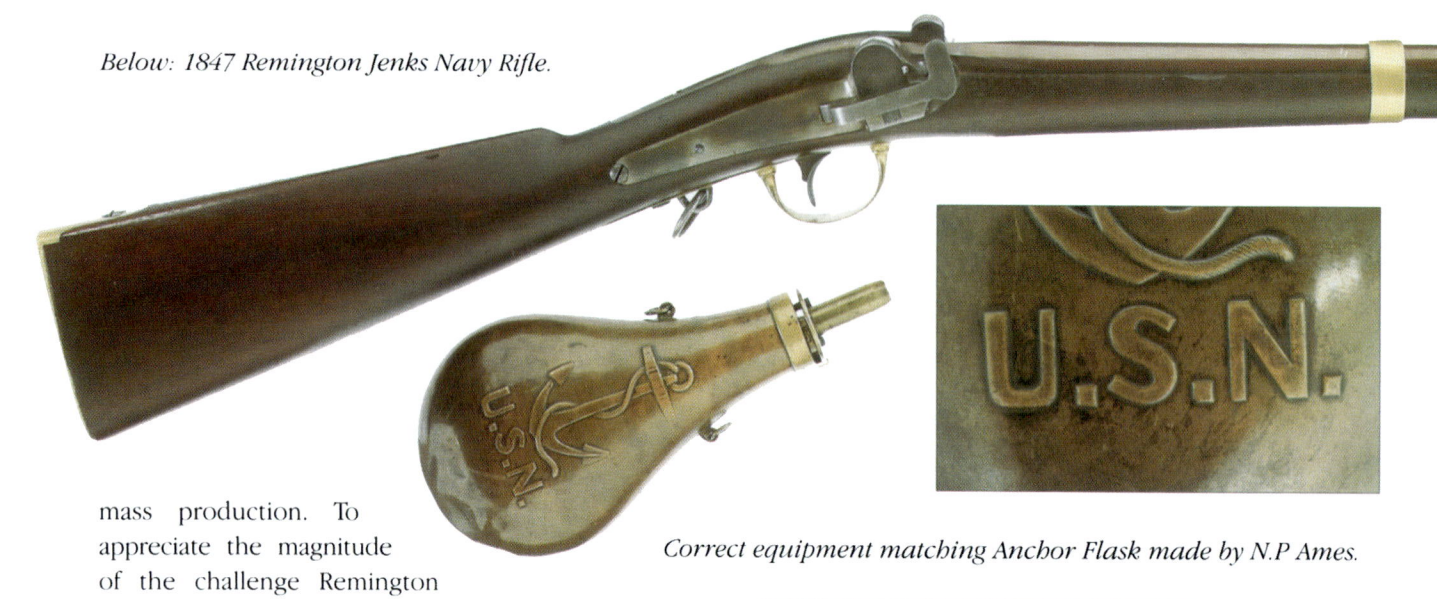

Correct equipment matching Anchor Flask made by N.P Ames.

mass production. To appreciate the magnitude of the challenge Remington faced, we must realize that mass producing rifles with true interchangeable parts had been fully realized by only a very few arms–producing establishments. The American System of Manufacture (as it was to be known) of fabricating interchangeable parts must be given to John Hall of the U.S. Rifle Works at Harper's Ferry. But it was Eliphalet Remington's efforts, which began in 1845, that helped make the American System the standard throughout the world. Remington understood the importance of the interrelationship of component parts and the tolerance bands necessary to achieve true interchangeability.

Remington combined the concept of interchangeable parts with progressive assembly methods and put the firm in an enviable position by the time of the Civil War. Government orders during the war gave rise to an

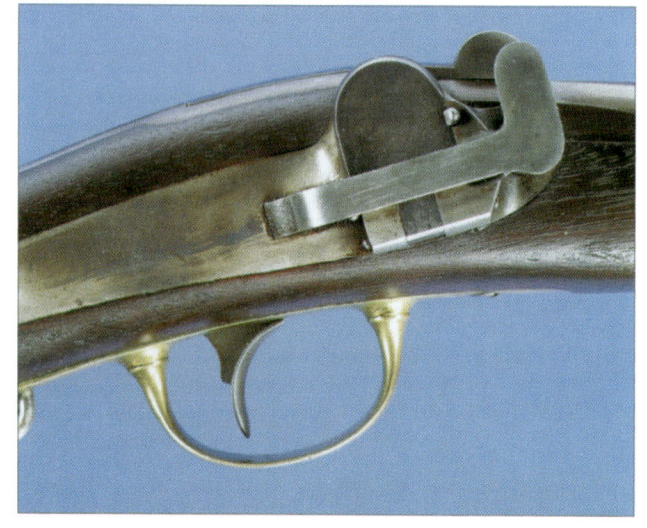

Both above: Remington Jenks contract carbine made for the U.S. Navy; and closeup view of the breech markings.

unprecedented expansion of plant, personnel, and production, employing upwards of a thousand workers in Ilion and nearby Utica. Remington's Armories reached a peak production of two hundred pistols and over one thousand rifles a day! In all, E. Remington and Sons supplied 40,000 muskets, 12,500 rifles, more than 144,000 revolvers, and 20,000 Remington carbines (subcontracted to the Savage Revolving Rifle Company) to the U.S. Army and Navy during the Civil War.

Above: The thriving village of Ilion—circa 1880s. E. Remington & Sons' Armory occupies a prominent position in the center of the village.

But Remington's contribution to industrial development extended far beyond firearms. When the war ended, the Remington factory was able to adapt to the rapidly expanding agricultural market of the West. In the years immediately following the Civil War, it was the Remington Agricultural Works that carried the firm, making all types of farm implements, iron bridges, and numerous other non–gun products including burglar alarms, safe doors and fire engines. Much later, the Remington name was found on bicycles, cutlery, cash registers, and other equipment.

When T. J. Jones of the Singer Sewing Machine Company could not convince his boss to adopt the refinements he had developed, he turned to Remington, and the company produced over a half a million sewing machines in the decades that followed. It was also Remington's support that brought to reality Christopher Latham Sholes' invention of a typewriter, and by 1882, over 2,500 typewriters a year were being manufactured by Remington. Although Remington was forced to sell that business in the 1880s, it continued to grow and prosper, buoyed by Remington's reputation for quality and innovation. Later the company became known as Remington-Rand, Sperry-Rand, Univac and Unisys.

Below: The rifle assembly room. Remington "rolling block" military muskets are observed throughout.

14 • The History of Remington Firearms

Right: Marcellus Hartley—circa 1880s.
Below: An early view of Remington's Armory along Otsego Street—circa 1872.
Bottom of page: Remington Custom Shop workers—circa 1890s. Shop superintendent L.N. Walker is center rear of photograph.

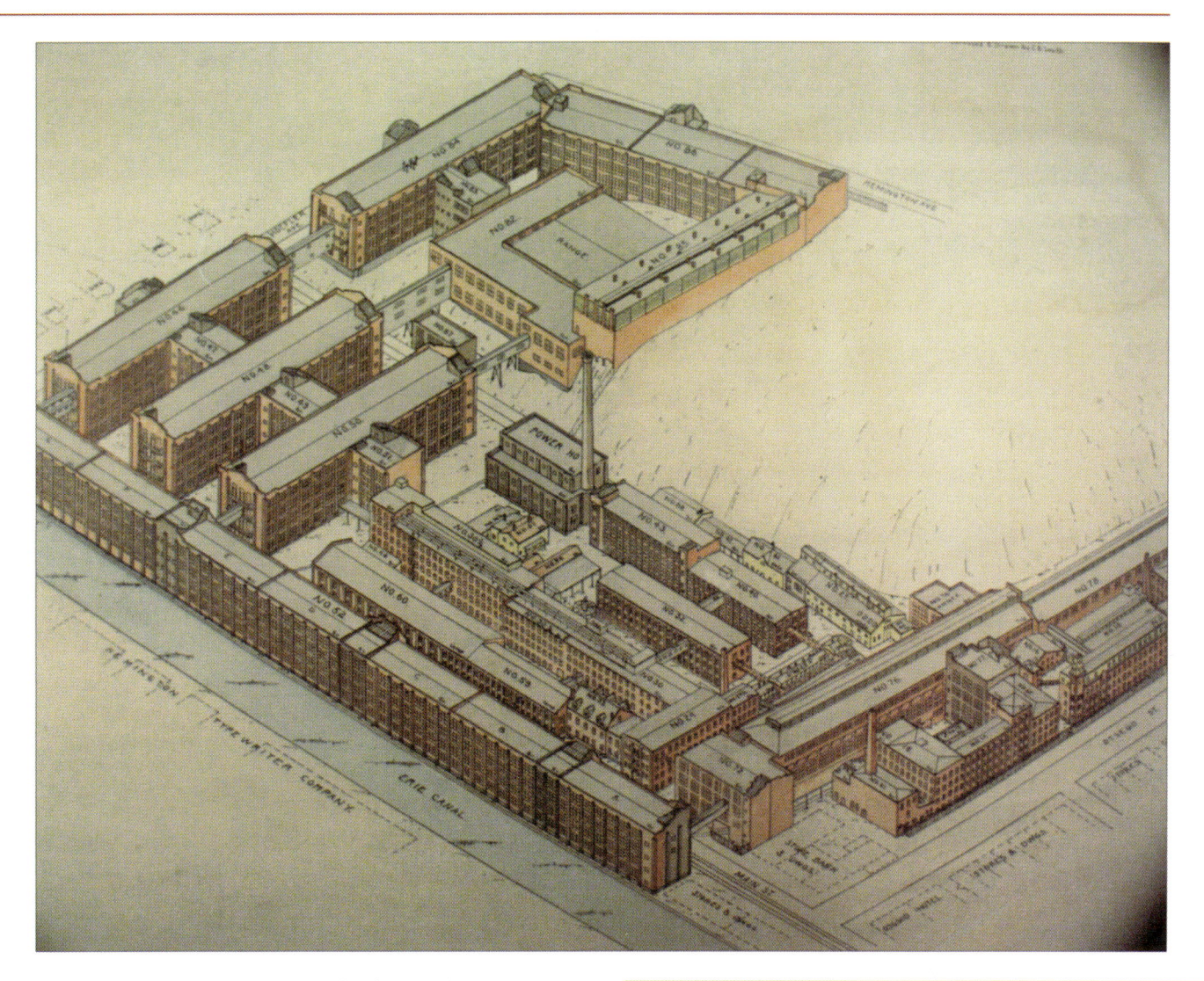

Above: Remington Arms–UMC facility in Ilion, New York—circa 1916. The factory was rebuilt in 1915 for the pending WWI arms production demands.
Right: E. Remington & Son's Armory buildings along Otsego Street—circa late 1870s.

In the field of ammunition design and manufacture, Remington was second to none. The company manufactured pistol, rifle and shotgun ammunition from 1871 until 1885. In 1888, the assets of E. Remington & Sons were taken over by Schuyler, Hartley & Graham, a NYC arms dealer that also controlled the Union Metallic Cartridge Company of Bridgeport, Connecticut (in operation since 1866). Marcellus Hartley took over control of both companies, and through his leadership seized a commanding position in the small–arms ammunition field that it has held ever since. During World Wars I and II, it was Remington that supplied more than half the small arms ammunition used by the allies!

In the period between 1865 and 1901, Remington fire–arms were awarded over twenty–two medals, including medals in the Paris Exposition of 1867, the U.S. Centennial Exposition of 1876, and the Chicago World's Fair of 1893. Remington continued to not only lure inventors and engineers to work for the firm, but also encourage that same entrepreneurship from its employees.

Among the gun inventors and designers who refined their ideas at Remington's plant were Joseph Rider, William Smoot, Arthur Savage, William H. Elliot, James P. Lee, John D. Pedersen, Crawford C. Loomis, Mike Walker and the greatest gun designer who ever lived, John Browning. Between the period of 1914 and 1948 alone, over one thousand patents were filed by Remington employees.

16 • THE HISTORY OF REMINGTON FIREARMS

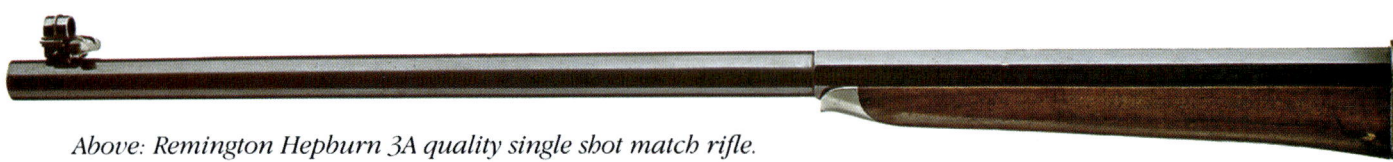

Above: Remington Hepburn 3A quality single shot match rifle.

Above: The winning American team members of the 1st International Match held at Creedmoor on September 26, 1874.
Right: Remington Arms Company factory, Ilion, New York—circa 1900.

Whenever the threat of war called for America to supply quality arms to equip our men, Remington was there. Almost overnight the company transformed itself from making sporting arms for civilians to meet the new challenge—building factories, retooling machines and training new workers. In the summer of 1914, the British approached Remington with an order for one million Enfield rifles. Working almost around the clock, Remington engineers designed the necessary machines and tools and supervised their construction and installation. Within a year after signing the contract, the first Enfields were tested successfully. A few months later, Remington's new factories reached their production goal of over two thousand finished rifles a day. In all, Remington made more than 1.5 million Enfield rifles.

REMINGTON COMPANY HISTORY • 17

Below and right: Two guns for very different purposes from the Remington Arms Company—the match rifle and the deringer.

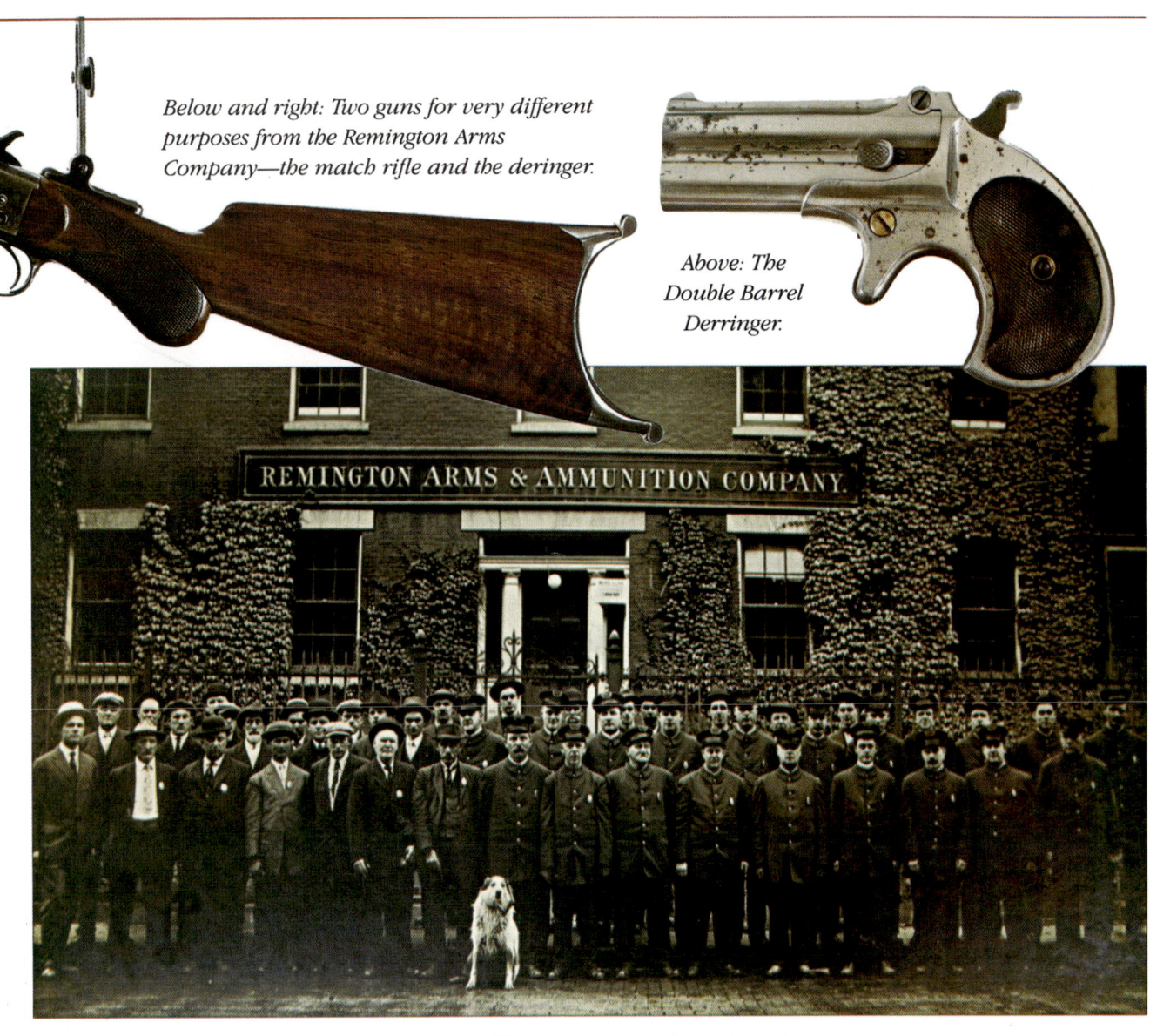

Above: The Double Barrel Derringer.

Above, Plant security and office personnel pose (with pet dog) in front of the office of Remington Arms & Ammunition Company—circa 1914.

18 • The History of Remington Firearms

Remington was able to gear up to produce better than three thousand rifles a day.

Concurrently, Remington's plants in Ilion, New York, Bridgeport, Connecticut, and Eddystone, Pennsylvania, produced millions of other weapons including Browning machine guns, Colt's M1911 pistols, Mark II signal guns, Mosin–Nagant rifles, Mdl 1907–15 rifles, Lebel *rolling block* rifles, and Pedersen Devices.

In World War II, the antiquated bolt–action Springfield rifle was once again called into service. Remington had to completely re–engineer the famous World War I firearm to make it lighter, more reliable, and easier to manufacture.

In the years that followed, Remington recognized that there were new "chipless" metal-working

Right: Ilion's Main Street cut squarely through the Remington plant until it was re-routed in the mid–20th Century. This photo is circa late 1920s.

All above: Salesmen examine a Remington cash register made at the Ilion plant in the 1920s. The company also manufactured the first effective typewriters (starting in 1874) and sewing machines.

REMINGTON COMPANY HISTORY • **19**

Top: Another view of Main Street cutting through the Remington factory—circa early 1950s.
Above: Hand checkering of shotgun stocks and forends— circa late 1930s.
Left: Main Street, Ilion, New York—circa early 1950s.

techniques that can make small parts with little or no secondary machining—like powdered metallurgy. When Remington was unable to purchase powdered metal parts to meet exacting specifications, the company developed superior processes and alloys to meet its

Above: Double-sided, cardboard store hanging sign advertising UMC ammunition.
Below: Late 1930s Remington advertisement.

needs. Since then, over 100 million powder metal components have been assembled into Remington products. In 1980, Remington was one of the pioneers in an advanced form of powder metallurgy known as metal injection molding, which produces geometrically more complex parts than those produced in conventional powder metallurgy. Remington has incorporated several million components produced through this process over the past decade.

BOB BARTLETT
FAMOUS ADVENTURER AND EXPLORER
says.."ONE THING I WANT ON MY GUNS ... THAT'S THE REMINGTON NAME"

"Whether it's polar bear in the Arctic or geese in Newfoundland ...I've found Remington guns and ammunition are right!"

In both powder metal and metal injection molding, Remington is recognized as a technical leader for supplying parts, not only for Remington firearms, but also for the automotive, computer, hand-tool, medical products, and firearms industries. Remington's commercial customers include General Motors, IBM, Kodak, Xerox, Snap-on-Tool, Smith and Wesson, and Colt Blackpowder Arms. Having set the standard of quality with the mass production of firearms with interchangeable parts, Remington is now coming full circle by merging precision machine tools with state-of-the-art computer technology to specialize in small volume production.

REMINGTON COMPANY HISTORY • 21

Above: The Remington factory constructed in 1915 was still in use in the 1960s.
Top right: Remington's Master Engraver Don Talbot working in his studio in 2004.
Both right: Two fine examples of Remington engraving and gold work.

In 1995, Remington opened a state–of–the–art R & D technology center in Elizabethtown, Kentucky. There, teams of some of the best engineers in the country are working to continue the tradition of innovation of firearms and ammunition well into the 21st century. Just like *"the inside contracting"* system introduced by Eliphalet Remington over 150 years ago, Remington is still relying on small technologically proficient teams to design, manufacture, and improve its products. For nearly 190 years, the name **REMINGTON** has stood for quality, innovation and advanced design of hundreds of products which benefit the sportsmen of America.

CHAPTER 2

Remington Pistols and Revolvers

America's peacetime economy of the 1850s meant that the U.S. military had little need for weapons from its own National Armories, and even less from private manufacturers. With no other orders for military weaponry on the horizon, Eliphalet Remington needed to maintain the operations of his establishment by fabricating non-military products that would keep revenues flowing into the Mohawk Valley. E. Remington & Sons continued to market rifle barrels of their own manufacture, as well as wholesale gun-related materials made by others, including fowling guns and percussion locks from Birmingham, wood blanks, butt plates, trigger guards, and lead shot and molded rifle bullets. Remington's Armory had successfully produced military weaponry, and it was only logical that his armory should also make arms for the civilian trade. However, having the capability to make guns, and having gun designs to make, are two distinctly different things.

By the mid-1850s, E. Remington & Sons did not have a gun designer in its employ. Fordyce Beals was the first to answer Remington's call. He was a talented gun designer and gunmaker, who had first come to Remington's Armory around 1847, staying for several years in various military rifle and carbine contract supervisory capacities. In 1854, however, Beals was enticed to go to the Whitneyville Armory near New Haven, Connecticut. There he developed a percussion revolver that was the initial flash of genius that led to the manufacture of tens of thousands of Remington revolvers for many years to come. U.S. Patent #11,715 was issued to Fordyce Beals on September 26, 1854, while he was living in New Haven, Connecticut, and working at the Whitneyville Armory. The proprietors at Whitneyville decided to market Beals' design for the civilian trade—the Whitney-Beals "Walking-Beam" Revolver. This unusual looking pistol did not infringe upon Colt's patented revolver, and at least fifty were made by Whitney in 1854 and 1855. Thereafter, the Whitneyville Armory entered full production and produced over 3,000 of these revolvers. Unfortunately for the proprietors, they were unable to induce Beals to remain with them.

1st Model Beals' Pocket Revolvers

Fordyce Beals returned to Ilion in 1856, and stayed there for the next two years. During this time, Beals helped E. Remington & Sons enter the civilian firearms market, a niche in which they have excelled ever since. Fordyce Beals perfected his Whitneyville design further, and on June 24, 1856, was awarded a new patent, #15,167, for what would become the first pistol made at Remington's Armory, the **1st Model Beals' Pocket Revolver**. Within a few years, this small, single-action, 5-shot, .31 caliber, cap & ball revolver underwent five design changes

Above: Remington Beals 1st Model Pocket Revolver.

(modern day collectors call them "variations"). More than 3,000 1st Model Beals' Revolvers were made over a three or four-year period. Initially they were manufactured for Beals by E. Remington and Sons and sold in non-labeled cardboard boxes (with black exteriors that simulate leather) complete with powder flask, bullet mold, nipple wrench and bullet seating tool (some had a spare cylinder added).

2nd Model Beals' Pocket Revolvers

Beals designed another pistol, this one having a spur-trigger rather than the ordinary trigger and trigger guard of the 1st model. It came to be known as the **2nd Model Beals' Pocket Pistol**. It has hard rubber grips, rather than the molded gutta-percha grips on the 1st Model Beals' Revolver. This single-action, spur-trigger civilian gun has a 3-inch barrel and bears both 1856 and 1857 Beals patent markings. Introduced about 1858, it is believed that fewer than 1,000 were made between 1858 and 1861.

Above: Remington Beals 2nd Model Pocket Revolver.

Above: Remington Beals 3rd Model Pocket Revolver.

3rd Model Beals' Pocket Revolvers

Just prior to the Civil War, Fordyce Beals designed a somewhat larger pistol which came to be called the **3rd Model Beals' Pocket Revolver**. Like the 2nd Model Beals, it also has a spur-trigger, and is a .31 caliber percussion gun. The 4-inch barrel is one inch longer than on the 2nd Model Beals. As many as 1,000 of these revolvers were made between 1859 and 1861. The 3rd Model Beals' Pocket Revolver was characterized by features that would become hallmarks of the large frame Beals' Army and Navy Revolvers that would follow. These included a pivoting rammer beneath the barrel and an enlarged, solid frame extension in front of the cylinder. One can readily see the transition that Fordyce Beals made in adopting these features into a large frame martial revolver.

Rider's Double-Action Pocket Revolvers

In early 1857, Joseph Rider, a gunsmith residing in Newark, Ohio, designed a spur-trigger, percussion revolver. Its patentable feature was the unique manner in which the cylinder was rotated. On August 17, 1858, Rider was awarded Patent #21,215. Unfortunately, no examples of this early Rider pistol are known. The following year, Rider applied again to the patent office, and on May 3, 1859, was issued U.S. Patent #23,861 for a double-action revolving pistol. Rider assigned a two-thirds interest in this patent to his two new Ohio business partners, John D. Martin and Andrew J. Dildine. They chose E. Remington & Sons Armory to manufacture their revolvers. Joseph Rider was given a per diem by his partners and was sent to Ilion to supervise Remington's work.

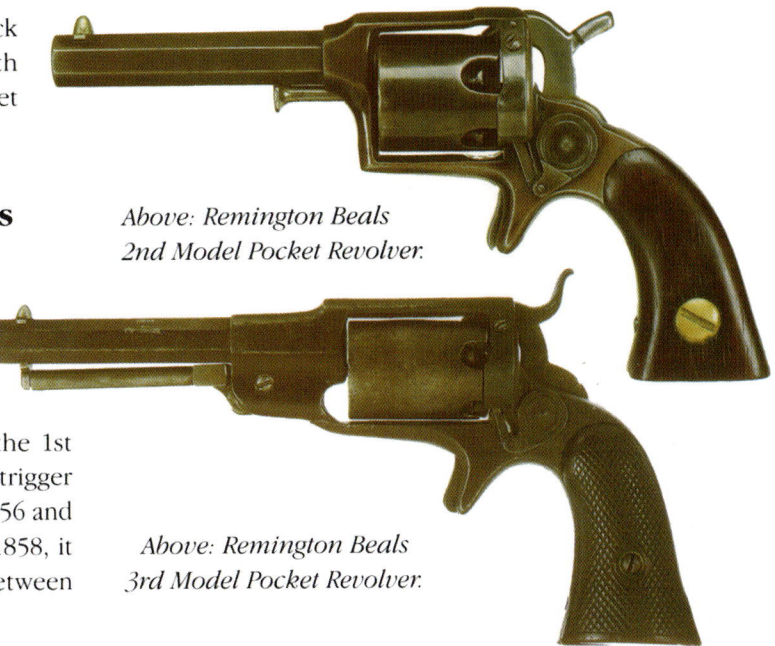

This pocket-sized civilian weapon was originally known as Remington's Pocket Revolver—Double Action or Self Cocking. Other contemporary advertisements refer to it as Rider's Patent Double Action or Self Cocking Pocket Revolver. Modern-day collectors, however, call it **Rider's Double-Action Pocket Revolver**. The manufacture of these revolvers was commissioned by the partnership of Rider, Dildine, Martin & Company. E. Remington & Sons were the manufacturers, and later became one of the distributers. These revolvers were mentioned in the E. Remington & Sons price list of October 1860, and as many as 20,000 may have been manufactured by Remington in the decade that followed.

In late 1861, Rider, possibly with Remington's financial help, re-acquired the two-thirds interest from

Above: Remington Rider Double Action Pocket Revolver.

Martin and Dildine, and assigned the entire patent right to his new employer, E. Remington & Sons. The distinctive features of Rider's double-action pistol are its "mushroom-style" cylinder, oversized trigger guard, straight trigger, and double-action mechanism. The pistols were packaged in cardboard boxes with loading

Left: Remington-Rider Double-Action Revolver.

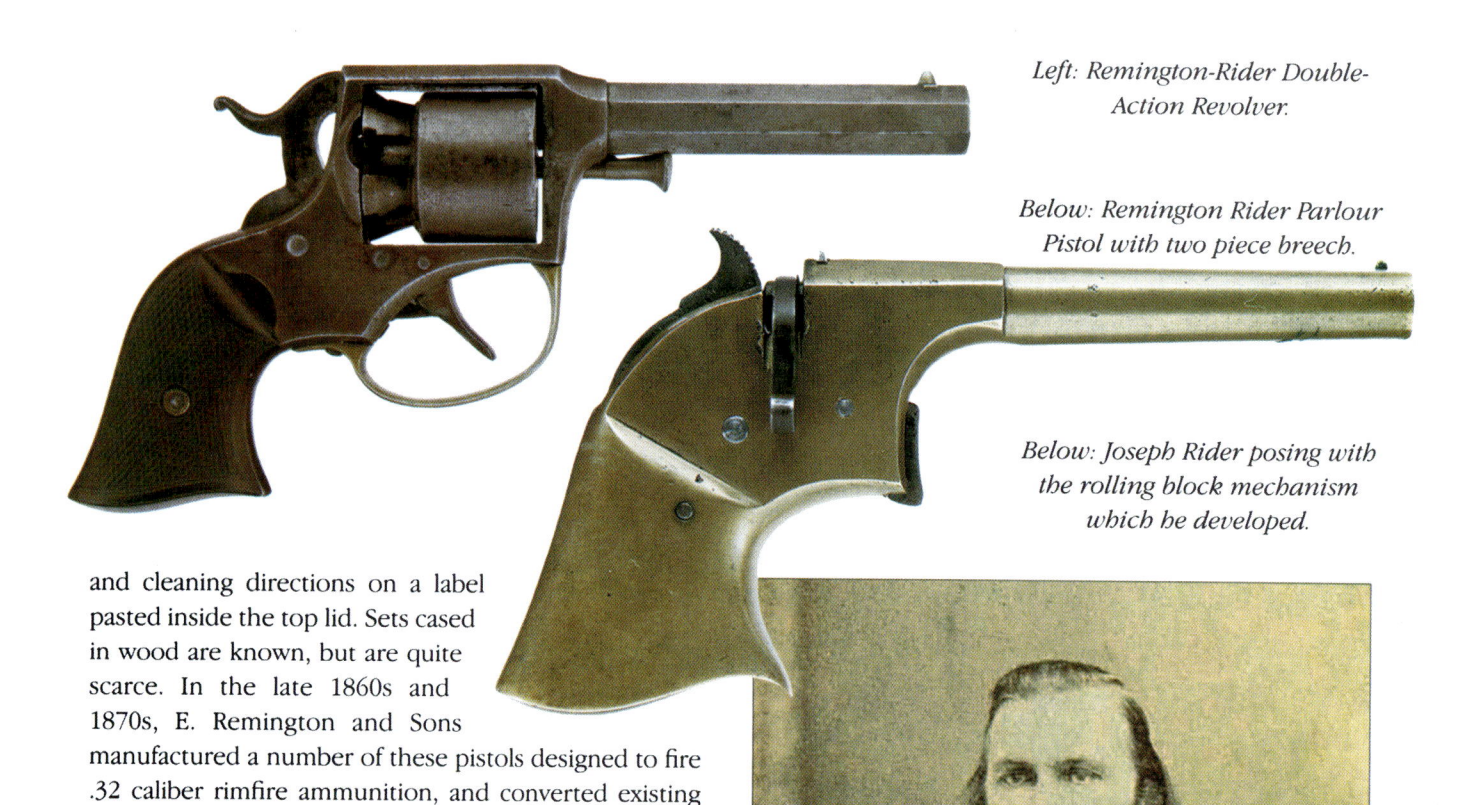

Below: Remington Rider Parlour Pistol with two piece breech.

Below: Joseph Rider posing with the rolling block mechanism which he developed.

and cleaning directions on a label pasted inside the top lid. Sets cased in wood are known, but are quite scarce. In the late 1860s and 1870s, E. Remington and Sons manufactured a number of these pistols designed to fire .32 caliber rimfire ammunition, and converted existing percussion pistols to rimfire.

Remington-Rider Parlor Pistols

In mid-1859, while working at Remington's Armory, Joseph Rider designed a single-shot parlor pistol, and on September 13th of that year was issued U.S. Patent #25,470. He immediately assigned part of the patent to E. Remington & Sons. This parlor pistol was marketed by Rider, Dildine, Martin & Company. Officially, it was known as Rider's Patent Parlor Pistol, but modern-day collectors call it the **Remington-Rider Parlor Pistol**.

This palm-sized, sand-cast, brass-framed, breech loading pistol was intended to be a parlor target pistol, not a defensive weapon. Its diminutive projectile, a .17 caliber lead ball, was propelled only with the fulminate from a percussion cap. With no powder used, the pistol developed minimal breech pressure and the projectile's velocity was very low, and ballistically suspect. Of the approximate two dozen authentic parlor pistols known, no two are alike, and many variations exist. The pistols were sold in tight-fitting cardboard boxes with the loading and cleaning directions on a label pasted inside the top lid. Both barrel and receiver/grip are one-piece brass. Two distinct types of breech mechanisms were made. The earliest is of one-piece construction with outside capping and the later was of two-piece construction with inside capping. Both types have smooth-bored barrels. While the total number produced during a one or two year period is not known, it is believed to be very low, possibly only a few hundred.

Remington Vest Pocket Pistols

Joseph Rider continued to work on the breech design on this parlor pistol and adapted it to produce a new pistol to fire a .22 caliber rimfire cartridge. The **Remington No. 1 Vest Pocket Pistol** was introduced by Remington sometime during the Civil War, but the exact date is not known. This single shot pistol bears a October 1, 1861, patent date. The pistols were intended to be concealable protection firearms, although their value as a defense gun is certainly disputable.

Above: Brass Frame Split Breech Pistol

Below: Remington Zig-Zag Pistol.

Above: Remington Elliot Ring Trigger Pistol.

Rider continued development on different breech loading designs, and sometime in 1863 perfected his first split-breech pistol. This concept was immediately adapted to a military carbine and after the war (1866) into two sizes of pistol: .32 caliber (**Remington's No.2 Vest Pocket Pistol**) and .41 caliber (**Remington's No.3 Vest Pocket Pistol**). These bear both October 1, 1861, and November 15, 1864, patent dates.

Elliot's "Zig-Zag" Pocket Revolvers

One more gun designer who came to Ilion to have his firearms made was Dr. William H. Elliot, a dentist from Plattsburg, New York. He was reputed to have designed more than thirty different dental inventions before turning his talented mind to firearms. He received more than fifty U.S. Patents for firearms from the 1850s to the 1880s, and even more thereafter. These patents included the basic design for the Colt Lightning rifle.

In 1858, Dr. Elliot came to Ilion, rented a small shop under the Ilion Citizen newspaper office, and equipped it with tools and gunmaking equipment. He was an independent gun designer and never became an employee of E. Remington & Sons. After some experimentation Dr. Elliot designed a revolving barrel pepperbox-type pistol and submitted specifications, a drawing, and a working model to the Patent Office. On August 17, 1858, he was awarded U.S. Patent #21,188 for what would eventually be called **Elliot's "Zig-Zag" Pocket Revolver**. The nickname "zig-zag" is a modern term given to this unique pistol because of the indentations at the rear of the barrel group that form a series of grooves. A pin connected to the trigger assembly causes the barrel group to rotate when the ring trigger is moved forward, then backward, to complete the firing cycle. The method is very complicated, and the mechanism is quite fragile.

Elliot's Ring-Trigger Pistols

On May 29, 1860, Elliot was issued patent #28,461 for the pistol most like the production Elliot Zig-Zag Pocket Pistols, which he commissioned E. Remington & Sons to make. Production guns have a barrel assembly group of six .22 caliber barrels that revolve around a center axis pin. As many as 1,000 Elliot Zig-Zag Pocket Pistols were made for Dr. Elliot in 1861. Production was interrupted by lagging sales, Dr. Elliot's redesign of an improved pistol, and Remington's need for gunmaking machinery for martial firearms during the Civil War. The inventor established Elliot's Arms Company in a store at 404 Broadway in New York City to sell his firearms, and it was maintained throughout the war years. Elliot's advertising in 1861, as well as box labels, refer to his gun as **Elliot's Pocket Revolver**.

The "zig-zag" pistol's greatest drawbacks were its complicated fire control mechanism and the revolving barrel group. Dr. Elliot and Rufus Howland corrected these deficiencies with an improved pistol design, which he also submitted for patent letters. On May 29, 1860, he was issued U.S. Patent #28,460 for his new design with stationary barrels and firing pin which rotated from chamber to chamber. This was the same day Elliot was issued his patent for his Zig-Zag pistol, which means that both pistol designs were available at the same time. Why Dr. Elliot opted to produce his Zig-Zag pistol first may never be fully known, but finally in 1862, he turned to Remington's craftsmen to produce his improved gun, later known in collecting circles as **Elliot's Ring-Trigger Pistols**.

E. Remington & Sons produced two versions of Dr. Elliot's pistol, which in the 1860s were called: Remington's New Repeating Pistol—Elliot's Patent No.1 (5-shot, .22 caliber rimfire with 3-inch barrels) and No.2 (4-shot, .32 caliber rimfire with 3-inch barrels). In all, about 12,000 of these pistols were made, although we may never know how many of each caliber were produced. Production continued until at least the late 1870s.

Beals' Large-Frame Revolvers

By 1860, Remington's armory was producing civilian pocket revolvers, cane guns and single-shot pistols. But, one type of weapon that Remington did not have was a military-size revolver. The answer lay in an improved version of Fordyce Beals' 3rd Model Pocket Pistol. In 1858, Fordyce Beals invented a spur-trigger, single-action, percussion revolver, and was issued U.S. Patent #21,478. The unique feature of his pistol was the manner of securing the cylinder pin with the loading lever. This arrangement would have far-reaching implications for Remington's large frame revolvers for years to come. His first successful martial revolver, which came to be known as the **Beals' Navy Revolver**, was an excellent weapon. Beals designed a 6-shot, .36 caliber, percussion revolver with a 7-inch octagonal barrel and walnut grips. This developmental work occurred in mid and late 1860, and the first weapons were ready for testing in the spring of 1861. The term Navy revolver refers to a .36 caliber weapon, while Army revolver refers to .44 caliber revolvers.

In early 1861 there was little doubt that a major conflict with the Southern States was coming. President Lincoln, inaugurated on March 4th, was soon-after

Above: Unidentified Confederate trooper poses proudly with his Remington Model 1861 revolver.

compelled to use his powers as Commander-in-Chief to call up 75,000 volunteers to augment his small standing army. This action resulted in a fever of enthusiastic recruiting throughout the North, and compelled manufacturers such as Eliphalet Remington to take notice. Samuel Remington journeyed to Washington, D.C., and showed Chief of Ordnance, Colonel James W. Ripley, a Beals' Navy Revolver. Ripley evidently liked what he saw, and immediately gave an order for 5,000 Beals' revolvers for $15^{00} each, however, these were to be made in .44 Army caliber, not .36 Navy. The official letter order was dated June 13, 1861, and called for these **Beals' Army Revolvers** to be delivered "with the greatest possible dispatch." Beals' military large-frame revolvers were weapons needed by Federal officers and cavalrymen alike.

The stress must have been enormous on everyone concerned, not the least of which was the proprietor, Eliphalet Remington. On July 12, 1861, the founder of Remington arms, passed into gunmaking history. Control of the company fell on his three sons, Philo, Samuel and

REMINGTON PISTOLS AND REVOLVERS • 27

Above: Remington Beals Navy Revolver.

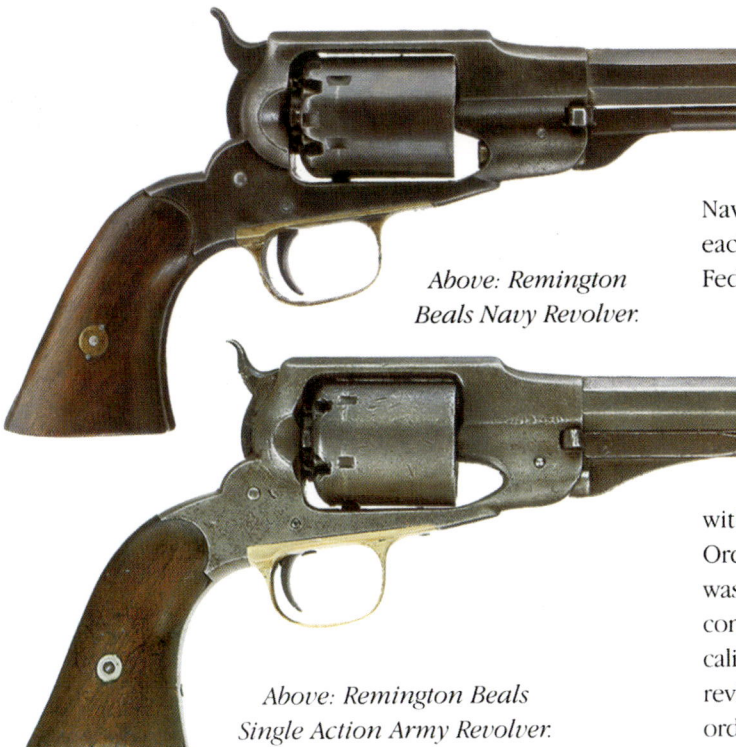

Above: Remington Beals Single Action Army Revolver.

1861 and May 1862. Between August 1861 and May 1862, E. Remington & Sons sold 7,250 Beals' Navy revolvers directly to the War Department, at $15⁰⁰ each. In all, nearly 13,000 Beals' Navy revolvers were in Federal service by the summer of 1862.

On August 17, 1862, E. Remington & Sons delivered the first 300 **Beals Army Revolvers** to the Army Ordnance Department on the original contract with Ripley. Samuel Remington testified before the Ordnance Commission in April 1862, and the end result was most favorable to the Ilion Armory—two new revolver contracts were awarded: one on June 13th for 20,000 .44 caliber Army revolvers at $12⁰⁰ each; and another as a revision of the initial order of July 29, 1861, this time ordering 5,000 Navy revolvers, also at $12⁰⁰ each.

Deliveries of the Navy revolvers were made between August and December 1862, and deliveries of the Army revolvers were made between July 1862 and June 1863. The total number of martially marked Beals' Navy revolvers accepted by the Ordnance inspectors during the Civil War is not known, but believed to be about 500 pistols. The number of Beals' Army revolvers made by Remington during the Civil War is estimated at about 1,900.

Eliphalet III. Out of respect, they retained the company name as it had been for many years. Under the brothers' management, a gunmaking establishment that had few rivals was built over the next four years.

Schuyler, Hartley & Graham, military goods dealers in New York City, were among the first to procure large numbers of these martial pistols. Other private dealers who procured pistols direct from Remington included Cooper & Pond, Palmer & Batchelders, and Tyler Davidson & Co. The Army Ordnance Department needed as many of these revolvers as possible to arm Federal troops in the Ohio and Mississippi River Valleys. In all, 4,586 Beals' Navy revolvers were procured for the Western Theater troops from dealers between August

Remington Model 1861, Elliot's Patent Army Revolvers

U.S. Patent #33,932 was issued to Dr. William H. Elliot on December 17, 1861, and covered an improved method of securing the base pin on the axle of the revolving cylinder, and the method of releasing the cylinder from

Left: Remington Beals Army Revolver.

Detail of blue steel finish and cartouche of William A. Thornton.

Above: Model 1861 Army Revolver

The initial delivery of **Remington Model 1861, Elliot's Patent Army Revolvers** to the Ordnance Department was made on August 3, 1862, with pistols made in Ilion. After Remington's Utica factory came into production in late 1862, subsequent deliveries of large-frame revolvers were made from there, and continued until March 1863, when they were discontinued in favor of the Remington New Model Revolvers. About 9,000 Model 1861, Elliot's Patent Army revolvers were delivered during this period.

The U.S. Navy Bureau of Ordnance ordered 120 Remington Navy revolvers in September 1862, and the armory sent them Beals' Navy revolvers. Later, the Navy ordered an additional 671 Remington revolvers in 1862, and these were also an assortment of Beals' Navy and Model 1861, Elliot's Patent revolvers.

Remington's Armory in Ilion was taxed beyond its ability to produce all of the revolvers contracted for by the Ordnance Department. Therefore, Remington went to nearby Utica, and struck a deal to acquire the vacant building that had formerly been occupied by the Utica Screw Manufacturing Company, located at the corner of Franklin and Fulton Streets. Necessary pistol-making machinery and tooling were procured and set up to manufacture Model 1861, Elliot's Patent revolvers. Production commenced in late 1862, and eventually, over 100 pistols a day were made here by workmen operating two 10-hour shifts daily.

Remington's Utica facility eventually took over the production of all large-frame military pistols during the

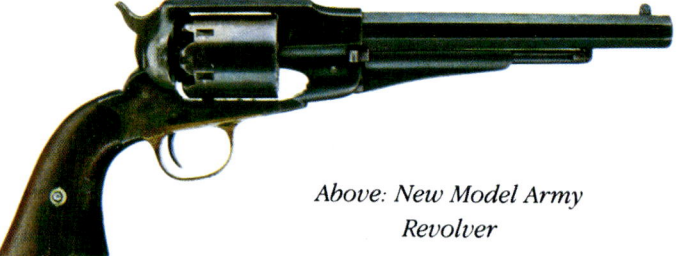

Above: New Model Army Revolver

Above: This Federal soldier poses in a photographer's studio with his Remington Model 1861 revolver.

the frame. When he testified before the Ordnance Commission in April 1862, Samuel Remington stated: "Our revolvers are made after a patent; those heretofore delivered are upon Beals' patent; those we propose to make in the future are in accordance with Elliot's patent."

remainder of the Civil War, including all New Model Army and Navy Revolvers. By 1865, Remington's Utica armory employed 150 men and 35 boys. Production continued under Samuel Remington's direction until the Utica facility was closed. Pistol-making machinery, tooling, raw materials, and in-process parts were transferred back to the Armory in Ilion.

Remington New Model Revolvers

In late 1862, the Army Ordnance Department received a number of complaints from army officers about Remington Model 1861, Elliot's Patent revolvers—notably the lack of safety notches on the cylinder, and a propensity of the cylinder to come loose. The Army Ordnance Department recommended that Remington return to the earlier loading lever and cylinder arbor design. Shortly after the final delivery of Model 1861, Elliot's Patent Navy Revolvers to the U.S. Army in late December 1862, Remington started making design improvements to their large frame Army and Navy revolvers. The new design reverted back to cylinders with safety notches. **Remington New Model Revolvers** were first delivered in March 1863.

On July 6, 1863, a new contract was signed with the Army Ordnance Department, calling for all the revolvers that "can be produced within the present year" up to 20,000 firearms, at $12^{00} apiece. Remington's Utica Armory eventually delivered 18,208 New Model Army revolvers on this contract, through January 2, 1864. A new contract was signed on November 21, 1863, for Remington to manufacture and deliver 64,900 Army revolvers at $12^{00} apiece. Eventually, Remington's Utica factory delivered about 57,000 New Model Army revolvers on this contract, and the Ordnance

Above: New Model Army Revolver.

Above: Remington Double Action Belt Revolver.

Department issued yet another contract, signed on October 24, 1864, for 20,000 additional revolvers for $15.50 each. Deliveries of New Model Army revolvers continued to the Ordnance Department throughout 1864 and into 1865, at a phenomenal rate that averaged about 1,000 revolvers a week.

On February 4, 1864, fire destroyed a major portion of Colt's Patent Fire Arms Company armory in Hartford, Connecticut, which had been used to manufacture pistols and revolving rifles, employing 900 workmen. The adjoining building (used to manufacture U.S. rifle muskets) was only slightly damaged. Remington's primary competitor was knocked out of the military revolver business for the remainder of the Civil War. By the close of the war, E. Remington & Sons had delivered a total of 116,765 Army revolvers (Beals' Army, M1861, Elliot's Patent Army, and New Model Army revolvers), and 16,736 Navy revolvers (all three varieties) to the Federal Government. In less than four years, the Remington brothers had built up a weapons-producing empire, acquiring hundreds of machines, tons of raw materials, and hundreds of skilled workmen.

Remington New Model Belt Revolvers

E. Remington & Sons decided to bring out a series of percussion revolvers intended to attract the civilian trade. Exactly when they were introduced is uncertain, but they were listed in newspaper advertisements in late 1865. Among them were Remington's **New Model Single-Action Belt Revolver** and the **New Model Double-Action Belt Revolver**—a six-shot, .36 caliber pistol with a 6-inch barrel. Upwards of 2,500 of each were made over a ten-year period. The New Model Belt Revolvers were slightly smaller than New Model Navy Revolvers, made popular in the Civil War. Some double-action New Model Belt Revolvers were made with fluted cylinders, rather than the plain round cylinders of most other Remington revolvers.

Remington also produced a somewhat smaller, single-action, .36 caliber **New Model Police Revolver** in various barrel lengths from 3-inches to 6-inches. In the decade that followed, at least 17,000 were manufactured.

Above: New Model Police Revolver.

Remington New Model Pocket Revolvers

Remington also designed a revolver to take the place of their 1st, 2nd and 3rd Model Beal's Pocket Revolvers, which had been introduced just prior to the war. The new gun was a single-action, .31 caliber, percussion, **New Model Pocket Revolver**, a 5-shot, "pocket-sized," spur-trigger pistol, available in 3-inch and 4-inch barrel lengths. As many as 26,000 New Model Pocket Revolvers were manufactured through the mid-1870s.

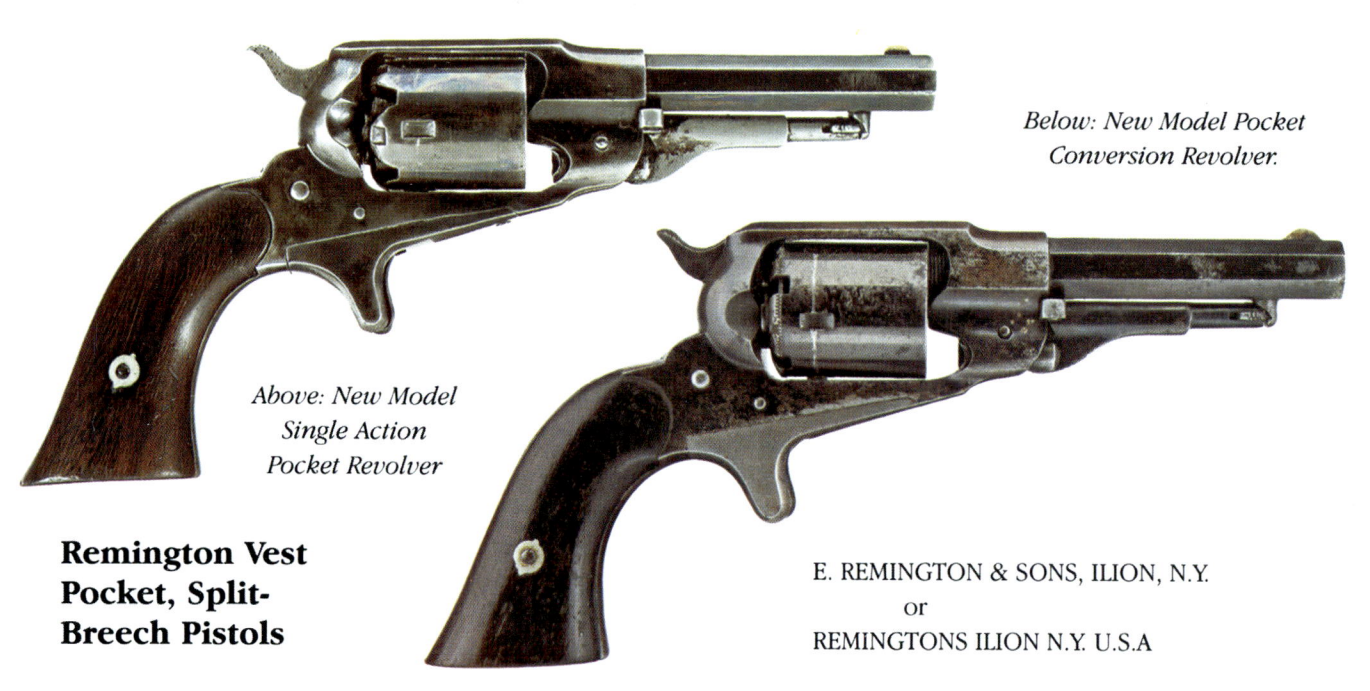

Above: New Model Single Action Pocket Revolver

Remington Vest Pocket, Split-Breech Pistols

Although the Rider split-breech design can be dated from mid-war, it was not until 1866 that Remington began offering split-breech pistols for the commercial market. **Remington Vest Pocket, Split-Breech Pistols** were chambered for either .32 caliber (designated the **No.2 Pistol**) or .41 caliber (**No.3 Pistol**) rimfire ammunition. A combined total of about 20,000 pistols in both calibers were made through 1875.

Remington Double Derringers

William H. Elliot was issued U.S. Patent #51,440 on December 12, 1865, for a double-barrel pistol, later to be known as the **Remington Double Derringer**. Superposed barrels held two .41 caliber rimfire cartridges. In all, more than 112,000 of these derringers were made, as production continued for the next 69 years, making it one of the longest produced firearms of all time.

- **First Model Double Derringer**—Serial numbered from 1 to at least 2141. Walnut or rosewood or ivory or pearl grips. All issues were marked on the opposite side rib (sometimes inverted):
    ELLIOT'S PATENT DEC. 12TH. 1865
1st Issue of the First Model Double Derringer dates from 1866, has no extractor, and side ribs are marked:
    MANUFACTURED BY E. REMINGTON &
    SONS. ILION. N.Y
2nd Issue derringer also has no extractor and side ribs are marked:
    E. REMINGTON & SONS, ILION, N.Y.
3rd Issue derringers are the first equipped with extractors and are marked:

Below: New Model Pocket Conversion Revolver.

    E. REMINGTON & SONS, ILION, N.Y.
    or
    REMINGTONS ILION N.Y. U.S.A

- **Second Model Double Derringer**—This model dates from 1868, and was made until 1887 when E. Remington & Sons was in receivership. Walnut or rosewood or ivory or pearl grips. An estimated 12,000 of this model were made in two runs of about 6,000

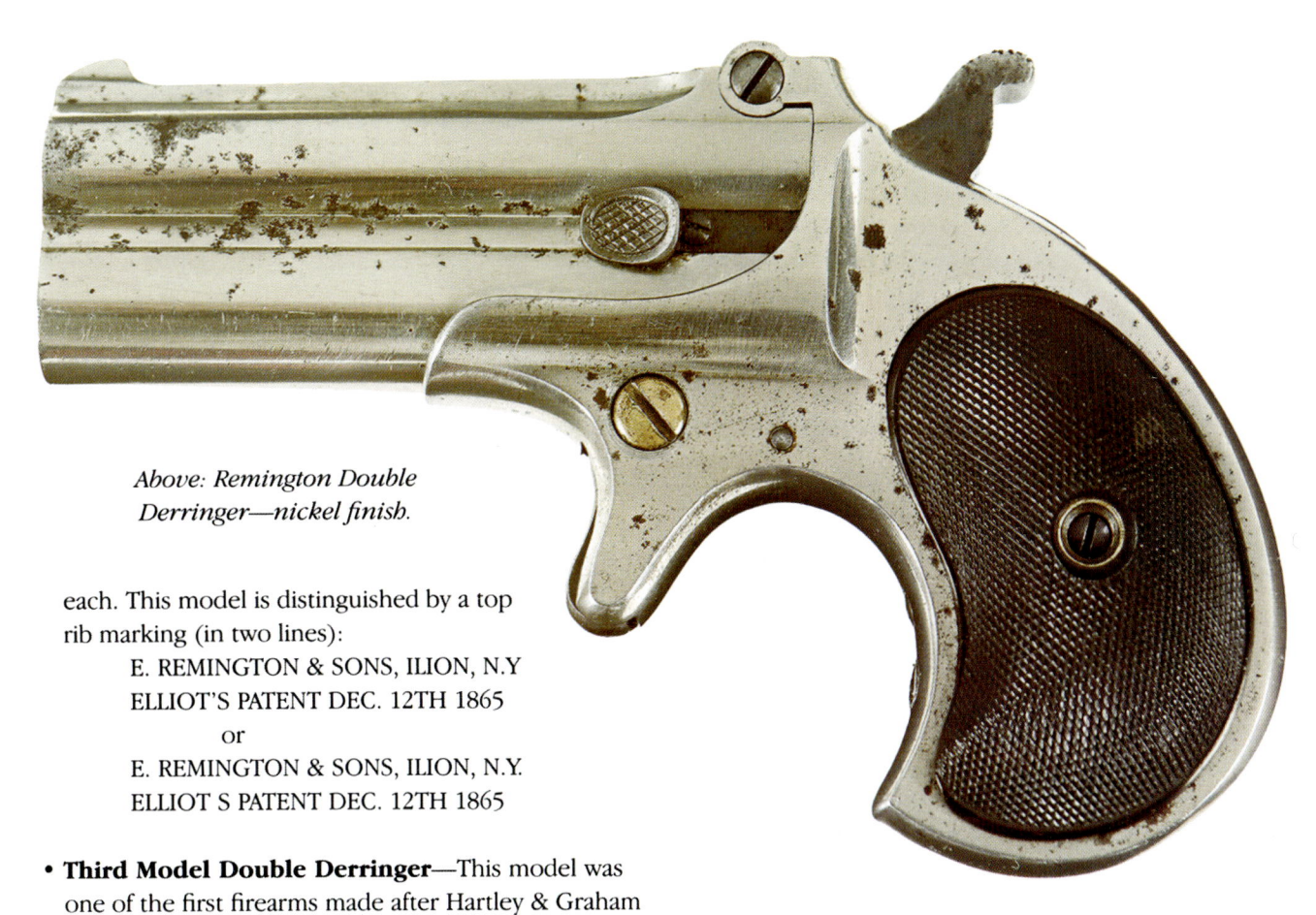

Above: Remington Double Derringer—nickel finish.

each. This model is distinguished by a top rib marking (in two lines):

E. REMINGTON & SONS, ILION, N.Y
ELLIOT'S PATENT DEC. 12TH 1865
or
E. REMINGTON & SONS, ILION, N.Y.
ELLIOT S PATENT DEC. 12TH 1865

- **Third Model Double Derringer**—This model was one of the first firearms made after Hartley & Graham and Winchester acquired the company, establishing

1st Issue marked
REMINGTON ARMS CO. ILION. N.Y.
2nd Issue marked
REMINGTON ARMS C O. ILION, N.Y.
3rd Issue marked
REMINGTON ARMS Co. ILION. N.Y.
4th Issue marked
REMINGTON ARMS Co. ILION. N.Y

- **Fourth Model Double Derringer**—This model was manufactured from 1911 (when the Rem-UMC marketing scheme was devised) to 1935, however sales are recorded at least through 1938, when the double derringer was discontinued. During that

Above: Double Derringer with blue finish.

Above: Double Derringer with nickel finish and ivory grips.

the Remington Arms Company in mid-1888. Remington manufactured 70,272 double derringers from 1888 to late 1910. Checkered, hard rubber grips are standard. All four issues of this derringer have the same top rib marking, although the letters vary by issue in font type and size:

24-year period a total of 27,914 double derringers were sold. Checkered, hard rubber grips are standard. Top rib marked:
REMINGTON ARMS-U.M.C. C.O. ILION, N.Y.
1st Issue double derringers—the first 2,000 or so were made without a letter prefix before the serial number.
2nd Issue first appeared in 1922. Serial numbers were preceded by the letter L, (believed to begin at

Above: Third Model Double Derringer.

Above: Fourth Model Double Derringer.

Above: The Model 95 Double Derringer.

L90001) and barrels were date coded. In 1923, Remington began referring to this as their No.95 Double Derringer, retailing for $11.65.

In 1930 this gun was first referred to as **Double Derringer—Model 95**. Sometime around 1931, Remington began making the monoblock version of this derringer without the rib between barrels, and a matte black finish. The last year this venerable derringer was advertised was in the Remington Price List of February 15, 1935, when it was referred to as **Remington Model No.95 Double Derringer**, selling for $13.45.

Remington-Elliot Single-Shot Derringer

On August 27, 1867, Dr. Elliot was issued U.S. Patent #68,292 for a single-shot, .41 caliber rimfire, derringer pistol, which was manufactured and marketed by E. Remington & Sons as the **Remington-Elliot Single-Shot Derringer**. A combination hammer and breechblock resulted in a simplified, very practical firearm design, ideal for a single-shot defensive weapon. Over a twenty-year period, more than 10,000 of these derringers were made.

Remington-Kittredge Conversion Revolvers

By the time the Civil War ended, it was clear that the era of percussion ignition firearms was over and the advent of cartridge arms was near. What stopped Remington, and most revolver manufacturers from adapting their weapons to fire rimfire cartridges was a compelling legal issue—Rollin White's U.S. Patent for the bored-through cylinder issued years earlier on April 3, 1855. On November 17, 1856, Smith & Wesson struck a deal, whereby their arms manufacturing firm would pay Rollin White 25¢ for every revolver made with a bored-through cylinder. Smith & Wesson effectively locked up the cartridge revolver market until 1868, producing more than two hundred thousand revolvers in the ten-year period. In February 1868, Smith & Wesson signed an agreement with E. Remington & Sons, allowing Remington to convert 4,575 New Model Army Large-Frame Percussion Revolvers to fire .46 caliber rimfire

REMINGTON PISTOLS AND REVOLVERS • **33**

Above: Remington Single shot Mississippi Derringer.

Above: Rollin White Patent conversion of Army Revolver.

Above: New Model Pocket Conversion Revolver.

percussion revolvers to fire rimfire or centerfire cartridges without fear of patent infringement. Remington waited until the White patent expired, and then set about converting many hundreds and later thousands of their percussion pocket, belt, police and large-frame revolvers to cartridge. These included:

- **New Model Large-Frame Army Cartridge Revolvers** in .44 and .46 rimfire and later .44 Remington centerfire, .44-40 Win centerfire, and .45 Colt centerfire, utilizing newly made cylinders;

cartridges. The work took place between September 1868 and April 1869. These were the first large-frame cartridge revolvers to be produced in quantity under Rollin White's patent. The newly made 5-shot cylinders were stamped: PATENTED APRIL 3D, 1855, the date of the Rollin White patent. When completed, the revolvers were shipped to Smith & Wesson for inspection and distribution. Of the total, 4,141 revolvers were sold to B. Kittredge & Company of Cincinnati, Ohio, between October 28, 1868, and April 1, 1869. Kittredge paid Smith & Wesson $3.36 per altered pistol. In turn, Smith & Wesson kept $1.00 per pistol, as royalty for allowing Remington to use the Rollin White patent to convert the revolvers. The remainder of the proceeds went to the Remingtons.

Remington Conversions of Percussion to Cartridge Revolvers

Since Federal protections of White's patent extended to 1869, Remington officials could not legally convert other

- **New Model Large-Frame Navy Cartridge Revolvers** in .38 long rimfire and .46 rimfire, utilizing new cylinders with separate recoil plates;
- **New Model Pocket Cartridge Revolvers** in .32 caliber rimfire;
- **New Model Belt Single-Action Cartridge Revolvers** in .38 caliber long rimfire;
- **New Model Belt Double-Action Cartridge Revolvers** in .38 caliber long rimfire; and
- **New Model Police Cartridge Revolvers** in .38 caliber long rimfire.

Remington Smoot Patent Revolvers

William S. Smoot was a gun designer who left his position as an U.S. Army Ordnance Officer to make his mark in Ilion, eventually becoming superintendent of Remington's manufacturing operation. Receiving full support from Remington, Smoot developed a pocket-sized cartridge revolver, and he was issued U.S. Patent #143,855 on October 21, 1873, for what would soon

Above: Remington No. 1 Smoot Revolver.

Above: Remington No. 2 Smoot Revolver.

Above: Remington No. 3 Smoot Revolver.

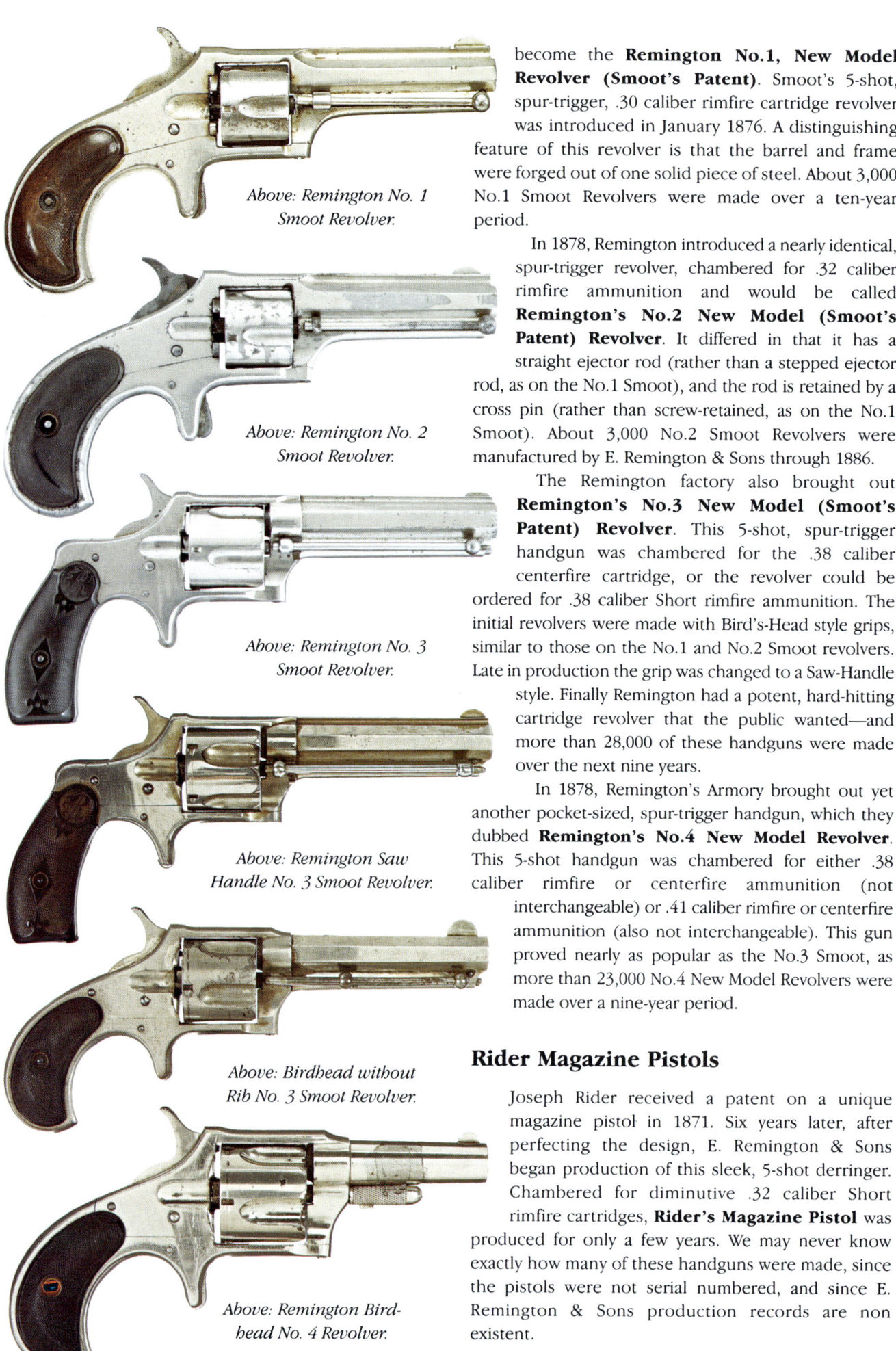

Above: Remington Saw Handle No. 3 Smoot Revolver.

Above: Birdhead without Rib No. 3 Smoot Revolver.

Above: Remington Birdhead No. 4 Revolver.

become the **Remington No.1, New Model Revolver (Smoot's Patent)**. Smoot's 5-shot, spur-trigger, .30 caliber rimfire cartridge revolver was introduced in January 1876. A distinguishing feature of this revolver is that the barrel and frame were forged out of one solid piece of steel. About 3,000 No.1 Smoot Revolvers were made over a ten-year period.

In 1878, Remington introduced a nearly identical, spur-trigger revolver, chambered for .32 caliber rimfire ammunition and would be called **Remington's No.2 New Model (Smoot's Patent) Revolver**. It differed in that it has a straight ejector rod (rather than a stepped ejector rod, as on the No.1 Smoot), and the rod is retained by a cross pin (rather than screw-retained, as on the No.1 Smoot). About 3,000 No.2 Smoot Revolvers were manufactured by E. Remington & Sons through 1886.

The Remington factory also brought out **Remington's No.3 New Model (Smoot's Patent) Revolver**. This 5-shot, spur-trigger handgun was chambered for the .38 caliber centerfire cartridge, or the revolver could be ordered for .38 caliber Short rimfire ammunition. The initial revolvers were made with Bird's-Head style grips, similar to those on the No.1 and No.2 Smoot revolvers. Late in production the grip was changed to a Saw-Handle style. Finally Remington had a potent, hard-hitting cartridge revolver that the public wanted—and more than 28,000 of these handguns were made over the next nine years.

In 1878, Remington's Armory brought out yet another pocket-sized, spur-trigger handgun, which they dubbed **Remington's No.4 New Model Revolver**. This 5-shot handgun was chambered for either .38 caliber rimfire or centerfire ammunition (not interchangeable) or .41 caliber rimfire or centerfire ammunition (also not interchangeable). This gun proved nearly as popular as the No.3 Smoot, as more than 23,000 No.4 New Model Revolvers were made over a nine-year period.

Rider Magazine Pistols

Joseph Rider received a patent on a unique magazine pistol in 1871. Six years later, after perfecting the design, E. Remington & Sons began production of this sleek, 5-shot derringer. Chambered for diminutive .32 caliber Short rimfire cartridges, **Rider's Magazine Pistol** was produced for only a few years. We may never know exactly how many of these handguns were made, since the pistols were not serial numbered, and since E. Remington & Sons production records are non existent.

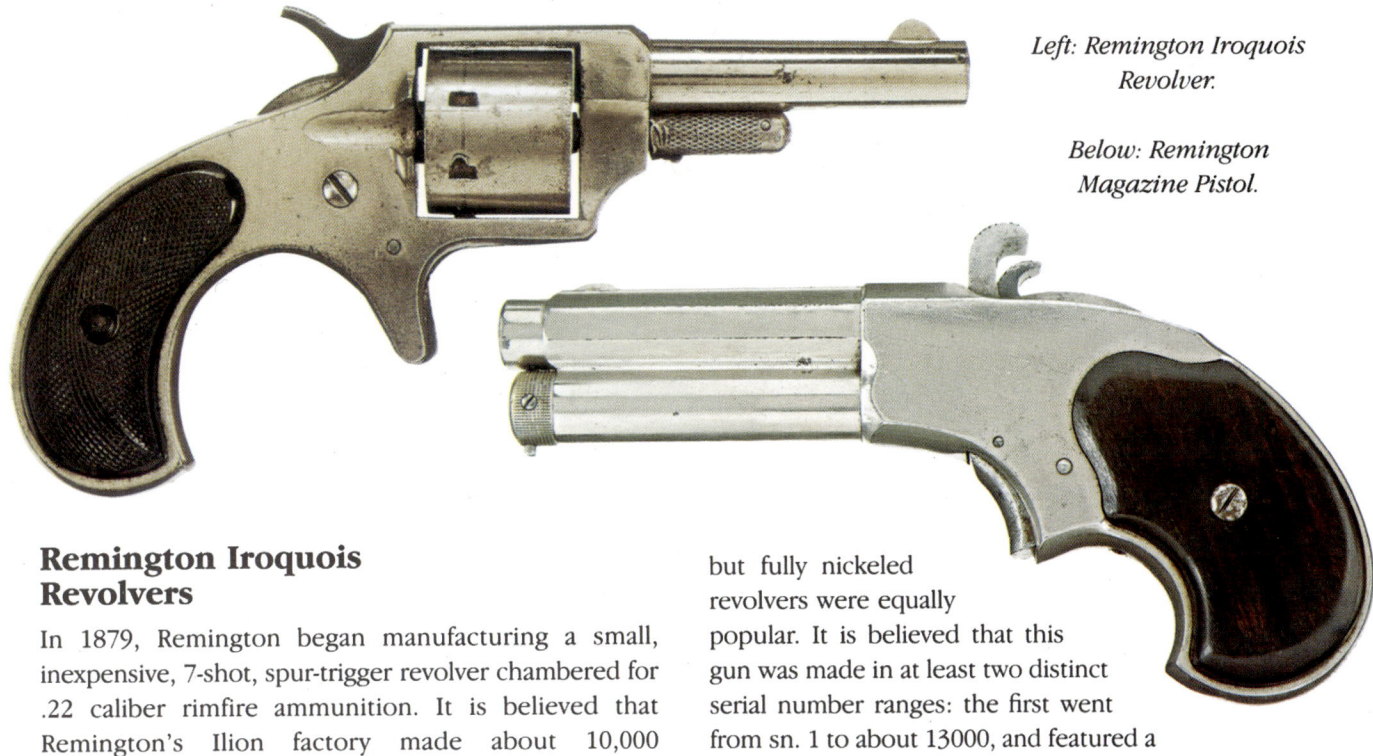

Left: Remington Iroquois Revolver.

Below: Remington Magazine Pistol.

Remington Iroquois Revolvers

In 1879, Remington began manufacturing a small, inexpensive, 7-shot, spur-trigger revolver chambered for .22 caliber rimfire ammunition. It is believed that Remington's Ilion factory made about 10,000 **Remington Iroquois Revolvers** over a seven-year period, with either plain or fluted cylinders.

Above: 1875 Army Revolver with Ivory Grips.

Remington Model 1875 Army Revolvers

In 1874, Remington developed a large-frame, single-action, .44 caliber cartridge revolver to compete against Colt's Model 1873 Single-Action Revolver. The Egyptian Government placed an order for 10,000 Remington Model 1875 Army Revolvers with E. Remington & Sons in 1874, and production commenced right away. After an undisclosed number of these hard-hitting revolvers were fabricated, Remington decided not to ship them, as the Egyptian Government still was behind on payments of several hundred thousand dollars for rolling block rifles and carbines.

Originally chambered for proprietary .44 Remington centerfire ammunition, these 6-shot revolvers were later available in .44-40 W.C.F. and .45 Long Colt calibers. These handguns were made with round 7-inch barrels, and although 5-inch barrels are known, they were never advertised by Remington. A blued finish was standard, but fully nickeled revolvers were equally popular. It is believed that this gun was made in at least two distinct serial number ranges: the first went from sn. 1 to about 13000, and featured a small, pinched front sight and no safety notch on the hammer; the second serial number range went from sn. 1 (again) and went to over 1837, and featured a tall, blade-type front sight and a safety notch on the hammer.

Unlike Colt's single-action revolvers, Remington Model 1875 Revolvers never gained popularity with the U.S. Cavalry, or with any other foreign power, except for Mexico. Equally telling was that this Remington revolver never became truly popular with America's civilian market. With a total production run of less than 15,000 revolvers over twelve-years, this model could not be relied upon to help E. Remington & Sons get through the difficult 1880s.

Remington Navy "Rolling Block" Pistols

Joseph Rider had developed the Remington split-breech system during the Civil War, adapting it to both small-frame and large-frame carbines. Concurrently, he continued to experiment with various methods of locking the breech and on December 16, 1864, submitted a new design to the patent office. On January 3, 1865, he was issued the first patent for what would evolve into the famous Remington rolling block action, #45,797. The term rolling block refers to a breech system comprised of a hammer piece that is brought to cocking position, and a semi-circular breechblock that is

Above: A Remington New Model revolver is held by one of these two Ute Indians—circa 1868.

rotated back to open the breech for extracting the spent shell casing and for inserting a new cartridge.

The Remingtons had a winner in Rider's rolling block, breech loading system. They encouraged Rider's developments and sought to interest Ordnance department officials in their new design. Finally news came that provided hope to the Remingtons and to other gun manufacturers. An Ordnance Board was to convene in Washington, D.C., in March 1866, as the U.S. Army wanted to adopt the very best breech loading rifle and carbine then available, and chose the most

REMINGTON PISTOLS AND REVOLVERS • 37

Right: Remington Model 1865 Rolling Block Pistol.

Right: Remington USN Model 1867 Rolling Block Pistol.

Above: Remington Plinker Rolling Block Pistol.

Above: Remington 1888 New Model Army Revolver.

Model 1871 Army pistol frames. The oridginal .50 caliber barrels were sleeved down to produce .22 rimfire, .25 rimfire and .32 S & W centerfire pistols. A number of these handguns were left at .50 caliber for centerfire ammunition.

appropriate method of converting hundreds of thousands of muzzle loading muskets to breechloaders. If only the U.S. Army would adopt a Remington System, this could be the solution to their immediate cash flow problems and the relative inactivity of their works.

Remington continued developmental work with rolling block pistols. A sample pistol was sent to the Navy Bureau of Ordnance in June 1866. Subsequently, an order for 5,000 such pistols was tendered on June 13th, and eventually signed by the Remingtons on November 16th. Eventually a total of 6,500 **Remington Model 1866 Navy Rolling Block Pistols** were made for the Navy Bureau of Ordnance; 5,000 pistols on the first contract were delivered between July and December 1867; and 1,500 more on a contract dated October 14, 1867, and delivered between January and May 1868.

Remington Model 1887 "Plinker" Pistols

In 1887, E. Remington & Sons fabricated approximately 800 rolling block pistols for "plinking", utilizing surplus

Remington Model 1888 New Model Army Revolvers

In 1889, Hartley & Graham offered a Remington New Model Pocket Army Revolver now referred to as the **Remington Model 1888 New Model Army Revolver**, which shares many features with the Remington Model 1875 revolver. This gun was never offered in any Remington catalog, and it is not known whether they were fabricated in Ilion, or at one of Hartley & Graham's subcontracted repair shops in New York City, utilizing left over M1875 revolver parts. These 6-shot revolvers were made for .44-40 W.C.F. cartridges, have 5-inch barrels, and were offered with blued or nickel-plated finishes for just $10.00. It is believed that fewer than 500 of these revolvers were made in 1888 and 1889.

Remington Model 1890 New Model Army Revolvers

In 1891, Remington Arms Company introduced the **Remington Model 1890 New Model Army Revolver**, a 6-shot handgun in .44-40 W.C.F., available with 5-inch or 7-inch barrels, and with either blued or nickel-plated finish. These single-action revolvers were not a popular selling item, as the styling was more than twenty years old. Remington was to sell only 2,020 Model 1890 revolvers between 1891 and 1894.

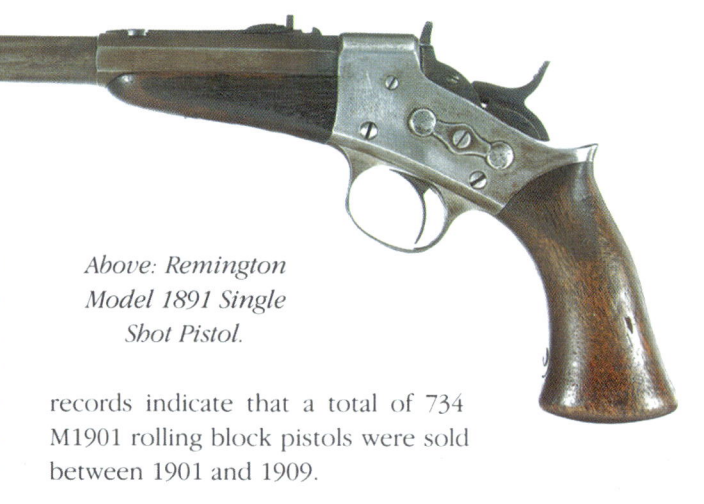

Remington Model 1891 Rolling Block Target Pistols

In 1892, Remington began selling the **Remington Model 1891 Rolling Block Target Pistol**, a single-shot pistol "for shooting galleries and target practice." They were made with left-over M1871 Army-frame receivers, 10-inch part-round/part-octagonal barrels, and chambered for a variety of .22, .25 and .32 caliber rimfire and centerfire cartridges. Remington began advertising this pistol for $10⁰⁰ in their 1894 catalog, and factory records indicate that only 116 were sold between 1892 and 1899.

Above: Remington Model 1891 Single Shot Pistol.

Remington Model 1901 Rolling Block Target Pistols

In 1901, Remington introduced the **Remington Model 1901 Rolling Block Target Pistol**, "for target and gallery practice." This well-made pistol utilized surplus Model 1871 Army-framed receivers, which were from military pistols repurchased from the U.S. Army years earlier. It is nearly identical to the Remington Model 1891 pistol, but the most distinguishing features are the sights (a Lyman fixed blade front sight with ivory bead, and a rear target sight, adjustable for both windage and elevation) and the checkered walnut, two-piece grips and fore-end. This pistol was chambered for .22 Short and .22 Long Rifle rimfire, .25-10 Stevens rimfire, or .44 Smith & Wesson Russian centerfire ammunition. Factory records indicate that a total of 734 M1901 rolling block pistols were sold between 1901 and 1909.

Colt Model 1911 Autoloading Pistols

On December 29, 1917, the Ordnance Department's Small Arms Division issued an order to Rem-UMC to manufacture 150,000 **Colt's Model 1911 autoloading pistols**. On March 21st, the Ordnance Department increased the order to 500,000 pistols, superseding the initial order for 150,000. The price was to be cost plus a 10% fixed profit, and delivery of the first firearms was to

Above and right: Customized and engraved Model 1901 Rolling Block Target Pistol.

Remington Pistols and Revolvers • 39

Above: The Model 1901 Rolling Block Target Pistol pictured in its presentation case.

begin on June 1, 1918. The first Rem-UMC produced Colt Model 1911 pistols were delivered to the U.S. Ordnance Department in August 1918. The Armistice was signed on November 11, 1918, and on December 17th, after only four months of production, the Ordnance Department's contract with Rem-UMC was suspended. Rem-UMC was permitted to continue manufacture until they completed a total of 21,513 M1911 pistols, which was fulfilled in February 1919. However, an additional 159, and later an additional 5 pistols were delivered, for a grand total of 21,677 pistols manufactured by Rem-UMC.

Mark III Signal Guns

20,460 "Mark III" signal pistols were made by Remington Arms—Union Metallic Cartridge Company, in its Bridgeport, Connecticut, facility. The Mark III signal pistol was issued with canvas holster and canvas cartridge belt with an assortment of 10 gauge signal shells.

Above right: 1901 Target Pistol in blue steel finish.

Above left: US M1911 Remington UMC Pistol.

Pedersen's Model 51 Autoloading Pistols

In 1913, John D. Pedersen began working on a new autoloading pocket pistol. Developmental work by Pedersen, which had been halted during the war, resumed in 1919, and Remington tooled-up to manufacture this autoloader for the civilian market. The first Model 51 pistols were ready in September 1919, selling for $36.30 each. The action is a unique combination blowback-recoil system—a hesitation or impinging action. Initially these 7-shot autoloaders were chambered for the .380 REM AUTOLOADING cartridge. Remington introduced a .32 ACP version in August 1921, with an initial selling price of $25.00. The magazine held eight rounds, one more than the .380 pistol magazine. Remington announced on August 18, 1926, that they were discontinuing the Model

51 autoloading pistol. In all, 64,796 pistols had been made in only seven years of production.

MODEL XP-100 PISTOLS

In the early 1960s, Remington decided to manufacture a high-power varmint pistol with a bolt-action based on the successful Model 40X rifle. The receiver and the bolt-assembly were shortened for weight reduction, and the new handgun would feature a DuPont Zytel nylon stock with an ambidextrous grip. After much testing, it was decided to chamber this pistol for a new .221 REM "Fire Ball" centerfire cartridge, with a 2,650 f.p.s. muzzle velocity. Production commenced on the single-shot Remington XP-100 Long Range Pistol in late 1962, and it was introduced to the public in early 1963. Initial advertising stated that the new pistol "shoots faster, flatter, farther and tighter than any handgun in history!" Initially it sold with a custom-fitted zipper carrying case. Variations of this bolt-action handgun, included:

Above: US Model 1911 seen from left hand side

- **Remington XP-100 Long Range Pistol**—This was the original single-shot design which was chambered for the .221 Rem "Fire Ball" centerfire cartridge. This nylon-stocked handgun had a ventilated rib 10-inch barrel (drilled and tapped for scope mounts), and was sold from 1963 to 1985.
- **XP-100 Silhouette Target Pistol**—This single-shot handgun was chambered for the 7mm BR [bench rest] Rem cartridge from 1980 to 1992, and for the .35 Rem cartridge from 1987 to 1992. It featured a Zytel nylon stock with universal grip, two-position thumb safety switch, match-type trigger, drilled & tapped receiver, and a 14-inch barrel.
- **XP-100 Silhouette Pistol**—This Custom Gun Shop, single-shot handgun was offered only in 1993 and 1994, and featured a solid American walnut stock with ambidextrous grip, 10-inch barrel, target-type sights, and was chambered for the 7mm BR Rem cartridge.
- **XP-100 Varmint Special**—This nylon-stocked, single-shot handgun had a 14-inch barrel and was chambered for the .223 Rem centerfire cartridge. It was available from mid-1986 to 1992. This pistol was also referred to as the **XP-100 Synthetic Pistol** in most of the later catalogs.
- **XP-100 Hunter**—This Custom Gun Shop, single-shot handgun was available only in 1993 and 1994, and featured an ambidextrous grip laminated stock, 14-inch barrel, no sights, and was chambered for .223 Rem, 7mm BR, 7mm-08 Rem, and .35 Rem centerfire ammunition.
- **XP-100 Custom Long Range Pistol—Walnut Stock**—This Custom Shop, single-shot pistol first appeared in 1986. It featured a sculpted American walnut stock and adjustable target sights, and was initially available in two chamberings. The 7mm-08 Rem version was "intended for metallic silhouette shooting," while the .35 Rem was "well suited for big game handgun hunting." A .223 Rem chambering was

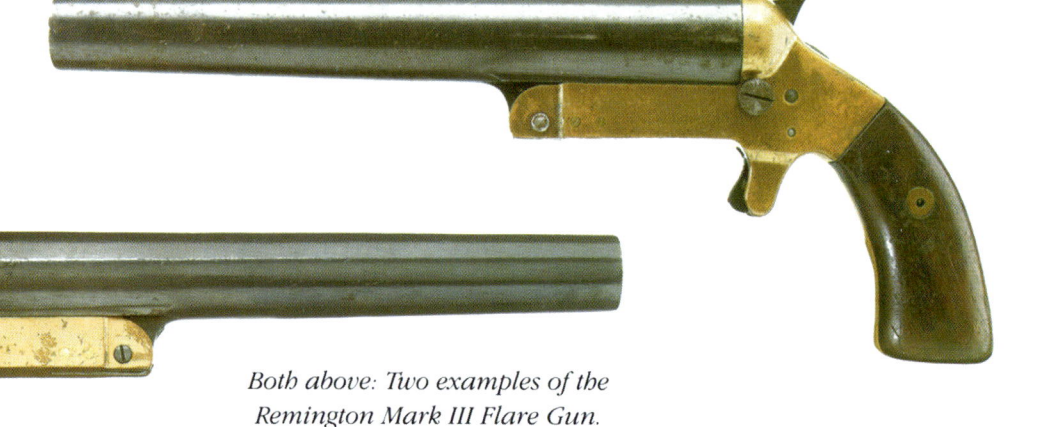

Both above: Two examples of the Remington Mark III Flare Gun.

Above: Pistol assembly room at the factory of E. Remington & Sons, Ilion, New York—circa 1874

Above: Remington XP-100 pistol with scope.

added about 1988, in an HB (heavy barrel) configuration. Right-hand and left-hand stocks were first offered in this custom gun in 1988. Additional calibers were added in 1989, including: .250 Sav, 6mm BR, and 7mm BR. In this same year, both standard weight 14-inch barrel and heavy weight 15-inch barrels were available in right-hand and left-hand versions. Heavy barrel guns came without sights or sight holes. In 1992, .22-250 Rem and .308 Win calibers were added.

- **XP-22R Rimfire Pistol**—This Custom Gun Shop handgun was a 5-shot, .22 rimfire clip repeater, and first appeared in the 1991 Remington catalog. It sported a Kevlar-reinforced stock and no sights. Only a few were made, but none were subsequently released to the public.
- **XP-100R Custom KS Repeater**—This Custom Gun Shop repeater sported a blind box magazine, an ambidextrous grip Kevlar-reinforced stock, 14-inch barrel, adjustable sights, and sling swivel studs at the front and rear of the stock. It was available from 1991 to 1994. Available calibers during this four-year period included .223 Rem, .22-250 Rem, .250 Sav, 7mm-08 Rem, .308 Win, .35 Rem and .350 Rem Mag. By popular demand this repeater was reintroduced in 1998, without sights, in the following calibers: .223 Rem, .22-250 Rem, .260 Rem and .35 Rem. It is now a regular production item and in contrast to the Custom Gun Shop version, does not have sights, sling or sling swivels.

CHAPTER 3

Remington Rifles and Carbines

U.S. Model 1841 Mississippi Rifles

By the late 1820s, the Remingtons experimented with the use of cast steel, a form of hardenable tool steel that was melted in the process of making barrels. This was later known as crucible steel. In February 1845, Samuel Remington appeared before the Ordnance Trial Board held at Washington Arsenal to urge the advantages of Remington cast steel barrels for military firearms. The Trial Board looked favorably upon the process and directed the Ordnance Department to conduct further tests. It should be recognized that Remington "cast steel" barrels are not barrels formed by casting! As it turned out, William Jenks (designer of the Jenks breech loading carbine) and Dr. Edward Maynard (inventor of the tape-priming system that would dominate ignition systems in U.S. small arms in the 1850s) were both at the Ordnance Trials. Young Samuel Remington probably conferred with them, which may have been the spark that ignited Remington Armory interest in entering the full arms manufacturing field.

Eliphalet Remington journeyed to Cincinnati, Ohio, in July 1845, where he negotiated the taking over of a contract to fabricate 5,000 U.S. Model 1841 rifles—which later came to be called Mississippi rifles. The initial contract had been given by the U.S. Army Ordnance Department to John Griffiths in December 1842, and he was to be paid $15.00 for each rifle delivered, but failed to produce any of the rifles under this contract. This failure to perform opened the door for Eliphalet Remington to enter the gunmaking business in a big way. Eliphalet came to terms with Griffiths quite quickly, and the deal included transferring specialized gun making machinery and tooling to Remington's Armory, none of which Eliphalet possessed. On July 14, 1845, Remington wrote to Ordnance Officer George Talcott, proposing that his company take over the Griffiths' contract. Just four days later, Talcott replied favorably to Eliphalet, who awaited his decision in Cincinnati. The Ordnance Department's approval of Remington's arrangement with Griffiths became final on September 8, 1845, and the government agreed to pay Remington $13.00 for each Model 1841 "Mississippi" rifle delivered. The official contract also permitted Remington to supply 1,000, of the 5,000 ordered with Remington "cast steel" barrels.

Prior to this date, Remington's Armory had only produced barrels for firearms and other metal goods, and did not possess the precision woodworking or metalworking machinery and tooling to make firearms. Acquiring such equipment would launch the company squarely into the gunmaking business. With the Mississippi contract, Remington was to acquire essential gunmaking machinery and precision tooling. Prior to acquiring both gunmaking contracts, Remington, the barrel maker, had few metalworking and no woodworking machines. If Remington was to enter the highly competitive field of military gunmaking, competing with experienced New England armories like North's, Whitney's, and Robbins & Lawrence's, he had to have modern machinery. These contracts gave him the opportunity to get that specialized machinery. However, the Remingtons waited in vain for the arrival of the gun making machinery and tooling from Cincinnati. Remington was unable to begin production on any of the rifles in 1846. Exactly when Griffiths delivered their equipment to Remington is not known.

In mid-1848, Remington's armory finally turned its attention to producing U.S. Model 1841 "Mississippi"

Above: U.S. Model 1841 "Mississippi" Rifle.

rifles. Many months were spent re-tooling Jenks machinery to produce the intricate metal and form-fitting wood parts for M1841 rifles. Finally in April 1850, the initial lot of 300 finished Mississippi rifles was shipped to the Ordnance Department. Lots of 500 at a time followed every 60 to 90 days thereafter, and the contract for all 5,000 rifles was fulfilled by September 1852. Buoyed by the success of their sojourn into gunmaking, E. Remington & Sons sought, and were awarded another contract for 5,000 Model 1841 rifles in November 1851. In all, Remington delivered a total of 10,000 Mississippi rifles by December 1854: 1,240 in 1850; 2,000 in 1851; 2,500 in 1852; 2,000 in 1853; and 2,260 in 1854.

Jenks Navy Carbines

At about the same time as Remington was talking to Griffiths, he began negotiations for another government contract for firearms. In 1841, William Jenks had signed a contract to supply the U.S. Navy with a large number of his patented breech loading, mule-ear carbines. Jenks subcontracted their manufacture under that and succeeding contracts to N.P. Ames & Co. of Chicopee Falls, Massachusetts, who eventually delivered 4,250 of these carbines to the Navy. Ames was known for excellent quality swords, and in the 1840s, also became known as producers of superior gunmaking machinery and precision tooling. On September 22, 1845, Jenks signed yet another contract with the U.S. Navy, this time to supply 1,000 of his carbines with Edward Maynard's patented tape priming mechanism, instead of with percussion cap ignition. Shortly thereafter, Eliphalet Remington contacted the proprietors of N.P. Ames, and after some negotiations, purchased their contract in late 1845. Eventually, Ames shipped the gunmaking machinery to Remington, along with the services of the carbine's inventor, William Jenks, and a promising gunmaker, Fordyce Beals. The first delivery of Jenks carbines to the Navy took place on April 5, 1848, and the whole lot of 1,000 carbines was completed and shipped by September, five months later. Even though they continued to produce thousands of gun barrels yearly for the civilian trade, E. Remington & Sons was squarely in the gun business, and has remained so to this very day.

The Maynard Tape-Priming Lock Contract

On November 9, 1853, Frankford Arsenal Commander, Major Hagner, received permission from the U.S. Ordnance Department to alter 20,000 old muskets. Since

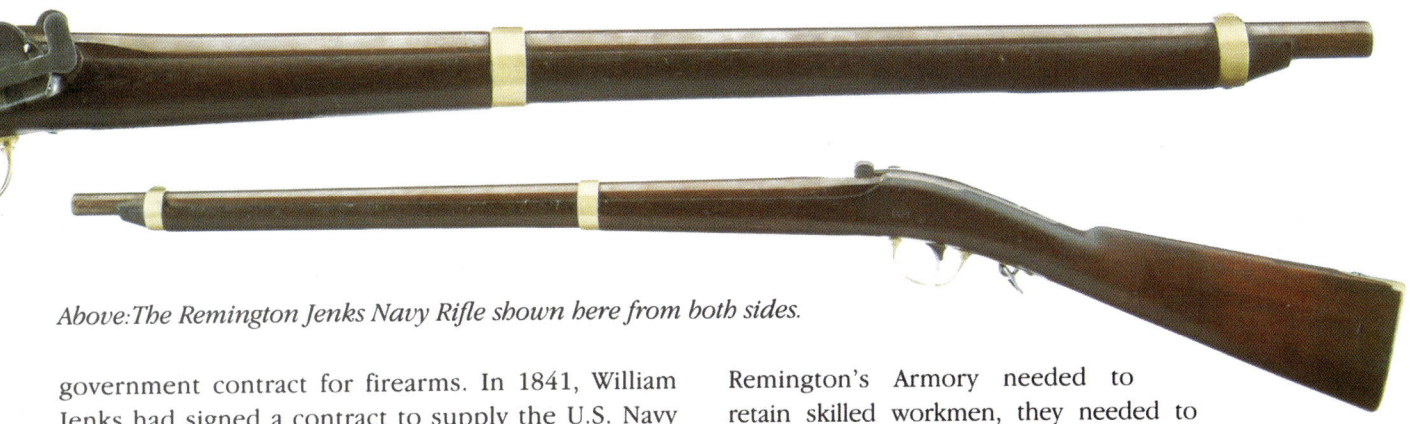

Above: The Remington Jenks Navy Rifle shown here from both sides.

Remington's Armory needed to retain skilled workmen, they needed to secure a new military order. On September 9, 1854, E. Remington & Sons signed a contract with the U.S. Ordnance Department to fabricate 20,000 percussion locks with Maynard tape primers for $3.15 apiece, complete with breech plugs.

After fabrication by Remington, these assemblies would be fitted by workmen at Frankford Arsenal to convert obsolete flintlock U.S. 1816 muskets to a more reliable form of ignition.

The finished lock and percussion bolster assemblies made at the Remington facility were shipped to the Frankford Arsenal where government workmen fitted the locks and breech plugs to the older muskets that were held in storage. The government workmen also added new front and rear sights, and 3-groove rifled the

Above: Remington Dog Head Percussion Cane Gun

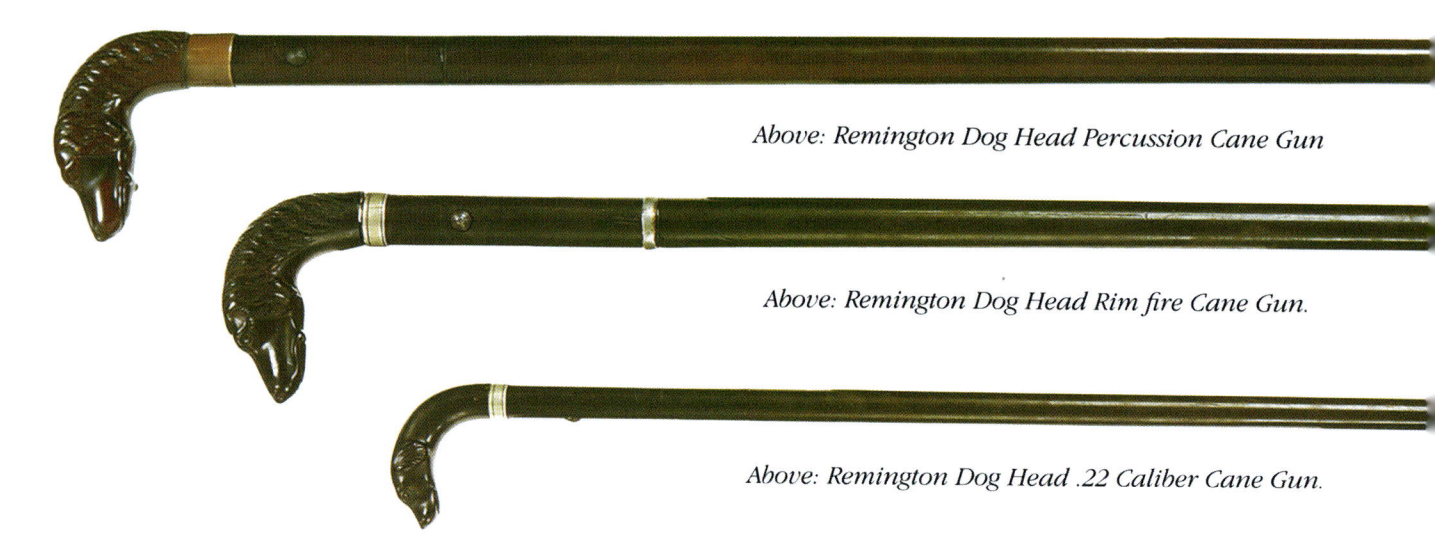

Above: Remington Dog Head Rim fire Cane Gun.

Above: Remington Dog Head .22 Caliber Cane Gun.

bores. Remington's Armory fulfilled their contract, and all 20,000 lock assemblies and percussion bolsters were shipped to Frankford: 50 in 1855, 1,500 in 1856, 10,000 in 1857, and 8,450 in 1858.

Remington's Thomas Patent Cane Guns

In the mid-1850s, cane guns were popular with gentlemen in American society. They served as protection, as well as being a gentleman's walking accessory. Never intended to be formidable weapons, cane guns protected their owners against stray dogs and the occasional advances of ruffians. Eliphalet Remington was on the lookout for new products for the civilian trade, and he had to look no further than a cane gun designed by John F. Thomas, an employee at his factory, who had previously been a gunsmith in Ilion. On February 9, 1858, Thomas, who later came to be master mechanic at E. Remington & Sons Armory, was issued U.S. Patent #19,328 for his percussion cane gun. Thomas assigned half of his invention to Samuel Remington in July 1859, and production is believed to have commenced sometime that year. Not only was this cane gun one of the first civilian firearms made by Remington, the firm was the only major gunmaker in America ever to offer a cane gun.

Initially, only .31 caliber percussion cane guns were manufactured and sold by Remington. Pre-Civil War advertising refers to them as **Remington's New Patent Gun Canes**, which were loaded with a .31 caliber lead ball. Serial numbers of the gun canes went from 1 to over 278. The iron, rifled barrel within the longer cane shaft measured only about 9 inches. Thereafter, the bullet traveled loosely through a brass tube to the muzzle, which was plugged for walking. In the years that followed, Remington (Thomas Patent) cane guns were made with a variety of handles, including ball & claw, dog's head (two sizes), full curve, curve with flat gripping area, bulbous-shape, and L-shape. The cane was covered with gutta-percha (a very fragile molded material that cracked easily) or vulcanized rubber. In the 1870s, ivory handles were offered. Various colors were available, including black, brown and coral. Many different handle, barrel, shaft and overall lengths (33-inches to 36-inches known) were made.

Production of percussion cane guns was interrupted during the Civil War years (1861 to 1865), and may have resumed in mid-1865. In the late 1860s, Remington's cane gun was re-designed to handle .22 caliber rimfire (called the **Remington No. 1 Rifle Cane**) and .32 caliber rimfire (**Remington No. 2 Rifle Cane**) ammunition. Remington's rimfire cane guns were first

Above: The beads of the Cane Guns were beautifully detailed.

Remington Rifles and Carbines • 45

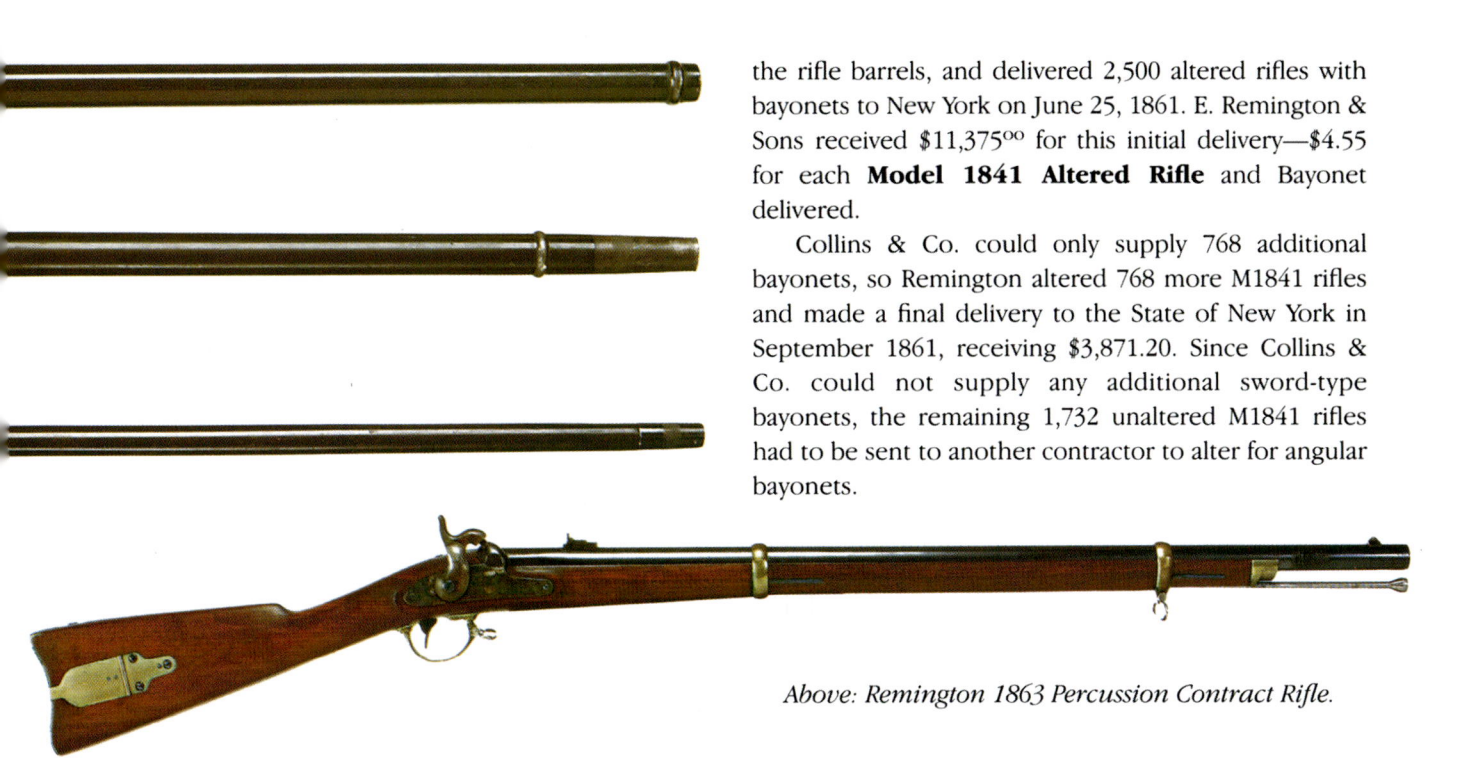

the rifle barrels, and delivered 2,500 altered rifles with bayonets to New York on June 25, 1861. E. Remington & Sons received $11,375.00 for this initial delivery—$4.55 for each **Model 1841 Altered Rifle** and Bayonet delivered.

Collins & Co. could only supply 768 additional bayonets, so Remington altered 768 more M1841 rifles and made a final delivery to the State of New York in September 1861, receiving $3,871.20. Since Collins & Co. could not supply any additional sword-type bayonets, the remaining 1,732 unaltered M1841 rifles had to be sent to another contractor to alter for angular bayonets.

Above: Remington 1863 Percussion Contract Rifle.

made with internal hammers, but were later improved with a rod driving the firing pin. Serial numbers for the rimfire cane guns started at 1 and went to over 1748. Production probably ceased sometime prior to 1886, when times were hard for E. Remington & Sons. The new proprietors, who named the company Remington Arms Company in 1888, saw no reason to resume production of cane guns. Not many Remington percussion and rimfire (Thomas Patent) cane guns were ever made—and fewer than 2,000 were produced over a 27-year period.

U.S. Model 1841 "Mississippi" Rifle Alterations

On April 25, 1861, the Ordnance Department sent 5,000 Model 1841 Mississippi rifles to the State of New York to arm its hastily assembled volunteer troops. All of the rifles were of Remington manufacture from the 1850s. Since the original Mississippi rifles had no provisions for bayonets, The New York Agency ordnance officials wanted them altered to take sword-type bayonets. Therefore, on May 30, 1861, New York signed a contract with E. Remington & Sons for "furnishing and fitting sword bayonets" to all 5,000 of the newly acquired Model 1841 rifles.

Remington went to Collins & Company of Collinsville, Connecticut, to procure 5,000 brass-handled, sword-type bayonets. Unfortunately, Collins was overtaxed in supplying bayonets to dozens of other arms contractors throughout New England, and could offer Remington only half what they needed. Nevertheless, Remington made the relatively simple alteration of attaching bayonet studs to the right sides of

Remington "Zouave" Rifles

On July 30, 1861, the Ordnance Department asked E. Remington & Sons to manufacture "10,000 stands of arms, .58 inch caliber, and to have three-leaf rear sight and a cupped ramrod, with sword bayonet stud similar to those of the Harpers' Ferry rifle model of 1855." This order arrived in Ilion during the funeral of Eliphalet Remington. Despite the sad times, the Remington brothers accepted the government's order, but were unable to deliver any rifles, as their machinery was tied up with fulfilling revolver contracts. When the Remington brothers saw that they were in danger of default, they requested a contract extension, which was granted. On August 11, 1862, this contract was re-issued for 10,000 **Harper's Ferry pattern rifles with sword bayonets**, caliber .58—all furnished with regular appendages—and packed 20 rifles and appendages in each box—at a cost of $17.00 for each arm, complete.

Remington acquired the machinery for the large job, and contracted with Collins & Co. to supply the sword bayonets and scabbards. The first delivery of 500 finished rifles and bayonets was made on April 18, 1863, and deliveries continued at a rate of one thousand rifles per month. In all 7,501 rifles were delivered on this contract before it expired.

On December 13, 1863, Remington was awarded yet another contract for Harper's Ferry rifles—this one for 2,500 rifles and bayonets at $17.00 for each arm, complete, with deliveries to be completed by January 8, 1864. All rifles, 2,500 rifles, including many 2nd class arms, were delivered between December 23, 1863, and January 8, 1864. Present-day collectors refer to these as **Remington Zouave rifles**, not Harper's Ferry rifles,

Above: Detail of lock from 1863 Percussion Rifle. It has US/Remington and federal eagle markings.

Above: Lock detail from Zouave Rifle dated 1863.

Above: Inspectors cartouches on left side of stock.

Above: Inspectors cartouches on left side of stock.

but the significance of this name change is not known. These rifles are often encountered in near-new condition, implying that most, if not all, were never issued to Federal troops during the Civil War.

U.S. Model 1863 Springfield-Pattern Muskets

Remington was awarded a contract on August 20, 1862, for 40,000 **Springfield Rifle-Muskets** at 16^{00} each. Unfortunately, this contract had to be abrogated, because Remington claimed that they could not deliver the muskets at the price specified. On December 14, 1863, E. Remington & Sons received a new contract from the Ordnance Department—for 40,000 Springfield-pattern rifle-muskets at 18^{00} each. More than twenty-one months would elapse until Remington was able to deliver their first muskets in late May 1864. When this contract expired on December 31, 1864, the Armory had delivered only 10,000 muskets—only one-fourth of the total contracted for. Remington petitioned for and received extensions on this contract, and managed to double production in 1865. Despite the cessation of hostilities in April 1865, Remington was one of the few armories that would be allowed to complete its contract. All 40,000 muskets were finally delivered by March 1866. Since the Ordnance Department contended that there were problems with the manufacturing quality, Remington was paid for five different classes of these arms, the lowest being 16^{00}. The order for 40,000 muskets was eventually worth over $700,000 to the Remington brothers and to Ilion's economy.

Remington Split-Breech Carbines

In the first years of the war, Remington had large-frame revolvers, but no proprietary long arms of its own to manufacture for the government. It would be Joseph Rider who would design a breech loading, single-shot long arm for Remington—later to be called the Remington Split Breech Carbine. Rider obtained U.S. Patent #40,887 on December 8, 1863, for a breech loading system with the block "swinging backward and downward". While it appeared similar to Leonard Geiger's U.S. Patent #37,501 issued on January 27, 1863,

Above: Remington Zouave Rifle.

Above: Remington 1863 Zouave Percussion Rifle with sword bayonet.

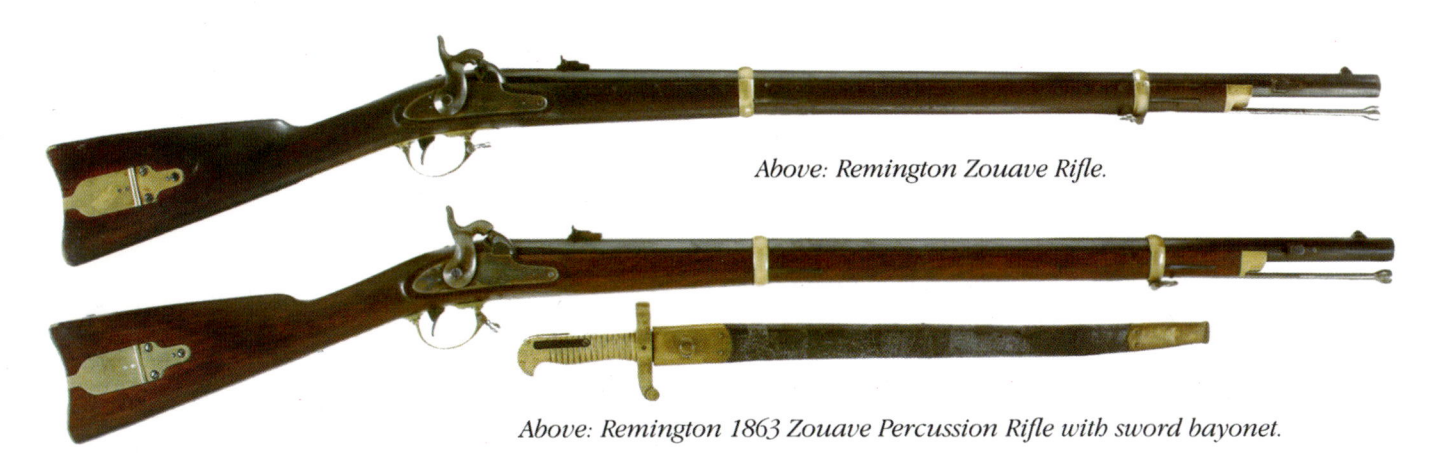

it was sufficiently different to warrant a separate patent. Even though Rider's patent drawings portray a split-breech pistol, Rider was encouraged to design a long arm on this unique breech system which would be saleable to the military. The result was a prototype carbine which the Remingtons brought to Washington, D.C., hoping to interest ordnance officials in its merit. There they were introduced to Samuel Norris, a Springfield businessman. Norris later recalled:

In Washington I was shown the first successful Rider arm by Samuel Remington, and I at once offered him three dollars royalty per arm, for the exclusive right to manufacture it. The firm gave me the exclusive right for two years, but I had to furnish the capital required.

The Remington factories in Ilion and Utica were so busy with work on percussion revolver, rifle and musket contracts, that they simply did not have the room, or machinery to devote to the manufacture of an entirely new firearm. Therefore, Remington allowed Norris to secure a contract with the government for Rider carbines, and then interest another manufacturer to make the firearms. This was a pretty tall order, and one fraught with risk for Norris. The Remingtons were given a contract for 1,000 carbines for further trial. Norris later said:

The policy of the Ordnance Department was to order 1,000 arms of all meritorious breech loading systems, and an order for that number of Remingtons was given. I gave the Savage Revolving Fire Arms Company of Middletown, Connecticut, an order for 10,000, as Savage required an order of importance before they would undertake the work. It was a risky thing to order so large a number of a new and untried arm, with only 1,000 ordered by the government, but my confidence in the arm was very great.

On March 13, 1864, Remington returned the signed contract for the .44 caliber **Remington Small-Frame, Split-Breech Carbines** to the Chief of Ordnance, Brigadier-General George D. Ramsay. The Remingtons, dutifully, gave Norris the go-ahead to engage the manufacturing capacity of the Savage Armory. Knowing that an increase in the government's order would increase their royalty profits, the Remingtons offered to supply the government 50,000 Remington-Rider carbines, a substantial increase on the original contract for 1,000. The Chief of Ordnance declined. Meanwhile, the Savage Revolving Arms Company began tooling up to manufacture 10,000 carbines for Norris. As only 1,000 of the 10,000 carbines were contracted for by the government, Norris must have worried about how he would pay for the unsold guns. Because of production delays the Ordnance Department extended the date for the initial delivery of carbines until December 31, 1864.

In September 1864, the Ordnance Department decided on a uniform rimfire cartridge for all future carbines made for Federal cavalry service. The cartridge was designated the Springfield caliber .50 rimfire cartridge, but we recognize it today as the 56-50 Spencer. The initial order for 1,000 Remington-Rider .44 caliber split-breech carbines was unaffected. On October 24, 1864, the Ordnance Department offered Remington a contract for 15,000 **Remington Large-Frame, Split-Breech Carbines**, .50 caliber at $23^{00} apiece—$345,000 for the entire contract. However, it would take the Savage Armory almost a year to make the first delivery of these large-frame carbines.

On October 14, 1864, E. Remington & Sons purchased half of Joseph Rider's patent rights for his upcoming new improvement in firearms—a true rolling-block design—U.S. Patent #45,123 of November 15, 1864. Two months later, on December 16, 1864, E. Remington & Sons purchased half of Rider's patent rights for another upcoming new improvement in firearms—#45,797, issued January 3, 1865, for a breech loading rifle. Not wishing any hint of infringement upon Leonard Geiger's U.S. Patent #37,501, issued January 27, 1863, for a rolling block type action, Remington struck up a deal on September 1, 1865, with Charles C. Alger, former partner of Leonard Geiger. A signed contract meant that Remington would pay a royalty of 50¢ for each Remington-Rider split-breech firearm made.

Since the Savage Armory was having problems with manufacturing the 1,000 small-frame carbines for the government, Norris thought it prudent to ask for a larger contract. As the Federal cavalry was much in need of quality carbines, the Army Ordnance Department accepted Norris's offer and gave him a revised contract for 5,000 small-frame, .44 caliber, split-breech carbines on January 19, 1865, at $17⁰⁰ apiece. The initial order for 1,000 was absorbed into this new contract, and all carbines were eventually delivered between March 30th and June 30, 1865.

None of these split-breech carbines were actually used in the Civil War, as all were delivered too late to see action. The Savage Armory completed the entire small-frame order before re-tooling their machinery to produce the large-frame carbines. In fact, the first large-frame carbines were not delivered until September 30, 1865. Despite less than favorable test reports, the Ordnance Department thought enough of the Remington large-frame, split-breech carbines to let the Savage Armory fulfill the entire order for 15,000. Many other private contractors did not fare as well, as the end of the war meant an end to the government need for weapons. Savage continued to ship carbines, the last of which were delivered on May 24, 1866.

Remington Revolving Breech Rifles

In 1865 Remington began the manufacture of **Remington Revolving Breech Rifles**, based on the design of the Civil War era .36 caliber and .44 caliber revolvers. These were newly made rifles, and did not share parts with the smaller-frame revolvers. These 6-shot rifles had octagon or part-round/part-octagon barrels of various lengths. As many as 750 of these unusual rifles were sold through the mid-1870s.

Remington-Beals Single-Shot Rifles

Fordyce Beals invented a single-shot, breech loading rifle that would bear his name—the **Remington-Beals Single-Shot Rifle**. The breech of this rifle is opened by lowering the under-lever, which slides the barrel forward. Two chamberings of this rifle were made between 1866 and 1872—.32 Long rimfire and .38 Long rimfire. Both iron (early production) and brass-framed receivers were made. This under-powered rifle was not very popular, and fewer than 900 were made in seven years of production.

Remington's Improved New Model Revolving Rifles

Besides these handguns, in the early 1870s, E. Remington & Sons also converted several hundred Remington Revolving .36 caliber and .44 caliber Percussion Rifles to fire .38 Long rimfire and .44 Long rimfire ammunition. Period advertising called these firearms **Remington's Improved New Model Revolving Rifles**.

Remington "Rolling Block" Rifles & Carbines

Joseph Rider had developed the Remington split-breech system during the Civil War, adapting it to both small-frame and large-frame carbines. Concurrently, he continued to experiment with various methods of locking the breech and on December 16, 1864, submitted a new design to the patent office. On January 3, 1865, he was issued the first patent for what would evolve into the famous Remington rolling block action, #45,797. The term "rolling block" refers to a breech system comprised of hammer piece that is brought to cocking position, and a semi-circular breechblock that is rotated back to open the breech for extracting the spent shell casing and for insertion of a new cartridge.

The Remingtons had a winner in Rider's rolling block, breech loading system. They encouraged Rider's developments and sought to interest Ordnance department officials in their new design. Finally news came that provided hope to the Remingtons and to other gun manufacturers. An Ordnance Board was to convene in Washington, D.C., in March 1866, as the U.S. Army wanted to adopt the very best breech loading rifle and carbine then available, and chose the most appropriate method of converting hundreds of thousands of muzzle loading muskets to breechloaders. If only the U.S. Army would adopt a Remington System, this could be the solution to their immediate cash flow problems and the relative inactivity of their works.

The Navy Bureau of Ordnance was firmly convinced of the merits of the Remington rolling block System. Therefore, it was only fitting that they would want rolling blocks when they needed carbines for shipboard service. On October 22, 1867, the Remingtons signed the contract to fabricate 5,000 **Remington Model 1867 Rolling Block Navy Carbines**, and they were delivered to the U.S. Navy between July 1868 and February 1869.

The Navy also needed 500 cadet-sized rifles for their midshipmen in Annapolis, and again they turned to Remington. On January 15, 1868, the Navy Bureau of Ordnance ordered 500 Remington rolling block breech loading systems from Remington. These were fabricated and then fitted to .50 caliber barrels sent from Springfield Armory. A total of 501 barreled-actions were shipped on June 25, 1868, where they were made by Springfield into finished **Remington Model 1867 Rolling Block Cadet Rifles**.

Above: USN Remington/Springfield Model 1870 Rolling Block Rifle.

On November 7, 1867, the Ordnance Department ordered 500 rolling block breech loading systems from Remington, at $7⁰⁰ apiece. At the time these were referred to as Remington Breech Loading Rifled Muskets, but today they are called **Springfield-Remington Transformed Rifle Muskets—Long**, because of their 39" long barrels. Nine days later Dyer ordered Springfield Armory to be prepared to receive these Remington Systems and use them to convert 500 Springfield rifle muskets to breechloaders. Remington convinced Dyer that they were better able to attach the 39-inch barrels to the systems than Springfield. The barreled-actions were completed in the spring of 1868 and shipped to Springfield Armory, where the conversions were completed. In August 1869, 500 of the original Springfield-Remington Transformed Rifle Muskets—Long had the barrels shortened to 36 inches and serial numbers were stamped on top of the breech–called **Springfield-Remington Transformed Rifle Muskets —Short**.

After the conclusion of the Civil War, southern states had no organized militias. In March 1869, South Carolina organized its first National Guard, and acquired a number of different weapons including 5,000 muskets transformed to breech loader with Remington rolling block actions. Dubbed **Remington Transformed Rifle Muskets—Long**, E. Remington & Sons made these 5,000 for South Carolina and an untold number for other buyers from the late 1860s through the 1880s. They are distinguished by the use of surplus Springfield Rifle Musket or Enfield Rifle Musket parts, including .58 caliber, 39-inch barrels. The transformed rifle muskets were chambered for .58 caliber centerfire ammunition, although some .58 rimfire weapons were also made. E. Remington & Sons also manufactured thousands of **Remington Transformed Rifle Muskets—Short**, which were identical to Remington Transformed Rifle Muskets—Long, but for their 36-inch long barrels.

Following a positive showing at the St. Louis Ordnance Board in 1869–70, the Army Ordnance Department decided to test a number of Remington rolling block carbines and rifles under actual field conditions. In late 1870, Springfield Armory assembled 313 carbines and 1,008 rifles, utilizing rolling block frames and breech pieces made by E. Remington & Sons. These **Springfield-Remington Model 1870 Trials Carbines and Rifles** were issued to cavalry and infantry units on the frontier, and field reports on these .50 caliber single-shot weapons were mostly favorable.

In early 1872, Springfield Armory fabricated 10,000 **Springfield-Remington Model 1871 Rolling Block Rifles**. Like the earlier Springfield–Remington M1870 Trial Carbines and Rifles, these were also chambered for the .50-70 Government centerfire cartridge.

Commencing in March 1869, the Navy Bureau of Ordnance tested dozens of weapons systems, and eventually settled on the .50 caliber Remington rolling block rifle as their choice to arm both the U.S. Navy and the U.S. Marines. Barrels were to be bright for the navy and browned for the marines. On December 6, 1869, the Chief of the Bureau of Ordnance ordered 10,000 Remington rolling block actions which Springfield Armory would use to manufacture **Springfield-Remington Model 1870 Navy Rifles—Type I**. After considerable dialog, it was decided in February 1870, that Springfield Armory would make the complete firearm, paying E. Remington & Sons a $1⁰⁰ royalty on each rifle made. Distinctive sword-type bayonets and scabbards were to be made by Ames of Chicopee, Massachusetts.

Poultney & Trimble, American agents for the French Government, acquired all 10,000 of these new rifles, as it was alleged that the rear sight was perilously close to the chamber, rendering the arms unsafe for U.S. Navy use. The rifles were actually acquired and shipped to arm the French infantry in the 1870–71 Franco-Prussian War. Realizing a tidy profit from this transaction, the Navy reordered an improved rifle and Springfield Armory made more than 12,000 **Springfield-Remington Model 1870 Navy Rifles—Type II** in 1871.

On November 16, 1871, the Governor of New York ordered 15,000 **Remington Rolling Block New York State Rifles** and bayonets for his state's National Guard infantrymen. The new rifles were chambered for the .50-70 Government centerfire cartridge, and are distinguished by a high-profile hammer spur and a locking-action, in which the hammer automatically drops to half-cock when the breechblock is closed. It must be brought to full cock to fire. On May 29, 1873, New York ordered an additional 4,500 rifles with bayonets and 1,500 **Remington Rolling Block New York State Carbines**.

Foreign Orders for Remington "Rolling Block" Military Firearms

No firearm system had such an economic impact on Remington as did their rolling block rifles, carbines, shotguns and pistols. This system brought E. Remington & Sons from near post-war bankruptcy to unprecedented prosperity. It would be the sales of hundreds of thousands of weapons to foreign governments that would result in a massive building effort in Ilion, and employment of more than 1,500 workers.

The first government to be shown the new rolling block rifle was the Austrian Grand Ordnance Commission on September 20, 1866. For nine days the rifle was subjected to the most grueling of trials, all which were successfully passed by Remington's new gun. The Commission recommended ordering 50,000 Remington rifles for adoption as the primary weapon for its troops, and the Emperor was invited to try the gun himself. Unfortunately, the Commission handed the Emperor rimfire cartridges made in their own facility, and the one loaded into the Remington rifle failed to fire. The shortsighted leader rebuffed the Remington firearm, opting to arm his troops with the Werndel system instead.

Denmark

Remington was informed that a Danish Ordnance Commission was coming to America to procure a large order of breech loading rifles for its infantry. Trials resulted in an order in April 1867 for 20,000 **Remington Model 1867 Danish Rolling Block Rifles** (at $13.42 each). This order represented Remington's first sizeable order for weapons since the cessation of the Civil War. On August 27th, Denmark ordered an additional 10,000 rifles and 1,800 **Remington M1867 Danish Rolling Block Carbines** (at $18.50 each). And finally in May 1868 an additional 10,000 Remington rolling block rifles were ordered. These three contracts would bring more than $570,000 to the Remingtons. Later, Danish Ordnance would be given a license by E. Remington & Sons to manufacture rolling block rifles and carbines in Denmark, bringing additional revenues to Ilion's economy.

Sweden and Norway

On November 15, 1866, the Swedish-Norwegian Ordnance Commission met to select new breech loading arms for its troops. After extensive trials the Commission selected the new **Remington Model 1867 Swedish**

Above: Lieutenant Colonel George Armstrong Custer with "The King of the Forest". This elk was killed with Custer's Remington "rolling block" sporting rifle during the Yellowstone Expedition - September 1873.

Rolling Block Rifles to re-arm its army. On May 8, 1867, the King approved the Commission's recommendation for 10,000 Remington rifles chambered for Swedish 12.17mm rimfire cartridges and additional 20,000 breech systems later used to convert Swedish muskets to breechloaders. Swedish Ordnance Officials sought and received a license from Remington to manufacture the rolling blocks in Sweden. Consequently, manufacturing facilities were established at Husqvarna Vapenfabriks and at Carl Gustafs Stads Gevarsfaktori. The factories made Model 1867/68 Swedish rolling block military rifles, followed by successive years of production of such weapons as the M1867/71 and M1867/75. Military rifles, musketoons and carbines were made in Sweden on Remington's Rolling Block System.

Egypt

In 1867, E. Remington & Sons captured the Silver Medal for firearms at the Paris International Exposition. It was here that Remington's European sales official, Samuel Norris, met Khedive (Prince) Ismail of Egypt. The Remington rolling block compared favorably against the Martini-Henry military rifle, culminating in a contract for 60,000 **Remington Egyptian Rolling Block Rifles** which was signed on June 30, 1869.

Work on this large order commenced immediately, and Remington spent many hundreds of thousands of dollars enlarging their Ilion facility and ordering large stocks of raw materials. To do this, E. Remington & Sons took out large loans. The initial contract was amended in 1870, with only 10,000 rifles having been delivered. The balance of 40,000 had been canceled by the Egyptian Government. The undelivered rifles were diverted to France for arming their troops in the Franco-Prussian War. Subsequent orders were received for an additional 55,000 Egyptian rifles in 1874, and later an order for Remington military carbines. It is believed that by 1880, more than 250,000 Remington firearms of all types had been shipped to Egypt, although payments had not kept up to products received. Much was at risk when Egyptian authorities began to default on payments. Egypt's debts escalated with concurrent military defeats in its war in Ethiopia. Egyptian stocks and bonds plummeted in value, loans dried up, and Egypt was unable to meet its financial obligations, including those to Remington's Armory. By 1877, Egypt's debt to Remington exceeded $1,000,000. Through the interaction of American Consulate Authorities Egypt eventually paid Remington about 66% of all monies owed, and the Khedive was eventually deposed in 1879. E. Remington & Sons would never recover from its disastrous dealings with Egypt.

The Papal States

In 1867, the Remingtons met the Nagant brothers, Emile and Leon, owners of Fabrique d' Armes Emile et Leon Nagant, in Liege Belgium. Soon thereafter, Remington licensed Nagant to manufacture weaponry based on Rider's rolling block system, receiving 4.5 francs royalty per rifle. In September 1867, Papal forces in Rome communicated with the Central Belgian Committee for the Defense of the Holy See to procure weaponry for its Zouaves Pontificaux armed forces. Concurrently, the Acting War Minister for the Papacy, General Ermanno Kanzler, was shown the new Remington rolling block system, and ordered the Commission to order 5,000 .50 caliber Remington-licensed Nagant Model 1868 Infantry Rifles equipped with sword-type bayonets—the modern term is **Nagant-made Remington Papal Guard Rolling Block Rifles**. All were delivered to Rome by October 1868, attesting to Nagant's incredibly efficient operation. Later musketoon-length rifles with the same bayonets were also shipped to Rome. In late 1869, the Papal Gendarmeria (the Papal police) were issued **Nagant-made Remington Papal Guard Rolling Block Carbines**, each equipped with bayonets.

Concurrently, the Papacy ordered 5,000 Remington rolling blocks from the arms manufacturer, Westley Richards of Birmingham, England, who were also licensed by Remington to manufacture rolling block arms. The cost of these weapons was underwritten by the French Catholic Organization, which did not want to place an order with a Belgian industry which was in direct competition with a French industry. All 5,000 British-made rifles equipped with long-blade yataghan bayonets were shipped to Rome, but were said to be of such inferior construction that "eight gunsmiths from Liege had to come to Rome to get them in working condition." No further orders for **Westley Richards-made Remington Papal Guard Rolling Block Rifles** were placed with the British firm.

Belgium

Although the Remington System was never adopted by Belgian military authorities, the Nagant Brothers Armory made many tens of thousands of rolling blocks for other countries. Besides the 10,000+ rifles, musketoons and carbines for the Papal forces, Nagant manufactured Remington–licensed weapons and sporting rifles and shotguns for others:

- The tiny country of **Luxembourg** purchased approximately 5,000 Remington-licensed military rolling block rifles from Nagant between 1869 and 1871. These rifles were chambered for the Swiss .41 caliber rimfire cartridge.
- In 1870, **The Netherlands** (Holland) adopted the Remington Rolling Block Carbine with which to arm its cavalry, sappers and mounted police force. These three distinctly different carbines (chambered for the 11.3x50R cartridge) were manufactured by Nagant under license agreement with E. Remington & Sons, and were delivered in 1873 and the following year, including the Cavalry Carbine (Cavalerie-Karabijn) made without provisions for bayonet, but with saddle rings; the Sappers Musketoon (Sapp-kar) with cruciform-bladed angular bayonet and sling swivels; and the Mounted Police Carbine (Marechaussee-Karabijn) equipped with folding bayonet, double saddle rings and sling swivels.
- The **Principality of Monaco** was armed with a quantity of Remington-licensed rolling block musketoon rifles manufactured by Nagant with the crest of the royal family.

Arms maker Francotte of Liege, Belgium was also successful in negotiating a license agreement with E. Remington & Sons to manufacture rolling block firearms. Francotte made military weapons for Uruguay and rolling blocks for sporting purposes.

Cuba and Spain

On March 28, 1868, Spanish authorities in Cuba signed a contract with Remington for 8,000 **Remington Civil**

Guard Rolling Block Rifles (later increased to 10,000 rifles). The two-band short rifles were intended for the Cuban Civil Guard, the official militia of this Spanish-possession island government. By 1872, 72,000 Remington .43 Spanish rolling block rifles and Civil Guard guns had been ordered for Cuban Civil Guard use.

The Royal Spanish Ordnance Commission conducted extensive trials in Spain which concluded in the summer of 1870. It was the Remington System that proved victorious. On March 24, 1871, the Commission recommended both Remington rifles and carbines, and therefore, subsequent Spanish rifles were referred to as **Remington Model 1871 Spanish Rolling Block Rifles and Carbines**. However, despite this acceptance Spain was not to order Remington rolling block firearms and bayonets until September 1873, when Samuel Norris secured an order for 50,000 rifles and carbines. This large order was completed in April 1875. Although contract order information for Spain is fragmentary, it is believed that Spanish Ordnance Authorities would eventually order 130,000 Remington rolling block rifles, Civil Guard guns and carbines directly from Remington.

Spain also negotiated a contract with E. Remington & Sons whereby Remington System rolling blocks could be manufactured in Spanish Arsenals. Many tens of thousands of Remington M1871, M1874, M1881 and M1871/89 infantry rifles, musket conversions, dragoon rifles, musketoon rifles, police short rifles, cadet rifles and cavalry carbines were made at Oviedo Arsenal, at Ritter Y Bock, and at other Spanish facilities.

Japan

In the summer of 1867, a Japanese Army Officer visited Remington's Armory in Ilion and took a liking to the new rolling block weapon system. Subsequently, Ordnance officials from the Imperial Japanese Government ordered a total of 3,000 **Remington Japanese Rolling Block Rifles**, the first 1,500 of which were shipped in July 1868. A surviving example in the Remington Museum collection has many of the characteristics of the M1867 Swedish/Norwegian Rolling Block Rifle. It's 32-inch barrel chambers the Swedish 12.15mm rimfire cartridge. No other orders for rolling blocks were forthcoming from Japan.

Greece

In 1869, despite a recommendation from Greek ordnance officials favorable to Martini rifles, War Minister Spiros-Milios placed an order for 16,000 **Remington Greek Contract Rolling Block Rifles** with E. Remington & Sons. Additional trials culminated in an increased order for 15,000 more Remington rifles. However, France's war with Germany resulted in Remington diverting 15,000 of these newly completed rifles to French Arsenals, instead. On June 12, 1871, the French Government agreed to pay Remington 100 francs for each Greek rifle. In turn, Remington paid the Greek Government 22 francs for each rifle diverted to France, or a total of 330,000 francs, promising to make new rifles for Greece at a later date. This was an order that would never come. The Remington Museum has a Remington Greek Contract Rolling Block Rifle which has three barrel bands, a 35-inch barrel with a large sword bayonet lug on the right side near the muzzle and a half-inch tenon on the opposing side, a dished breechblock and linear extractor.

France

Although the French Government never adopted the Remington rolling block as its official arm, their relationship with E. Remington & Sons was to funnel hundreds of thousands of military weapons into the country in the years prior and during the Franco–Prussian War of 1871. Despite exhaustive trials of Remington rolling block weapons in 1866, '67 and '68, the French selected the Chassepot with which to arm its troops. Remington was persuaded to divert a large order of rolling block rifles which were being manufactured under contract to Egypt and to Greece, shipping them to French forces instead. Schuyler, Hartley & Graham also shipped many tens of thousands of weapons during this frantic one-year period.

Chile

In 1874, the Republica de Chile ordered 12,000 Remington rolling block rifles.

Peru

Peru ordered 5,000 Remington .43 caliber rolling block rifles from E. Remington & Sons in 1874. These were used five years later when Peru was at war with Chile between 1879 and 1883.

Puerto Rico

While a Spanish Colony, Puerto Rico ordered 10,000 Remington rolling block rifles from E. Remington & Sons in 1874.

Argentina

Argentina purchased an undisclosed quantity of Remington .43 Spanish and .50-70 Export Rolling Block Rifles in the early 1870s, and they were used with effectiveness in the Battle of Naembe on January 26, 1871.

Remington Rifles and Carbines • 53

Above: Studio photograph of "Touch-The-Clouds, Minneconjou chief, taken in 1879. Speculation has it that it was Custer's rifle taken at the Little Big Horn in June 1876.
Top of page: Above Rolling Block Carbine with photo of Mexican 'Rurales' circa 1910.

Later, a quantity of Remington .50-70 Spanish Export Rolling Block Carbines was received for Argentine cavalry troops. In 1876, more export rifles were ordered and it was evident that the ordnance officials were pleased with the simplicity and ease of handling of the Remington weapons. It was decided that Argentina would standardize the military arms for its infantry and cavalry by purchasing specially designed Remington rolling block rifles and carbines. The result was an order in 1879, for 20,000 **Modelo Argentino 1879 Rifles** (equipped with German-produced sword-type bayonets) and 5,000 **Modelo Argentino 1879 carbines**, both chambered for the .43 Spanish bottle-neck centerfire cartridge.

Mexico

Between 1869 and 1873, the Republic of Mexico acquired an assortment of 6,268 Remington rifles, carbines and revolvers. It is believed that a number of these were rolling block conversions of muskets to breechloaders. In 1874, Mexico purchased 10,000 **Remington Mexican Model 1871 Rolling Block Rifles**, which were said to be the first "modern arms" ordered for its poorly armed military forces. Later the same year Mexico ordered another 40,000 rifles and carbines.

On September 7, 1877, a contract was signed by General Pedro Ozagon, Mexican Secretary of War and Navy (sic) to acquire 3,000 **Remington .43 Spanish Rolling Block Rifles** with angular bayonets, 1,000 **Remington .50 caliber Rolling Block Carbines**, and a large number of cartridges for both from E. Remington & Sons. Yet another contract was signed on June 25, 1879, but the details are not known at this time. In 1881,

Above: The firing line at Creedmoor during the third International Match, September 1876. Note the unusual back firing position by the shooter.

Mexico established Fabrica Nacional De Armas to produce military weaponry, and secured a licensing agreement with E. Remington & Sons to manufacture rolling block firearms. A number of weapons were made here, including an 11mm rolling block rifle, the Ramirez lever-action rifle, and the M1884 rolling block rifle. By 1881, it was reported that Mexico had received over 100,000 Remington rolling block weapons. Yet another contract with Remington was signed on May 12, 1884, the details of which are not known.

Other South and Central American Countries

Remington established effective marketing and sales forces throughout the United States and the principal countries of Europe. Having no such establishment in Central and South America, Philo, Samuel and Eliphalet III turned to the New York City military goods purveyor Schuyler, Hartley & Graham. Starting in the 1870s, the New York City establishment was to sell more than 144,000 Remington rolling block rifles and carbines to government military forces, rebel contingents, commercial organizations and to individual buyers. Tens of thousands of orders were efficiently handled by Schuyler, Hartley & Graham, who sold weapons on consignment from Remington, as well as those which they owned outright. Countries known to use Remington rolling block weapons included Bolivia, Brazil, Chile, Columbia, the Dominican Republic, Ecuador, El Salvador, Guatemala, Honduras, Nicaragua, Panama, Paraguay, Peru, and Puerto Rico.

In the decades that would follow, Schuyler, Hartley & Graham contracted with arms establishments such as Starr's Armory, J.R. Frazier, and Wm. F. Coxford, to repair some arms and to modify others. The quality of the work done by these

Below: Heavy Barrel Rolling Block Rifle.

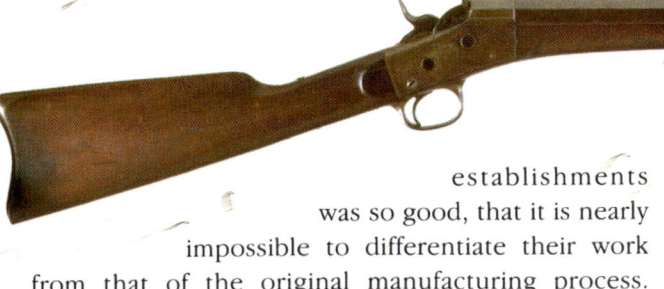

Above: Remington Rolling Block Sporting Rifle.

establishments was so good, that it is nearly impossible to differentiate their work from that of the original manufacturing process. Remington transformed muskets were made into carbines, export rolling block carbines were fitted with sabre-bayonet lugs, barrels in the white were browned, and surplus rolling block pistols were made into cadet rifles. Anything and everything was possible, which will be the bane of the modern-day collector who has thought that his unusual weapon was a Remington prototype—not so, as it probably was a Hartley & Graham modification.

Remington No.1 Sporting and Target Rifles

While Remington put most of their effort into producing military rolling block rifles and carbines, it was only logical that the action could be utilized in a sporting rifle configuration. It would not be until 1868 that Remington rolling block sporting rifles were first made on what would later be called their **No.1 action**. In all, Remington made about 13,000 **No.1 Sporting and Target Rifles** in a nineteen-year period.

No.1 Sporting and Target rifles were made with a great variety of optional features, offered at extra cost, including: fore-end and pistol-grip checkering; Beach combination front sights; Buckhorn and/or Rocky Mountain rear sights; single-set triggers; longer barrel lengths; fancy stocks; sling swivels; and various patterns of engraving.

E. Remington & Sons also manufactured a number of specialty rolling block sporting rifles, including:

- **Short Range No.1 Sporting Rifle**
  Manufactured 1877 through 1886, chambered for rimfire or short-range centerfire ammunition, octagonal or part-round/part-octagonal barrel, short range tang-mounted rear sight with or without rear barrel sight, blade-type or globe front sight, single or single set-trigger.

- **Mid-Range No.1 Sporting Rifle**
  Manufactured 1877 through 1886, chambered for centerfire ammunition, octagonal or part-round/part-octagonal barrel, mid-range tang-mounted rear sight with or without rear barrel sight, blade-type or globe front sight, single or single set-trigger.

- **Long Range "Creedmoor" No.1 Sporting Rifle**
  Manufactured from 1873 through 1886, chambered for .44-90, .44-100 and .44-105 bottleneck and straight-case cartridges, part-round/part-octagonal barrel, globe front sight, long-range tang-mounted sight, pistol-grip stock, shotgun-style butt plate, and single trigger.

- **Hunter's Rifle**
  Manufactured from 1877 to the 1880s, with plain open sights, standard sporting stock and fore-end, .38, .40, .44 or .50 caliber rimfire or centerfire ammunition.

- **Black Hills Rifle**
  Manufactured only from 1877 to 1878, with No.1 military-style receiver, pinched front sight and step-adjustable rear, standard sporting stock and fore-end, round 28-inch barrel, .45-60 or .45-70 centerfire ammunition.

- **Adirondack Rifle**
  First advertised in 1871 by Schuyler, Hartley & Graham. Chambered for the .45-50 Peabody sporting centerfire, bottlenecked cartridge, fixed sights, straight stock, 34-inch octagonal barrel, and rounded butt plate.

- **Buffalo Rifle**
  Manufactured only in 1872, utilizing military rolling block action and round barrel. Offered only in .50-70 Govt caliber. Open sights. Wood snaubel on forend tip.

- **Deer Rifle**
  Manufactured since 1873, with 24-inch round barrel, sling swivel, and chambered for .46 Long rimfire ammunition.

Above: Remington Rolling Block Creedmoor Rifle.

Above: Remington Model 1-½ Rolling Block Rifle.

Remington No. 1½ Sporting Rifles

Remington's Rolling Block No.1½ Sporting Rifle was a smaller variation of the No.1 sporting action, as it had a thinner receiver and resulting lower weight. The No.1½ Sporter was first offered to the public in the 1885 E. Remington & Sons Sporting Arms Catalog, as sold by D.H. Lamberson & Co., Chicago. This rifle was intended for lower power rimfire and centerfire cartridges, from as small as the .22 caliber rimfire to as large as the .44-40 W.C.F. It was an inexpensive rifle, and the only options were extra sights, longer barrel lengths, single-set trigger, and part-round/part-octagon barrel.

Production of the No.1½ was interrupted briefly during E. Remington & Son's period of receivership (1886–88). Production resumed by mid-1889, and continued through 1897. At least 4,200 No.1½ Sporting Rifles were made over a ten-year period.

Remington No.2 Sporting Rifles

The **Remington Rolling Block No.2 Sporting Rifle** was first listed in the March 1873 Price List of E. Remington & Sons, intended to be a lightweight alternative to the No.1½ Sporting Rifle. This rifle was made in a variety of rimfire (.22 to .38 caliber) and centerfire (.22 Maynard Extra-Long to .38-40) cartridges. Its primary distinguishing characteristics are its smaller-sized frame, the curved rear sides of the frame where it joins the stock, and a "perch-belly" stock. Except for the tangs, the No.2 rolling block receiver is nearly identical to that of the Remington Model 1871 Army Pistol. At least 42,700 No.2 Sporting Rifles were made over a thirty-seven-year period, interrupted only during the two-year company receivership.

Remington-Keene Rifles & Carbines

Remington realized that they needed to develop a repeating rifle to compete in military trials against other repeaters in the 1870s, and to compete in the civilian market against the formidable Winchester Model 1873 rifle. John W. Keene was a Newark, New Jersey, inventor who began work on a bolt-action, magazine-fed repeating rifle in the early 1870s. In the years that followed, Keene perfected his rifle, receiving nine separate U.S. Patents for his gun.

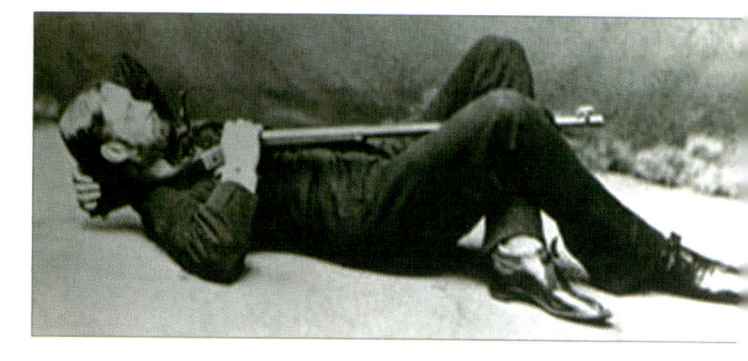

Above: A long range shooter firing a Remington No.1 "Creedmoor" target rifle in the unusual "back position".

Below: Remington Keene Sporting Rifle.

Full manufacturing commenced in 1879, even though the rifle's inventor, John W. Keene, died unexpectedly on October 4th. By mid-1880 a variety of military and sporting Keene rifles and carbines were offered for sale, including:

- **Remington-Keene Repeating Carbine**—with 20-inch round barrel and straight-grip stock and a fore-end held by a single barrel band. The tubular magazine held six .45-70 GOVT centerfire cartridges. In 1880, the Keene Carbine cost $22.00 each.
- **Remington-Keene Repeating Army Rifle**—with 32-inch round barrel and straight-grip stock and a fore-end held by two barrel bands. Cleaning rod on left side of fore-end. The tubular magazine held nine .45-70 GOVT centerfire cartridges. In 1880, the Keene Army Rifle cost

Remington Rifles and Carbines • 57

24^{00} with angular bayonet, and 22^{00} without.
- **Remington-Keene Repeating Navy Rifle**—with 29-inch round barrel and straight-grip stock and a fore-end held by two barrel bands. Cleaning rod on left side of fore-end. The tubular magazine held nine .45-70 GOVT centerfire cartridges. In 1880, the Keene Navy Rifle cost 26^{00} with sword-type bayonet, and 22^{00} without. On April 16, 1880, the U.S. Navy Bureau of Ordnance ordered 250 of these rifles.
- **Remington-Keene Frontier Rifle**—with 24-inch round barrel and straight-grip stock and a fore-end held by a single barrel band. The tubular magazine held eight .45-70 GOVT centerfire cartridges. In 1880,

additional chambering for .40-60 centerfire sporting ammunition. The number of Keene firearms made during the 1880s is not known, complicated by the absence of E. Remington & Sons production and shipping records. Relatively few were produced, and unsold Keene firearms remained in inventory when the company went into receivership in 1886. The complicated Keene mechanism was difficult and thereby expensive to produce, adding to the company's woes. Many tens of thousands of dollars had been tied up in machinery, tooling, materials, labor and advertising, all to no avail. Rather than help Remington's bottom line, Keene firearms drained it.

Above: Remington Hepburn 3A quality match rifle.

Above: Remington Hepburn Single Shot Rifle.

this Keene rifle cost 22^{00} each. In April, July and August 1880, Remington delivered a total of 600 of these rifles to the U.S. Interior Department for arming the Indian Police on reservations in the west, at a cost of $17.50 apiece.
- **Remington-Keene Hunter's or Sporting Rifle**—with 24-inch barrel and half pistol-grip stock and a fore-end held by a single barrel band. The tubular magazine held nine .45-70 GOVT centerfire cartridges. Four grades were offered, each with different sporting features, including: round or part-octagonal/part-round barrel; checkering; iron or hard rubber butt plates; and a variety of sporting or target sights. Prices were from 27^{00} for A Grade, to 60^{00} for D Grade rifles.

Beginning in 1882, Remington produced their Remington-Keene Army Rifle, Navy Rifle, and Carbine in both the .45-70 GOVT centerfire, and .43 Spanish centerfire ammunition. The Remington-Keene Frontier Rifle continued to be chambered for the .45-70, but the Remington-Keene Hunter's or Sporting Rifle had an

Remington-Hepburn No.3 Rifles

Lewis L. Hepburn was a New York gunsmith who left his shop to work at E. Remington & Sons Armory in the early 1870s. Hepburn's most famous contribution to his employer was the **Remington-Hepburn No.3 Rifle**. On October 7, 1879, Hepburn was issued U.S. Patent #220,285 for a unique falling block which was the basis for all Remington-Hepburn No.3 Rifles that would follow. The breechblock is lowered by a lever affixed to the right side of the receiver—a very strong action, capable of handling the most powerful of centerfire, black powder cartridges (and later, smokeless powder, high-power ammunition).

The Hepburn rifle was made in a variety of calibers, grades and configurations, including hunting, sporting and target rifles These were chambered only for centerfire ammunition, including those in .32, .38, .40, .44, .45 and .50 caliber. The types of Hepburn rifles that were available during the 1880s include:

- **Remington-Hepburn No.3 Hunter's or Sporting Rifle**—about 8,000 of these rifles were produced from 1880 to 1887, and from 1889 to 1904. Over this 24-year period, these rifles were chambered for 27 different centerfire, blackpowder cartridges. Rifles were available in a variety of fixed and adjustable front and rear (barrel-mounted) sights. In 1889, Remington Arms Company resumed production of several varieties of these rifles. Thirteen centerfire calibers were offered, from .32-20 Win to .45-90 Win. The rifles were priced from $15.00 to $17.00, and the only optional features were double-set triggers and extra-sights. Sales continued until 1904.

- **Remington-Hepburn No.3 Short Range Rifle**—a relatively small number of No.3 Short-Range Rifles were produced between 1880 and 1883, chambered for .38-40 centerfire ammunition. This rifle was offered with open sight or short-range target sight, including wind-gauge front sight with spirit level and tang-mounted, short-range Vernier sight. Swiss-Schuetzen-style butt plates were optional. Production of these popular, short-range, off-hand target rifles had slowed during receivership (1886–87), but resumed in earnest in 1889. Available in both A and B Quality, the price ranged from $23.00 to $40.00. The distinguishing features on this rifle are Swiss Schuetzen-style butt plates, and wind-gauge, spirit-level front sight and Vernier rear tang sight. Remington Arms Company sold these target rifles through 1903 in six different calibers from .32-40 Ballard & Marlin to .40-65 Rem straight centerfire.

- **Remington-Hepburn No.3 Mid-Range Rifle**—these rifles were produced between 1880 and 1887, with production resuming again from 1889 to 1904. They were chambered for nine different varieties of .38, .40 and .45 caliber, centerfire ammunition, and the rifles were offered with open sights or mid-range target sights, including wind-gauge front sights with spirit level and tang-mounted, short-range or mid-range Vernier sights. Production also resumed on these target rifles in 1889, which were intended for short and mid-range target shooting between 200 and 600 yards. Chambered for .40-45 and .40-65 Rem straight centerfire cartridges, they were offered with open or target sights, and cost $32.00 or more, depending on optional features. They were offered to the shooting public through 1904.

- **Remington-Hepburn No.3 Long Range Creedmoor Rifle**—only a few hundred of these specialty rifles were produced in the 1880s, as they were intended for long-range target shooting at Long Island's 1,000-yard target range. These rifles were specifically designed to conform with the National Rifle Association's Long-Range Creedmoor rules, including having barrels no longer than 34", a maximum weight under 10 pounds, and a single trigger. These precision target rifles were chambered for massive .44-77, .44-90 or .44-100 straight-case or bottleneck, centerfire cartridges. The rifle was offered in three grades, all with wind-gauge front sight with spirit level and tang-mounted, long-range Vernier sight. If desired by the shooter, a sight base could also be mounted on the rear butt stock top.

- **Remington-Hepburn No.3 Long Range Military Rifle**—this rifle was intended for long-range military Creedmoor matches, and was produced in very small quantities only from 1885 to 1887. Built in a military configuration, this rifle was chambered for Remington .44-85 centerfire ammunition, and was available with military-style or target-type sights. A military-configuration stock and full-length fore-end is held to the barrel with two barrel bands. Both straight-grip and pistol-grip variations were made.

- **Remington-Hepburn No.3 Match Rifle**—in 1882, E. Remington & Sons came out with a Hepburn target rifle intended for short-range, off-hand target shooting. This was a popular selling rifle for the company, as several thousand were produced through 1903, with production interrupted briefly by company receivership between 1886 and 1887. This target rifle was equipped with Vernier rear tang sight, a wind gauge, spirit level front sight, a Swiss-Schuetzen-style butt plate, and a two-piece stock with high cheek-piece.

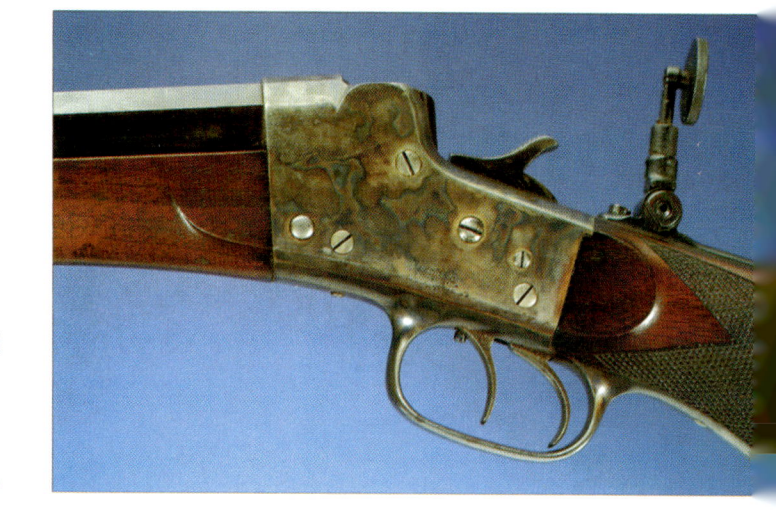

Top: Remington Model 3 Hepburn Single Shot Rifle.
Above: Detail of Rolling Block action and fitted tang sight.

Above: Remington Hepburn Single Shot Rifle.

Above: Remington-Lee 1882 Magazine Bolt Action Rifle.

These rifles were chambered for a variety of .25, .32, .38, and .40 caliber short-range and mid-range centerfire cartridges during nearly twenty-years of production.

E. Remington & Sons brought out the Hepburn rifle at a most difficult economic period for the company. Remington was overextended by manufacturing too many different products, and several legal decisions went against the corporation at the worst possible time. The popularity of the Hepburn rifle was rekindled after the company was sold in 1888. Surviving shipping records indicate that nearly 3,000 Hepburn rifles were made in the years following receivership. In 1903, Remington came out with a Hepburn No.3 Sporting Rifle capable of shooting modern, smokeless powder cartridges. The following year, Remington's Custom Shop produced an expensive, off-hand short-range Walker-Hepburn Rifle intended for the then-popular Schuetzen matches. Remington-Hepburn rifles were last advertised in 1904, with diminished sales through 1907. In all, more than 10,000 Hepburn rifles of all types were made over a 24-year period.

Remington-Lee Rifles & Carbines

James P. Lee was to become one of the 19th Century's greatest gun designers. He first became acquainted with E. Remington & Sons during the Civil War when 1,136 carbine-length barrels were made for Lee's company. Later, Lee traveled east to do developmental gun work at E. Remington & Sons Armory. On May 21st a contract was signed by Lee whereby his recent Martini-like gun patent was assigned to the Remingtons. Several of Lee's forthcoming patents were also assigned to the Remingtons for further improvements in the Martini-like action, and for a cartridge extractor, trigger lock and sling swivel.

Upon returning to Milwaukee, Lee designed a box magazine for which he was issued U.S. Patent #162,481 on April 27, 1875. Meanwhile, he continued work on a variety of firearms, and in mid-1878, submitted a bolt-action, magazine gun to the U.S. Ordnance Repeating Small Arms Trials at Springfield Armory. Unfortunately, Lee withdrew it from the trial before it could be evaluated. Importantly, this was the first mention of a Lee bolt-action gun. Lee returned to Ilion, and continued experiments with his bolt-action concept. On September 6, 1878, Lee was issued U.S. Patent #221,328 for a design that would become the famous Lee bolt-action rifle. Following months of correspondence with the Sharps Rifle Company of Bridgeport, Connecticut, in early 1879 Lee decided that he would set up his own company, the Lee Arms Company of Bridgeport, Connecticut, to market this arm. Since the Sharps company was very short of working capital, they could not give Lee the attention that was needed to manufacture and market a new firearm. The situation worsened through 1880, and by November the Sharps factory production department was shut down, leaving 300 incomplete Lee rifles.

Lee turned once again to the Remingtons for help, and on April 1, 1881, the Lee Arms Company entered into a manufacturing agreement with E. Remington & Sons to complete 300 Model 1879 Lee bolt-action Navy Rifles for the U.S. Navy. On April 5th, a second contract extended the relationship beyond the 300 partially finished rifles. The Lee Arms Company was to remain the selling agent. Remington workmen took Lee receivers made by Sharps, and military rolling block rifle parts made by Remington, and assembled finished rifles. Remington-Lee rifles include:

- **Model 1879 Lee Magazine Navy Contract Rifles**—Approximately 7,500 of these rifles were manufactured by E. Remington & Sons between 1881 and early 1884. Three hundred with angular bayonets were delivered to the U.S. Navy on January 12, 1882, in fulfillment of a contract signed years earlier. Many have called this the first modern military rifle. Blued, 29-inch barrels were stamped with various naval inspection marks, including an anchor. Each has a 5-round Lee-Diss detachable box magazine with 2 grooves on the side. Most of these rifles were chambered for the .45-70 GOVT cartridge, but some 4,000 were intended for foreign sales and made in .43 Spanish centerfire. All 4,000 were eventually sold to the Chinese Government on June 18, 1884.

- **Model 1882 Remington-Lee Magazine Military Rifle**—More than 32,000 of these rifles were

Above: US Navy Remington-Lee 1885 Bolt Action Rifle with Bayonet.

Above: Model 1899 Remington-Lee Magazine Bolt Action Rifle with bayonet.

manufactured from late summer 1884 to 1885. The first lot of 750 rifles in .45-70 were made for the U.S. Army, and had been recommended for trial by the 1882 U.S. Army Ordnance Board. A large contract for more than 15,000 rifles was signed with the Chinese Government, and were delivered from late 1884 to early 1885. The order was filled with both .45-70 GOVT and .43 Spanish rifles.

- **Model 1882 Remington-Lee Magazine Military Carbine**—An unknown number of these carbines were manufactured in 1884 and 1885, most going to the Chinese, in fulfillment of the large contract for military weapons.
- **Model 1882/85 Remington-Lee Military Conversion**—Between 1885 and 1887, an estimated 500 M1882 rifles and carbines were converted by Remington to take an improved M1885 Rem-Lee bolt with separate bolt head. The conversions include both .45-70 GOVT and .43 Spanish rifles and carbines, all of which have a 5-round Lee-Diss detachable box magazine with 2 grooves on the side.
- **Model 1882/85 Remington-Lee Sporting Rifle**—Although never cataloged by Remington, a very limited number of these rifles were made in 1885, with 30-inch part-octagon/part-round barrels chambered for .45-70 ammunition. One-piece sporting stocks have a fleur-de-lis pattern of checkering on the straight-wrist and fore-end.
- **Model 1885 Remington-Lee Magazine Military Rifle**—Despite Remington's entry into receivership, production commenced on this model in mid-1886. About 5,000 rifles in both .45-70 and .43 Spanish were fabricated before all firearms production was halted by April 1887. Three hundred of these rifles were purchased for the British Ordnance Trials in April 1887. New Zealand purchased 500 rifles on July 29, 1887. Later, the U.S. Navy and various Naval Militias throughout the U.S. purchased over 4,000 M1885 rifles from the Remington Arms Company, including those with the improved design.

Remington Arms Company produced 8,086 **Remington-Lee Model 1899, Small Bore, Box Magazine Rifles** with 29-inch barrels between 1899 and 1909. The State of Michigan ordered 2,001 of these rifles (chambered for .30-40 GOVT ammunition) and short-knife bayonets to arm the Michigan National Guard, and Remington delivered them in 1899 and 1900. In 1904, the Cuban Government ordered about 400 of these rifles and about 2,600 **Remington-Lee Model 1899 Box Magazine Carbines** (chambered for .30-40 GOVT ammunition, and with 20-inch barrels) for arming Cuban Rural Guard troops. This constituted nearly the entire production of this carbine, as Remington production records list a grand total of 2,693 carbines that were made between 1900 and 1907.

Concurrently with the production of military

Above: Remington-Lee Model 1882 Bolt Action Rifle.

firearms, Remington began manufacturing **Remington-Lee Model 1899 Sporting Rifles**. Inexplicably, these were the first production sporting Lee firearms made, even though Lee bolt-action guns had been made since the 1870s. These 5-shot sporting rifles were available with 24-inch, 26-inch or 28-inch barrels, and could be chambered for 7mm Spanish Mauser, 7.65mm Belgium Mauser, .236 Remington, .30-30 WIN, and .30-40 GOVT centerfire ammunition. The rifles had one-piece American walnut stocks with checkered semi pistol-grips and grooved fore-ends. When introduced in 1899, the rifles cost $30⁰⁰. In 1903, this rifle was also produced in .44-77, .43 Spanish, .45-70 and .45-90 centerfire, black powder cartridges, priced at $20⁰⁰. In the same year, a deluxe edition sporting rifle was introduced, priced at $60⁰⁰, featuring a part-round/part-octagon barrel, select English walnut stock, a variety of sporting sights, and chambered for several new smokeless powder cartridges. In all, Remington Arms Company sold just 1,446 Rem-Lee M1899 Sporting Rifles between 1899 and 1909, although production had ended in 1905.

Remington "Light Baby" Carbines

The proprietors of the Remington Arms Company were ever vigilant for new guns which were easy to manufacture and would assure steady sales. Remington found such a gun in their rolling block, **Light-Baby Carbine**. These saddle-ring carbines were light, weighing only 5 pounds, maneuverable, and fun to shoot with .44-40 W.C.F. ammunition—the same round chambered in many thousands of M1875 and M1890 single-action Remington revolvers. They were available with either 18-inch or 20-inch barrels, and the carbines cost $13.25 for a blued barrel gun, or $14⁰⁰ nickel-plated. Production commenced in 1889, with initial sales coming the following year. Production continued without interruption until 1898, with diminishing sales through 1910. In all, Remington Arms Company manufactured and sold 3,480 Light Baby Carbines over a twenty-one year period.

Remington No.4 Rolling Block Rifles

Remington's first true "boy's rifle" was the **Remington No.4 Rolling Block Rifle**, introduced in 1890. This single-shot rifle was available with either a 22-inch or 24-inch full octagon barrel, weighed a scant 4lbs/4oz, and cost only $9⁰⁰. The rifle was initially chambered for .22 caliber or .32 caliber rimfire ammunition. This turned out to be one of the best-selling sporting guns ever made by Remington, or any American gunmaker. From the beginning it could be ordered with standard open sights, or tang-mounted peep sights and/or Beach combination front sights. The first No.4 rifles had barrels securely screwed into solid frames and were not "take-down." In 1898, .25-10 Stevens rimfire was added. It is believed that a total of 157,595 "solid frame" No.4 sporting rifles were made over a twelve-year period from 1890 to 1901.

In 1902, Remington improved their No.4 rifle by making it "take-down," whereby the barrel could be easily removed from the receiver by a twist of a lever on the right side of the frame. Despite this additional feature, the rifle's cost was lowered to $8⁰⁰. Beginning in 1906, the rifle was also available in smooth-bore for

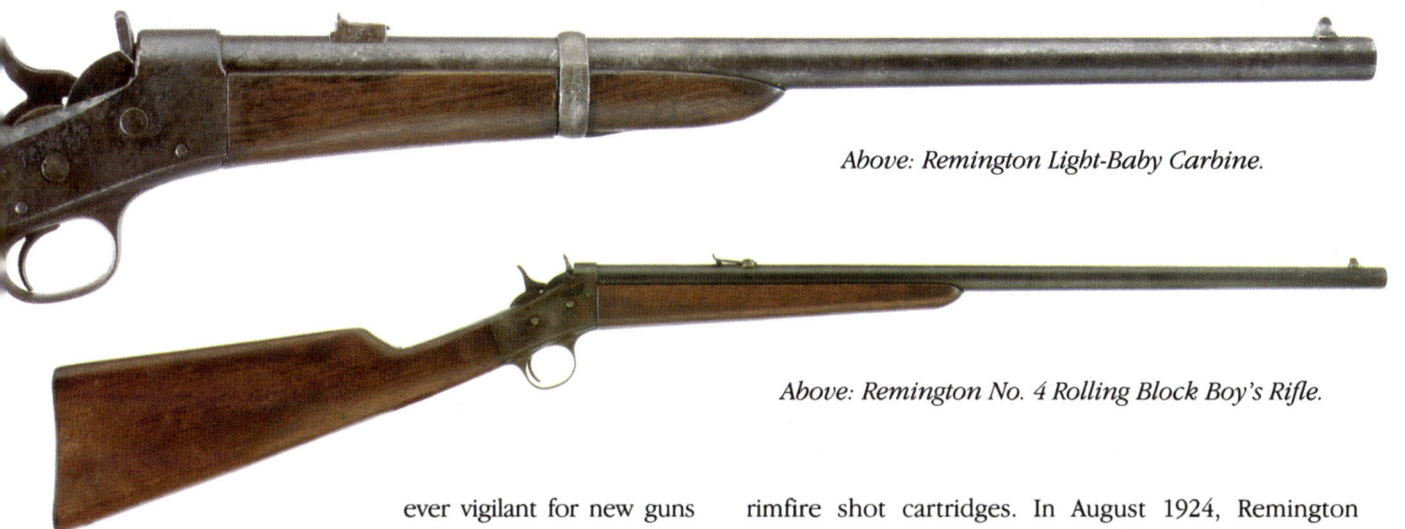

Above: Remington Light-Baby Carbine.

Above: Remington No. 4 Rolling Block Boy's Rifle.

rimfire shot cartridges. In August 1924, Remington announced an **Improved Model 4 Rifle** with a 22-inch round barrel (octagonal barrels were discontinued), screw-adjusted elevating rear sight, shotgun style butt plate, and a take-down screw with a large slotted head to lock the barrel to the frame (to replace the take-down lever). In all, Remington sold more than 356,000 No.4 Boy's Rifles between 1890 and 1932.

Above: Remington Model No. 4 Rolling Block Rifle.

Above: Remington Model No.4 Rifle.

In 1913, Remington introduced a military-style rifle for Boy Scout use, based on their No.4 action. The **Remington No.4S Boy Scout Rifle**, leather sling strap, bayonet and leather scabbard were offered for $8⁰⁰. The 28-inch barrel was chambered only for .22 caliber Short rimfire ammunition. Remington advertising boasted that this rifle was "the Official Arm of the American Boy Scouts." This organization (formerly known as the United Boy Scouts) split from the Boy Scouts of America in 1913, and sought a single-shot, military-style rifle for training purposes. On July 1, 1913, an Arms Selection Committee chose this rifle over samples supplied by Winchester, Ridabeck & Company, and by the J.C. Stevens Arms & Tool Company. This rifle was offered by Remington only in 1913 and 1914, and was replaced by a nearly identical **Remington No.4S Military Model Rifle** in 1915, with no price change. The front sight has a shorter blade than that on the No.4S Boy Scout Rifle. It was chambered for .22 Short, Long and Long Rifle rimfire ammunition, while the No.4S Boy Scout Rifle was chambered only for .22 Short cartridges. The No.4S Military Rifle was manufactured from 1915 through 1923. Remington made an estimated 6,000 Boy Scout and Military Model rifles over this 10-year period.

Remington Cadet "Rolling Block" Rifles

The 1890s was also a popular era for military academies for young men, who were taught scholastics and military discipline. Over the next twenty years, military academies in the east and south trained thousands of boys and needed cadet-sized firearms for drill purposes. Academies turned to Hartley & Graham and to the Remington Arms Company to supply them with these rifles. Remington shipping records indicate that 1,987 rifles were manufactured and sold to military academies between 1893 and 1905. These hybrid **Remington Cadet Rolling Block Rifles** were made utilizing surplus Navy rolling block pistol actions or No.1 and No.2 sporting rifle receivers.

Remington Model 1897 Military Rifles & Carbines

The era of the modern cartridge began in the 1890s, with the development of smokeless powder. Remington was one of the first arms manufacturers to adopt smokeless powder cartridges to its firearms, introducing their Remington New Model Small-Bore Military Rifle in 1896. This rifle was the first to feature a re-designed rolling block action made of alloy steel to withstand the increased breech pressures of the new smokeless powder ammunition. The rifle featured a 30-inch barrel, a tall blade-type front sight, a cleaning rod, and full-length fore-end held by two barrel bands. This military-style rolling block rifle with "knife-bayonet" and scabbard cost $15⁰⁰ when introduced. In 1898, the name of this rifle was changed to **Remington Model 1897 Rolling Block Small-Bore Military Rifle**. Over a five-year period ending in 1900, a total of 28,198 of these high-power rifles were produced, including 7,702 rifles produced in 7mm Spanish Mauser for the Mexican Government and delivered in 1899 and 1900, and 94 rifles chambered for .30-40 GOVT ammunition and sold between 1897 and 1900.

Remington also fabricated a smokeless powder carbine during this period, which they called the **Remington Model 1897 Rolling Block Small-Bore Military Carbine**. Most were made with sling swivels mounted on the right side of the barrel band and on the right side of the stock. In all, a total of 9,438 of these carbines were produced between 1898 and 1900, including 7,010 carbines in 7mm Spanish Mauser for the Mexican Government and delivered in 1900.

Remington Model 1901 Rolling Block Military Rifles & Carbines

In 1901, Remington improved their single-shot, M1897 rolling block military rifles by banding the front sight to the barrel, by strengthening the wood hand guard, by improving the rear sight, and changing from a sliding extractor to a rotary one with power ejector. A total of 46,449 **Remington Model 1901 Rolling Block Military Rifles** were made between 1901 and 1910.

At the same time, Remington also improved their M1897 rolling block military carbines in the same manner. A total of 11,434 **Remington Model 1901 Rolling Block Military Carbines** were made between 1901 and 1910, chambered for 7mm Spanish Mauser ammunition.

Remington No.5 Sporting & Target Rifles

In 1898, the Remington Arms Company introduced the **Remington No.5 Sporting & Target Rifle**, a rolling block hunting firearm intended for smokeless powder ammunition. This sporting rifle was initially chambered for .30-30 WIN, 7mm Mauser and .30-40 GOVT centerfire ammunition but in 1901, .303 British. Offered at $18^{00}, these simple but aesthetically pleasing hunting rifles never caught on with the turn-of-the-century shooting public which preferred repeating firearms. Only 198 of these rifles were ever sold over a six-year period ending 1903.

Remington No.6 "Falling Block" Rifles

In 1901, Remington Arms Company introduced a new "boy's rifle" that was even less expensive than their No.4 Sporting Rifle—the **Remington No.6 Rifle**—with a falling block action. This lightweight .22 caliber rimfire rifle weighed a scant 3 pounds, had a 20-inch round barrel, and was "take-down" by unscrewing the barrel/fore-end from the receiver. With American walnut stock and fore-end, and case-hardened frame, it cost $5^{00} in 1901. Beginning in 1903, the Remington No.6 rifle was available with an inexpensive, stamped steel rear tang sight, and was also made in .32 rimfire. In September 1928, Remington began shipping an **Improved Model 6 Rifle** with a 24-inch barrel and a frame made from one solid piece of steel. Coil springs replaced flat springs, a longer fore-end was added, and a new safety feature was included whereby the rifle could only be loaded at the half-cock position. This was a popular firearm, as Remington sold a total of 497,222 No.6 Boy's Rifles in the thirty-two, year period between 1901 and 1933.

Remington No.7 "Rolling Block" Target Rifle

In 1903, Remington introduced the Remington No.7 Target

Above: Remington Model 1897 Military Rolling Block Rifle.

& Sporting Rifle. Utilizing surplus M1871 Rolling Block Army-framed receivers, these well-balanced rifles feature a checkered, full pistol-grip stock and fore-end of polished, imported walnut, part-round/part-octagonal barrel (24-inch, 26-inch or 28-inch in length), Beach combination front sight and Lyman tang-mounted rear sight. Various calibers were offered, including .22 Short, .22 Long Rifle and .25-10 Stevens rimfires. Optional features were a Swiss Schuetzen-style butt plate, and a wind-gauge front sight, with or without spirit level. Remington No.7 rifles were offered at $24^{00}, and factory records indicate that only 350 rifles were sold between 1903 and 1910.

Remington Walker-Hepburn Schuetzen Rifles

Without a doubt, the finest target rifle ever offered by Remington was originally known as Remington-Schuetzen Match Rifles—New Special Model, but modern-day collectors refer to them as **Remington Walker-Hepburn Schuetzen Rifles**. These hand-made, short-range Schuetzen target rifles were manufactured in Remington's Custom Gun Shop, under the direction of Louis N. Walker. This rifle was illustrated only in the Remington Arms Company catalog dated 1904–05, and in the 1904 M. Hartley Company Illustrated Catalog. Distinguishing features include a Remington-Hepburn No.3 receiver modified with a scroll-shaped, Schuetzen-style under-lever which opens the falling block action, double-set triggers, 30-inch or 32-inch half-round/half-octagon barrel, hooded front sight, tang-mounted Vernier rear sight, checkered, Schuetzen-style butt stock with high cheek-piece and Swiss butt plate, and straight or pistol-grip. Prices varied from $60^{00} to $87^{00} or more, depending on optional features, including palm-rests for off-hand shooting, and testing "for guaranteed group within 2 " circle at 200 yards." Originally chambered for .32-40 Ballard & Marlin centerfire cartridges, but other short-range calibers from .22 to .40 could be furnished. For the purist, this rifle

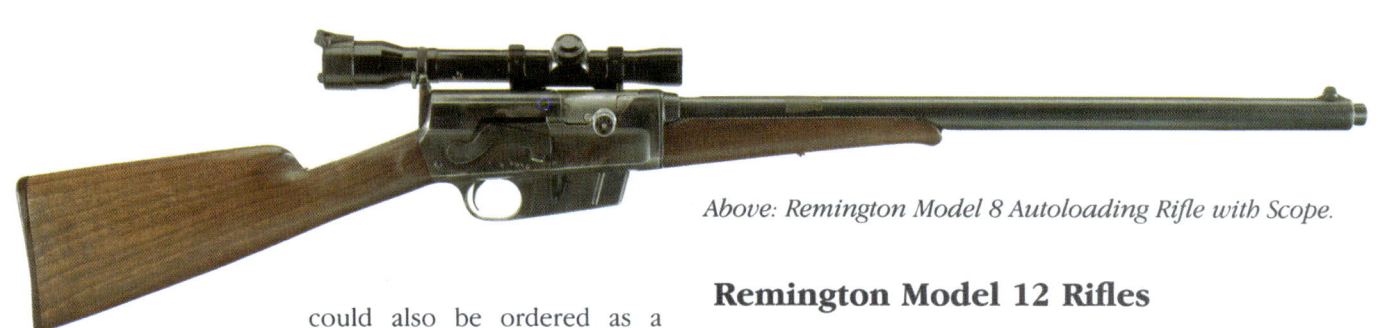

Above: Remington Model 8 Autoloading Rifle with Scope.

could also be ordered as a "muzzle—loader" with false muzzle and bullet-starter–the shooter inserted a primed and loaded shell into the chamber, closed the action, and then seated the bullet through the false-muzzle. Only 23 of the specialized, expensive rifles were ever sold, including 10 in 1904, 1 in 1906, 11 in 1907, and 1 in 1908.

Remington Model 8 Autoloading Rifles

Designed concurrently with his autoloading shotgun was Browning's autoloading, high-power rifle. The first production Remington Autoloading Repeating Rifles—No.1 Standard Grade were ready for delivery in October 1906. The Model 8 rifle is a semi-automatic, hammerless, solid-breech rifle, and was designed for .25 REM, .30 REM, .32 REM and .35 REM centerfire, rimless cartridges. A 22-inch round barrel recoils within a fixed, metal barrel jacket. A straight-grip American walnut stock and fore-end was standard, but pistol-grip stocks were an optional feature. The rifle has a fixed, 5-shot box magazine which can be single-loaded, or loaded by clip. These were simply called Remington Autoloading Repeating Rifles for many years, and the designation, Remington No.8 (and later **Remington Model 8 Autoloading Rifles**) was not given until 1911. Remington continued to sell Model 8 rifles through 1937, and the following year the factory brought out an improved gun—the Model 81. In all, Remington sold 69,514 Model 8 sporting rifles over a thirty-one-year period dating back to 1906.

Remington Model 12 Rifles

In October 1907, Pedersen turned his inventive genius toward designing a pump-action .22 caliber rifle for Remington. In September 1909, the first Remington Model 1909 Repeating Rifles (later to be renamed **Remington Model 12 Repeating .22 Caliber Rifles**) were ready for shipment at $12.65 each. This is a slide-action, solid breech, hammerless, take-down, side-ejection, .22 caliber rifle. The early rifles held 14 Short, 11 Long or 10 Long Rifle rimfire cartridges, but within a few months the factory changed the tubular, below-barrel magazine to hold one more of each. Variations of the Model 12 include the **Model 12A** (the basic rifle with round, 22-inch barrel and straight-grip stock), the **Model 12B** Gallery Special (first offered in 1910, with 24-inch octagonal barrel, pistol-grip stock and optional extended magazine holding 25 .22 Shorts), the **Model 12C Target Rifle** (first offered in 1910, with 24-inch octagonal barrel, straight-grip and later pistol-grip stock), the **Model 12CS, DS, ES** and **FS** (first offered in 1914, chambered for .22 REM Special cartridges, and with increasing quality of finish), **Model 12D Peerless Grade, E Expert Grade**, and **F Premier Grade** (first offered in 1910, chambered for .22 caliber rimfire ammunition, and with increasing quality of finish), and **Model 12C N.R.A. Target Grade** (first offered in 1923, chambered for .22 Long Rifle ammunition only, with Lyman tang sight and globe front, and sling strap). Pedersen's rifle would prove to be one of the best-selling guns ever produced by Remington, as 831,737 rifles were made in a 27-year period through 1936.

Above: Factory engraved Model 12 Slide Action Rifle.

Above: Remington Model 12 Slide Action Rifle.

Above: Remington Model 12 Gallery Special Rifle.

Above: Model 14 Slide Action Rifle.

Above: Model 14 Slide Action Rifle.

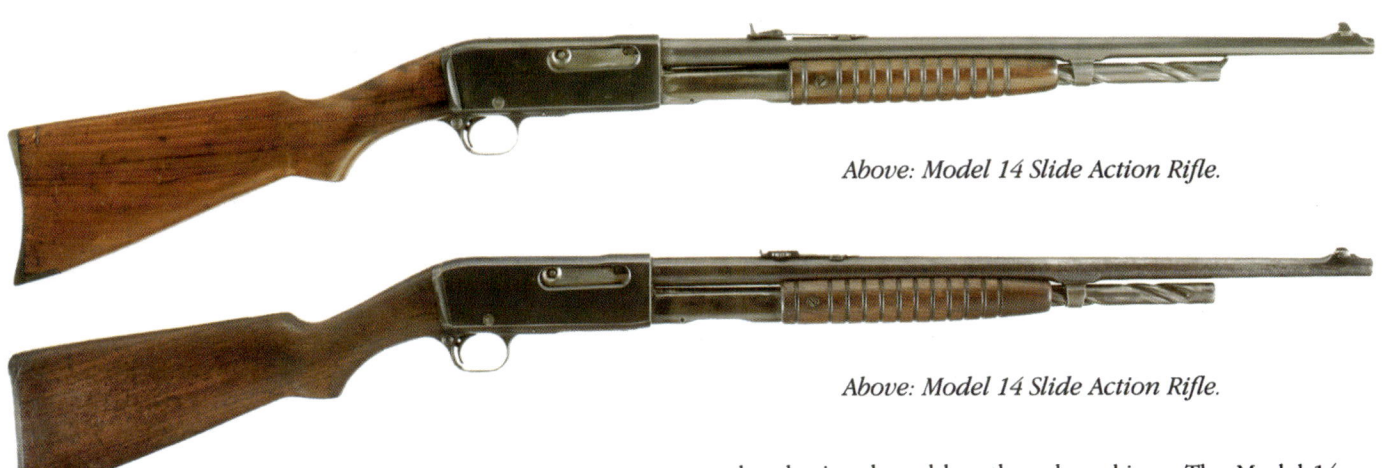

Remington Model 14 Slide-Action Rifles

John D. Pedersen began working on a high-power, pump-action sporting rifle for Remington in September 1908. Remington's Crawford C. Loomis assisted Pedersen, and the **Remington Model 14 Slide-Action Rifle** was introduced in August 1912. Initially chambered for .25 REM, .30 REM and .32 REM rimless centerfire ammunition, .35 REM was soon added to the line. The 1913–14 Remington catalog offered the hunting rifle in six grades: No.14A Standard Grade (with 22-inch barrel and pistol-grip stock) for $20.00; No.14C Special Grade for $35.00; No.14D Peerless Grade for $55.00; No.14E Expert Grade for $70.00; No.14F Premier Grade for $105.00; and No.14R Carbine (with 18-inch barrel, straight-grip stock, and saddle ring) for $18.00. In October 1919, Remington announced several design improvements to their Model 14 rifles and carbines, including a breechblock located safety. This durable hunting rifle was offered in five grades with retail prices ranging from $34.90 for the basic Model 14A Standard Grade Rifle, to $172.30 for the Model 14F Premier Grade Rifle. Other variations included the Model 14C Special Grade, 14D Peerless Grade, 14F Premier Grade, and 14R Carbine. The Model 14 rifle was chambered for the same ammunition as Remington's Model 8 rifle. Remington sold a total of 125,056 Model 14 and Model 14 rifles and carbines between 1912 and 1935.

Remington Model 14½ Slide-Action Rifles

The **Remington Model 14½ Slide-Action, Sporting Rifle** was introduced a year after the Model 14 rifle. Remington's retail price list dated January 12, 1914, offered the No.14 A Standard Grade Rifle (with 22-inch barrel and pistol-grip stock) for $17.25 and the No.14 R Carbine (with 18-inch barrel, straight-grip stock, and saddle ring) for $16.75. Both were chambered for .38-40 W.C.F. or .44-40 W.C.F. ammunition. The Model 14½ was nearly identical to the Model 14, except for the chambering, barrel length and markings. The Model 14 was last advertised in 1931. The exact number of Model 14 firearms sold is not known, as the factory production figures were combined with Model 14 rifles and carbines.

Remington Model 16 Autoloading Rifles

Remington's Charles H. Barnes began conceptual work on a .22 caliber, autoloading rifle in 1909. In September 1914, the factory shipped the first **Remington Model 16, .22 Caliber Autoloading Rifle**. Remington's 1915–16 Catalog listed four grades, including: No.16A Standard Grade for $20.00; No.16C Special Grade for $28.00; No.16D Peerless Grade for $48.00; No.16F Premier Grade for $85.00. The Model 16 rifle is a solid breech, hammerless, take-down, autoloading repeater which holds fifteen .22 REM autoloading rimfire cartridges in a butt stock magazine. This rifle was never a very popular gun for Remington, as only 13,764 rifles were made through 1919. A grand total of 17,716 Model 16 rifles were made in thirteen years of production, through 1928.

Remington Model 1914 Lebel "Rolling Block" Military Rifles

When Germany declared war against France on August 3, 1914, French ground troops were ill-equipped and much in need of quality rifles and small-arms ammunition. On November 19th, the French Republic ordered 100,000 **Remington Model 1914 Lebel Rolling Block Military Rifles**, French Model 1914 sword-bayonets and steel scabbards from the Remington Arms and Ammunition Company of Ilion, New York. These single-shot rifles were chambered for the smokeless powder, French 8mm Lebel rimmed cartridge. Work commenced on these rifles on March 2, 1915, and Ilion workmen eventually achieved a production rate of 200 rifles per day. In all, Remington made a total of 100,291 M1914 Lebel Rolling Block Rifles, including 45,611 in 1915, 54,413 in 1916, and 267 in 1917.

Above: Pattern 1914 Magazine Rifle.

Mle 1907-15 Berthier Military Rifles

France later ordered 200,000 **Mle 1907-15 Berthier Military Rifles** from Remington, which were also chambered for the 8mm Lebel rimmed cartridge and were loaded with 3-shot Mannlicher-style clips. These rifles were manufactured at Rem-UMC's Bridgeport armsmaking facility, not at Ilion. While the exact details of this contract are not presently known, it is believed that Rem-UMC manufactured only half the amount ordered.

Magazine Rifles, .303 inch, Pattern of 1914

On November 24, 1914, Remington received a contract from the British Government to manufacture 200,000 military rifles—**Magazine Rifles, .303 inch, Pattern of 1914** and Pattern 1913 sword-bayonets with Pattern 1907 metal scabbards. Work on these rifles began in Ilion in early 1915, and on February 10, 1915, Remington received a second contract from the British Government for 200,000 more of these rifles. On September 27, 1915, Remington received a third contract from the British Government to supply 600,000 additional Pattern 14 military rifles. On March 25, 1916, work began in Ilion on the rifles for England. An average rate of production of 1,000 rifles per day was eventually achieved, with the greatest rate of production of 2,000 rifles in one day on March 10, 1917. Production ceased in mid-1917.

Even though plans were underway to enlarge Ilion's manufacturing capacity, M. Hartley Dodge decided in 1914 to organize the Remington Arms Company of Delaware, and leased factory space from the Baldwin Locomotive Works at Eddystone, Pennsylvania. This factory, located near Philadelphia, was earmarked as one of two manufacturing facilities for the $60,000,000 contract to manufacture Enfield Pattern 14 military rifles for Great Britain. Eventually, the Eddystone plant would fabricate 604,941 Pattern 14 rifles for Great Britain, while the Ilion plant would manufacture 403,193 rifles.

Remington-made Mosin Nagant Military Rifles

Remington received their largest single order for military rifles during World War I from Czarist Russia on November 3, 1916. The contract called for the delivery of one million Mosin-Nagant Military Rifles and bayonets, at a cost of $30^{00} each. **Remington-made Mosin Nagant Military Rifles** are 5-shot, bolt-action weapons which were nearly identical to their Russian-made counterparts. Hundreds of thousands of rifles were fabricated in 1916, and into 1917. In February 1917, Czar Nicholas II was overthrown, and the Provisional Kerensky Government took over. Despite the turn of events, Remington continued to fabricate Russian rifles. As late as November 1917, Rem-UMC's Bridgeport facility was producing between 4,000 and 4,200 Russian rifles per day, which is an astounding 100,000 rifles per month.

Of the 750,000 Mosin-Nagant rifles manufactured by Remington, only 469,951 had been delivered to Russia by February 1917. Facing a horrific economic loss after

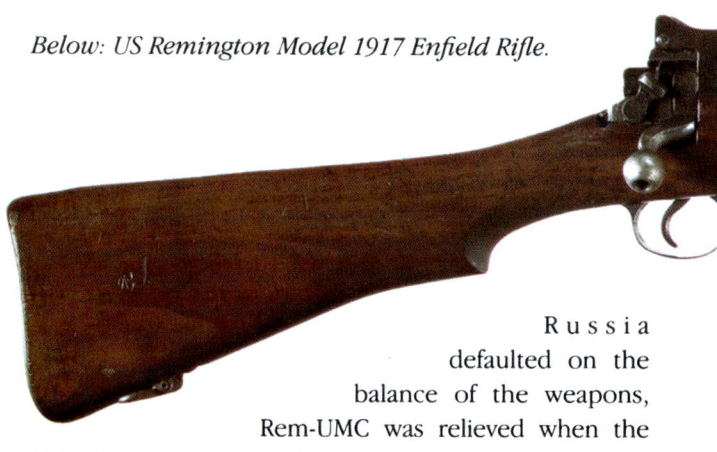

Below: US Remington Model 1917 Enfield Rifle.

Russia defaulted on the balance of the weapons, Rem-UMC was relieved when the U.S. Government purchased most of the remaining, completed rifles. Many were used for military training purposes, and some were used to arm the A.E.F. troops which were dispatched to Murmansk, Archangel and Vladivostok in 1918 and 1919.

Remington Rifles and Carbines • 67

U.S. Rifle, Caliber .30, Model of 1917

In January 1917, the War Department turned to Rem-UMC to manufacture Springfield M1903 rifles. Unfortunately, the tools, jigs and fixtures which contracted with Remington for 300,000 rifles, officially known as the **U.S. Rifle, Caliber .30, Model of 1917**. Manufacturing went on in a hurried pace, and on October 9, 1918, Remington was given a contract for an additional 250,000 rifles. Eventually,

Above: Remington Model 1903-A3 Military Rifle.

Above: Model 1903-A4 Remington Bolt Action Sniper Rifle.

Above: Model 1903-A3 Bolt Action Rifle.

Above: Model 1903-A4 Remington Sniper with Weaver telescopic sight.

Remington had used to manufacture Pattern 14 Rifles, were unsuited to making Springfield rifles. It was decided that Remington could modify their Pattern 14 rifle machinery, and produce an entirely new military firearm which had been designed by Major P.T. Goodsal at the Birmingham Small Arms factory in England. The new weapon would fire the .30-06 Gov't. cartridge, and the first sample rifle was ready in April. On July 12, 1917, the Ordnance Department

Remington's Ilion plant would manufacture 646,444 of these rifles before production ended on December 23, 1918.

Remington's Eddystone facility also made M1917 Enfield rifles. Pattern 14 rifle production at Eddystone had ceased in late 1916, and the plant had re-tooled to begin making the new rifles. An astounding 1,181,908 of these rifles were made in the months to come, before production halted on January 9, 1919.

Above: Browning machine gun on tripod.

Browning Machine Gun, Model of 1917, Caliber .30

In 1917, American Expeditionary Forces had no heavy machine guns to speak of, and were issued insufficient quantities of European-made, 2nd-class guns. While working at Colt's Armory, John M. Browning developed a rapid-fire machine gun, capable of achieving a cyclic rate of fire in excess of 600 rounds a minute. Officially, this deadly weapon became known as the **Browning Machine Gun, Model of 1917, Caliber .30, Water-Cooled**. It is classified as a heavy, recoil operated and belt-fed machine gun, and weighs 30 pounds. It became apparent that no single manufacturing plant in the U.S. was capable of producing all the machine guns that were needed by its armed forces. Colt's agreed to sell these rights to the U.S. Government for a royalty consideration.

Colt's received an initial contract in July 1917 to produce 10,000 Browning heavy machine guns. Remington Arms-Union Metallic Cartridge Company was given a contract in September 1917, to manufacture 15,000 Browning machine guns. On January 10, 1918, New England Westinghouse was given a contract to construct 20,000. However, it was the middle of May 1918, before Rem-UMC's arms plant in Bridgeport, Connecticut, was able to deliver completed weapons.

After June 1918, American troops that sailed for the European Theater were armed with Browning M1917 heavy machine guns. When the Armistice was finally signed on November 11, 1918, Rem-UMC, Westinghouse and Colt's armory had delivered nearly 43,000 Browning heavy machine guns, including 30,150 by Westinghouse, 12,000 by Rem-UMC, and 600 by Colt's armory. The dates of delivery were far too late to be of any significant influence on the battlefield against a nearly defeated enemy. American and Allied officers alike agreed that the war's best heavy machine gun had not been adequately battle tested.

Pedersen Devices

On March 16, 1915, independent gun designer John D. Pedersen wrote a letter to the Vice President of Remington Arms and Ammunition Company, stating that he had designed a prototype, autoloading military rifle. Remington then began a series of negotiations with the Ordnance department, culminating in a go-ahead for full, top-secret development. On October 8th, Chief of Ordnance General William Crozier, a few Ordnance Officers and some Congressmen, all sworn to secrecy, attended Pedersen's first official demonstration of his invention—an automatic bolt which changed the Springfield M1903 from bolt-action to autoloading. This would later be known as the **Pedersen Device**, but in late-1917, it was a top-secret weapon.

To maintain the highest levels of secrecy, a misleading name was given to the device, and it was officially adopted as the **Automatic Pistol, Caliber .30, Model 1918, Mark I**. An order was subsequently placed with Rem-UMC for 100,000 Pedersen Devices on March

26, 1918, and it was soon-after increased to 133,450 devices. On June 27, 1918, Pedersen was ordered to adapt his device to the M1917 Enfield Rifle, and it became known as the **M1918 Pistol, Mark II**. On September 20th, the Ordnance Department ordered Remington to manufacture 500,000 Mark II devices once the original Mark I contract was completed.

The Pedersen Device replaced the standard Springfield bolt, which the soldier would place into a canvas pouch on his equipment belt. Removing the Pedersen Device from a metal container hanging on the belt, the soldier would insert it into the open breech, and lock it in place by the rifle's magazine cut-off. Then the soldier would take a long, black magazine holding forty pistol-sized cartridges and snap it in place, it protruding from the right side of the breech at a 45E angle. The soldier then had a 40-round, autoloading weapon that could fill the air with bullets. Each time the trigger was pulled, the Pedersen Device mechanism fired a round.

Production of the Mark I Devices commenced in secrecy at Remington's Bridgeport facility in 1918, and continued even when the Armistice was declared on November 11, 1918. On December 17th, the Ordnance Department canceled the Mark II contract, however production of the Mark I Devices continued until the order for cancellation was issued on March 1, 1919. Rem-UMC had completed and delivered exactly 65,001 Mark I receivers and other parts from Model 1917 Enfield rifles which Remington had built during the war. Like the military configuration, the Model 30 rifle was chambered for the versatile .30-06 SPRG centerfire cartridge. Higher quality versions with fine wood, checkering and engraving were available, upon request. Because of its high cost—$64.15, its heavy weight—eight pounds, and its somewhat clunky lines, the Model 30 did not sell well. Only about 2,500 Model 30 rifles were sold between 1921 and 1925 when it was replaced by an improved version.

Remington introduced an improved version of the Model 30 rifle in 1926, calling it the Remington Model 30 Express Rifle. Besides the .30-06 cartridge, this new gun was also chambered for the same rimless cartridges as the Model 8 Rifle—.25 REM, .30 REM, .32 REM and .35 REM centerfire ammunition. The rifle weighs 7lbs/4oz, the barrel was shortened to 22-inches, the action cocked upon the opening of the bolt (not upon closing, as was the M30), the trigger-pull was lightened, the fore-end and pistol grip were checkered, but the price remained the same as its predecessor—$45.75. Optional features included a micrometer rear sight, and an adjustable web-type sling strap with hooks. In June 1931, Remington began offering this rifle in 7mm MAUSER, and in 1936, the .257 REM-ROBERTS was added.

In March 1930, Remington brought out a higher quality version of the Model 30 Express Rifle, the

Above: Remington M1903 Bolt Action Rifle.

Above: Remington Model 30 Express Bolt Action Rifle.

Devices and some 65,000,000 cartridges by this date. Springfield Armory continued modifying Springfield rifles until March 1920, at which time about 145,000 M1903, Mark I Rifles had been fabricated.

Remington Model 30 Bolt-Action Rifles

In April 1921, Remington announced the **Remington Model 30 Rifle**. Remington designers utilized left-over

Remington Model 30S Special Grade Bolt Action Rifle. This rifle featured a high-comb stock (adapted to scope), full pistol-grip, shotgun-style steel butt plate, Lyman No.48 rear micrometer sight, gold bead front sight on matted ramp, 22-inch barrel, and chambered for either .30-06 SPRG, 7mm MAUSER, or .25 REM calibers. When introduced, it cost $60.00. In 1935, .257 REM-ROBERTS was added with 24-inch barrel. In 1937, Remington changed the designation of the M30S Special

Above: Remington Model 24 Autoloading Rifle.

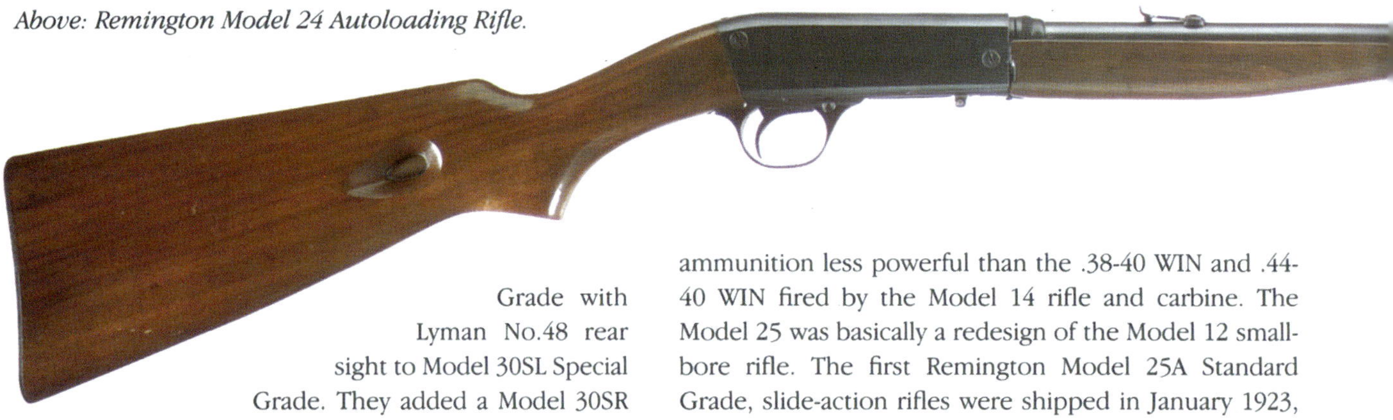

Grade with Lyman No.48 rear sight to Model 30SL Special Grade. They added a Model 30SR with Redfield No.102R rear sight, and Model 30SX without rear sight, but with a step-adjustable open rear sight on the barrel. In 1939, Remington added the Model 30SM Rifle with Marble-Goss receiver sight.

In October 1927, Remington introduced the **Model 30R Express Carbine**, which sold for $42.15. It shared the same characteristics as the M30 Express rifle except for the shorter 20-inch round barrel, finger grooves in forestock instead of checkering, and plain pistol-grip stock, shotgun-style, steel butt plate, and weighing 7 pounds.

Model 30A Express Rifles, M30R Carbines, and M30S Special Grade Express Rifles were last offered in 1940, replaced the following year by Remington Model 720 High-Power Rifles.

Remington Model 24 Autoloading Rifles

In April 1922, Remington announced a new .22 caliber, autoloading rifle, based on John M. Browning's patents. When introduced, the new autoloader sold for $28⁰⁰, and was initially chambered for .22 Short rimfire ammunition. The **Model 24A Standard Grade Rifle** was loaded through an opening on the right side of the stock just behind the semi pistol-grip, and the internal magazine held 15 cartridges. Initially, the M24 rifle was made with a 19-inch round barrel, measured 37-inches overall, and weighed just 4lbs/12oz. Later, the barrel length was increased to 21 inches, the overall length became 39 inches, and the rifle weighed in at five pounds. In 1923, Remington began offering this autoloader in either .22 Short or .22 Long Rifle (not interchangeable), and in several other grades: Model 24C Special Grade; Model 24D Peerless Grade; Model 24E Expert Grade; and Model 24F Premier Grade. Remington sold a total of 130,415 Model 24 Autoloading Rifles in a thirteen-year period between 1922 and 1935.

Remington Model 25 Slide-Action Rifles

In early 1922, Remington began work on a lightweight, centerfire, slide-action rifle which would shoot centerfire ammunition less powerful than the .38-40 WIN and .44-40 WIN fired by the Model 14 rifle and carbine. The Model 25 was basically a redesign of the Model 12 smallbore rifle. The first Remington Model 25A Standard Grade, slide-action rifles were shipped in January 1923, with 24-inch round barrel in .25-20 W.C.F. or .32-20 W.C.F. calibers. The tubular magazine beneath the barrel holds 10 cartridges, loaded through the door on the right side of the solid receiver. It has a semi pistol-grip stock fitted with a steel, rifle-style butt plate. This take-down hunting rifle weighs a scant 5lbs/8oz. Several other grades were offered, including the Model 25C Special Grade, the Model 25D Peerless Grade, the Model 25E Expert Grade, and the Model 25F Premier Grade. These had increasing quality of wood and more intricate hand engraving.

Concurrently, Remington introduced a 6-shot **Model 25R Carbine** with 18-inch barrel, straight-grip stock and shotgun-style butt plate, weighing only 4lbs/8oz. Production of Remington Model 25 rifles and carbines continued uninterrupted through 1936, and a total of 31,828 Model 25 rifles were made during this 13-year period.

Remington Model 26 Repeating Air Rifles

In March 1927, Remington, began working on the company's first and only air rifle—the **Model 26**, and finished rifles were ready for shipment on October 1928. Remington's initial air rifles had a black painted finish on all exterior metal parts, and a plain wood stock with simple pistol grip, no butt plate, and a grooved wood fore-end. To cock the action, a boy needed only to pull back the pump handle and then push it forward. Initially, the air rifle fired only .177 caliber lead shot, however an improved version was released in 1932 which would shoot either lead or steel shot. Remington sold 19,646 Model 26 Repeating Air Rifles between 1928 and 1934, when production was discontinued.

Model 33 Bolt Action, Single-Shot, .22 Caliber Rifles

In July 1931, Remington's first bolt action 22 rifle was ready for shipment. Remington's **Model 33A Standard Grade Rifle** was simply made, inexpensive to produce, affordable in a difficult economic era, easy to shoot, and a perfect "first gun" for any youngster. The opening of lengthened, and grasping grooves were cut into both sides of the fore-end. The bolt was simplified, and the angle and finish of the bolt handle was changed. The trigger was shimmed in profile, and the edges of the trigger guard were somewhat rounded. This "improved" rifle is now referred to as a Model 33, Type 1933 Rifle.

In February 1933, Remington introduced the **Model 33 N.R.A. Junior Target Grade Rifle**, equipped with Lyman No.55R adjustable rear peep sight and a Patridge-type front sight, and no barrel-mounted rear sight. This rifle had a wide adjustable leather sling strap and swivel hooks.

In early 1934, Remington brought out the Model 33A with a Lyman No.55R adjustable rear peep sight. In 1935, Remington began calling this rifle the **Model 33P**, designated by the peep sight.

The company manufactured the Model 33 Boy's Rifle only through 1935, and sold a total of 263,547 rifles in the six-year period through 1936, when it was replaced by the Remington Model 41A Rifle.

Model 34 Bolt Action, Repeating .22 Caliber Rifles

Concurrently, Remington began work on a tubular magazine, bolt action repeating .22 rifle—**Remington Model 34A Standard Grade Rifle**, and the first rifles were delivered in July 1932. It features a tubular magazine beneath the 24-inch barrel which holds 22 Short, 17 Long or 15 Long Rifle rimfire cartridges, interchangeably. The rifle weighs just 5lbs/4oz.

In March 1933, Remington introduced the **Model 34 N.R.A. Junior Target Grade Rifle**, equipped with a Lyman No.55R adjustable rear peep sight, Patridge-type front sight, and adjustable leather sling strap and swivel hooks.

Above: Remington Model 34 Bolt–Action, repeating rifle.

the bolt extracted and ejected the spent .22 shell. A new cartridge was loaded by hand into the awaiting chamber, and the bolt closed. As a safety feature, the young shooter still had to pull back the bolt plunger by hand to cock the action. Other features of the rifle include a 24-inch round barrel, 4lbs/8oz weight, one-piece American walnut stock, and low cost—$5^{00} when introduced in 1931. The Model 33 was also produced with a smooth-bore barrel intended for .22 caliber shot cartridges.

In 1932 and 1933, Remington redesigned several features of the Model 33, improving the gun and reducing production cost. The one-piece stock was

Beginning in early 1934, Remington offered the Model 34A with a Lyman No.55R adjustable rear peep sight. The following year Remington named this rifle the **Model 34P**. Eventually, Remington sold 162,922 Model 34 repeating rifles in the five-year period between 1932 and 1936, when it was replaced by the Remington Model 341A.

Model 37 Rangemaster Target Rifle

In the latter months of 1932, Remington decided to produce a bolt action, .22 caliber target rifle to compete with Winchester's Model 52. The first prototype target rifles were ready for trial in mid-1936, and a number of guns were sent out to small-bore marksmen for competitive tests at Camp Perry. After heeding the advice and making last minute design changes, Remington finally announced the **Model 37 "Rangemaster" Bolt Action Target Rifle** to the public in mid-1937.

Characteristics of Remington's first bolt action, small-bore target rifle include: a heavy, full-floating, 28-inch barrel; chambered for .22 Long Rifle rimfire ammunition; bolt action; adjustable trigger pull; dual extractors; 5-

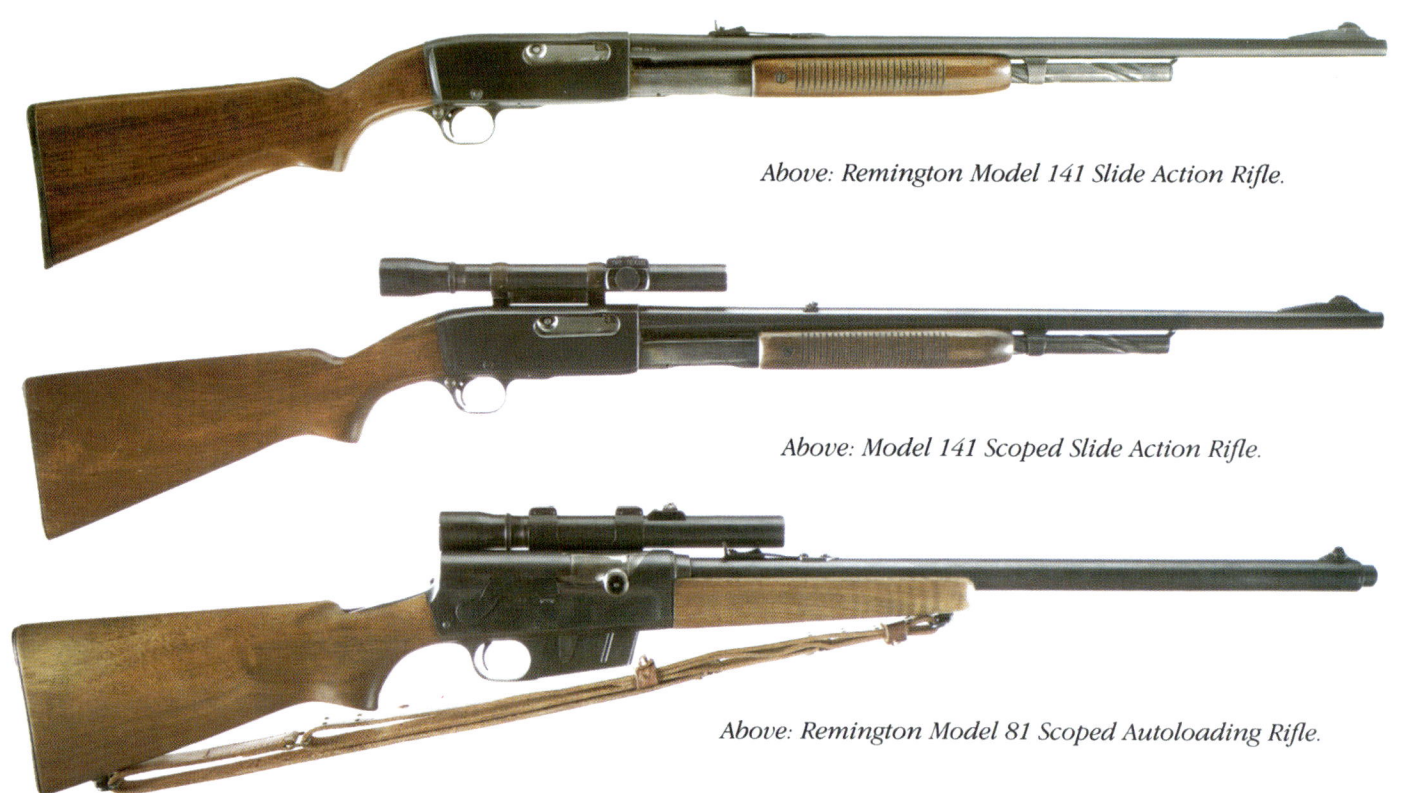

Above: Remington Model 141 Slide Action Rifle.

Above: Model 141 Scoped Slide Action Rifle.

Above: Remington Model 81 Scoped Autoloading Rifle.

cartridge removable clip magazine; full target-style American walnut stock with semi-beavertail fore-end and adjustable front sling swivel; Remington micrometer rear sight and Redfield hooded front sight with changeable inserts; Carney leather shooting sling; and 12 pound weight. Only 1,788 of these precision target rifles were sold between 1936 and 1939.

In January 1940, Remington announced an improved **Remington 1940 "Rangemaster" Model 37 Target Rifle** with a new stock (with higher and thicker comb, reshaped pistol grip, and wider and longer beavertail fore-end), and an improved adjustable trigger. Variations of this improved target rifle include the **Model 37AR** (with Remington rear micrometer sight and Redfield front sight); **Model 37AS** (same as M37AR except without sling strap); **Model 37AF** (without rear sight, but with Redfield front sight); **Model 37AX** (without sights); **Model 37AV** (with Wittek Vaver receiver sight and Redfield front sight); and **Model 37AM** (with Marble Goss receiver sight and Redfield front sight). Remington eventually sold 2,032 of the 1940 variation of the Improved Model 37 Target Rifles between 1939 and 1942, when production halted due to Remington's wartime commitments.

Model of 1934 Military Bolt Action Rifles

In 1933, Remington fabricated the first prototype Remington Model of 1933 Miliary Rifle in 7mm Mauser caliber utilizing an Enfield M1917 action and other parts. The following year Remington received a contract to make 3,000 of these military bolt action rifles for Honduras, each chambered for 7x57mm Mauser centerfire ammunition, and these were called **Model of 1934 Military Rifles**. About 500 were fabricated in 1934, and 2,500 in 1935, utilizing the same receivers as those in Remington Model 30S Express Rifles. Each were

Above: Remington 1934 Bolt Action Rifle.

fitted for the standard Springfield-pattern bayonet. Soon after, Nicaragua placed a large order for these rifles in .30-06 SPRG caliber, but the contract was never consummated.

Remington Model 141 "Gamemaster" Rifles & Carbines

The design of the Remington Model 14 slide-action rifle was reviewed in February 1935, and cosmetic improvements were made to improve its appearance. The result was the introduction of the **Remington Model 141 Slide-Action rifle** and **carbine** in 1935—dubbed the **Gamemaster**. This rifle was chambered for .30 REM, .32 REM, and .35 REM rimless centerfire cartridges. Rifles have 24-inch barrels and carbines have 18-inch barrels. Improvements included a longer barrel, a semi-beavertail fore-end, and a restyled stock with shotgun-type steel butt plate. In 1936, variations of this firearm included the **Model 141A Standard Grade Rifle**, the **M141C Special Grade**, the **M141D Peerless Grade**, and the **M141F Premier Grade**. The Remington Model 141R Carbine was also introduced in 1936, but chambered only for .30 REM and .32 REM ammunition. The M141R carbine was discontinued after 1945. Remington manufactured the Model 141 Gamemaster through 1950, and in that period sold 76,881 rifles and carbines. In 1952, the M141 was replaced by the Remington Model 760 Gamemaster Slide-Action Rifle.

Remington Model 81 "Woodsmaster" Autoloading Rifles

In November 1935, Remington began work on improving the Model 8 high-power rifle. Seven months later, in June 1936, Remington introduced the **Model 81 "Woodsmaster" Autoloading Rifle**, chambered for .30 REM, .32 REM and .35 REM centerfire ammunition. Differences between the Model 8 and the new Model 81 were more form over substance. The new rifle sported a beefier stock with full pistol-grip, a thicker semi-beavertail fore-end, and a shotgun-style steel butt plate. The Model 81 Woodsmaster was offered in M81A Standard Grade, M81C Special Grade, M81D Peerless Grade, M81E Expert Grade, and M81F Premier Grade.

In 1939, the designation M81C was changed to M81B. In August 1940, Remington began offering the Model 81 autoloader in .300 SAVAGE. Manufacturing continued into 1942, and then was interrupted by Remington's commitment to the war effort. In 1946, Remington ceased making this rifle in .32 REM. Remington last advertised the Model 81 Woodsmaster in the 1949 catalog, although production continued into 1950. In all, Remington manufactured 55,581 Model 81 rifles in this fourteen-year period.

Remington Model 241 "Speedmaster" Autoloading Rifles

Remington began looking at the Model 24 autoloading rifle in January 1935, with the intent to modify and improve its function and look. Five months later, Remington announced that the new **Model 241 Autoloading .22 Caliber Rifle** would be available by August. Remington advertised "a man-sized gun that is

Above: Remington Model 241 Speedmaster Rifle.

bigger, heavier and better than the gun it replaced." Other changes included a longer 24-inch barrel, better finish of internal fire control parts, a new device that locked the barrel and receiver tightly, and a re-designed stock. The variations offered include: M241SA or M241LA Standard Grade ; M241SC or M241LC Special Grade; M241SD or M241LD Peerless Grade; M241SE or M241LE Expert Grade; and M241SF or M241LF Premier Grade. The letter immediately following the model designation indicates the cartridge for which the rifle is chambered. S indicates .22 Short and L indicates .22 Long Rifle. The .22 Short magazine holds 15 cartridges, and the .22 Long Rifle magazine holds ten. Ammunition was not interchangeable.

Remington later offered several gallery variations of this gun, including the **Model 241SA Gallery** or **M241LA Gallery** rifles with either regular sights or "course" sights with a slightly wider notch in the rear sight. Also offered were **M241SA** and **M241LA Full Nickel Gallery Guns** (with nickel plated receiver, trigger plate, barrel and all exposed metal parts), the **M241SA** and **M241LA Nickel Trim Gallery Guns** (receiver and trigger plate are Chrome plated), and **M241SA** and **M241LA Gallery Guns** (fitted with screw eyes for counter fasteners).

In the late 1930s, Remington offered Model 241 autoloaders with Routledge bored barrels, chambered for .22 Long Rifle shot cartridges. These proprietary barrels are smooth bore, but the forward 15-inch to 17-inch of the barrel have been enlarged to about .375 inches in diameter. These were special order guns, and were not a Remington catalog item.

Model 241 autoloading rifles were sold from 1935 through 1941, and then again from 1945 to 1951, although they were last listed in the 1949 Remington catalog and price lists. This model was eventually replaced by the Model 550 autoloading rifle.

Remington Model 341 "Sportmaster" Bolt Action Repeating Rifles

Remington's popular Model 34 bolt action, .22 repeating rifle introduced in 1932, was one of the first products re-evaluated in mid-1935 by Remington, with the result being the **Model 341 Sportmaster Rifle**, introduced in February 1936. In the months to come the following variations were made available:

- **Model 341P Sportmaster**—had the same features as the Model 34 Rifle it replaced, plus these improvements: a new Remington Point Chrometer rear adjustable sight with two interchangeable discs; a new hooded front sight with four reticles; a newly-configured stock; a re-styled bolt handle; a new military-style safety; a heavier target barrel; and 6lbs/4oz weight.
- **Model 341PT Special**—same as the M341P, except that the rifle is drilled & tapped for a 4-power Weaver No.344 scope and #3 mount.
- **Model 341A Standard**—same as the M341P, except that it had a step-adjustable rear sight and white metal bead front sight, and weighed 6 pounds. It initially retailed for $13.90.
- **Model 341AT Special**—same as the M341A Standard, except that the receiver is drilled & tapped for a 4-power Weaver No.344 scope and #3 mount.
- **Model 341SB Smooth Bore Rifle**—intended for .22 caliber Long Rifle shot cartridges only. This rifle had a white metal bead shotgun-style front sight and

no rear sight. Remington offered a Lyman #422 "Expert" 4-power scope for the M341 in 1938, retailing for $8.25, when ordered with the rifle.

The Model 341 was discontinued in late October 1940, scarcely four months after it was introduced. There were runoff sales through 1941, and in all, 131,604 M341 Sportmaster Rifles were sold. The M341 Sportmaster was replaced in 1940 by the Remington Model 512 Sportmaster.

Remington Model 121 "Fieldmaster" Slide-Action Rifles

In September 1936, Remington introduced the **Model 121 Fieldmaster** slide-action rifle. It differed from its predecessor in that it had a larger stock with pistol grip, a checkered steel butt plate, semi-beavertail fore-end with lateral grooving, larger recoil shoulder on breech block, increased capacity magazine tube (14 L.R., 16 L or 20 S.), Model 34-style front and rear sights, 24-inch round barrel, and heavier weight. Variations offered included: M121A Standard Grade; M121D Peerless Grade; M121E Expert Grade; and M121F Premier Grade. Remington also marketed the M121S Remington Special Grade (firing the .22 REM Special {W.R.F.} rimfire cartridge); and M121DS, ES and FS grades.

In February 1939, Remington introduced the **Model 121SB Smooth Bore** with non-rifled barrel, white metal bead front sight, no rear sight, and magazine holding 14 Long Rifle rimfire shot cartridges. In February 1939, Remington began shipping **Remington Model 121A Standard—Routledge Boring Rifles** with 23-inch round barrel bored to Routledge specifications for shot cartridges, and with white metal bead front sight and no rear sight. The Routledge guns were special-order rifles and were not listed in any factory catalog. Remington also introduced the **Model 121 Skeetrap Rifle** with 25-inch barrel bored to Loewi specifications, white metal bead front sight, and no rear sight.

In January 1951, Remington discontinued production of M121S and M121SB rifles. In April 1954, M121D, E & F grade rifles were discontinued, and in December 1954 all remaining models were dropped. In all, the factory had shipped 199,891 Model 121 slide-action rifles.

Remington Model 41 "Targetmaster" Bolt Action Rifles

In March 1936, Remington introduced the **Remington Model 41 Targetmaster**, a .22 caliber, bolt action target rifle:

- **M41P Grade** with 27-inch round barrel, one-piece American walnut stock with pistol-grip and semi-beavertail fore-end, shotgun-style butt plate, a hooded front sight and a Remington receiver-mounted peep sight. This gun weighed 5lbs/4oz, and a leather sling strap was optional.
- **M41A Grade** was identical to the M41P, except it had a white metal bead front sight and a step-adjustable sporting rear sight. It was also available with a smooth-bored barrel.

In 1937, Remington began offering the Model 41 rifle in .22 REM Special (W.R.F.): the **M41PS Grade rifle**, and the **M41AS**; otherwise, the rifles were identical to M41P and M41A rifles. In 1938, Remington introduced the **M41SB**, the smooth bore version which was first offered in 1936 without a model designation. The Model 41 rifle was also available with a Lyman No.422 Expert 4-power scope with micrometer click mounts. Only three years after inception, all varieties of the Model 41 Targetmaster were discontinued in December 1939, after 306,880 were sold.

Remington Model 411 Bolt-Action Rifles

One of the least known Remington small-bore rifles of the 1930s was the Model 411. This was essentially the same rifle as the single-shot Model 41, except it was chambered only for .22 caliber CB Cap rimfire ammunition. The low-cost M411 had a one-piece barrel and receiver assembly, one-piece stock, a self-cocking bolt, an extractor but no ejector (spent shells fell through the bottom of the receiver into a discharge tube), 24-inch barrel, blade and bead front sight and non-adjustable, wide V-groove rear sight. The M411 was never a catalog entry, as all 1,003 made in 1937, 311 in 1938 and 2 in 1939, were intended for one customer—Steel Materials Corporation of Detroit, Michigan. These rifles were utilized in a self-contained shooting gallery enclosure that Steel Materials called the "Bang-a-Deer."

Remington Model 510 Bolt-Action Rifles

In the late-1930s, Remington developed a plan to produce a family of sporting guns in which many parts would be interchangeable. In this manner, parts would be mass-produced in large quantities, thereby reducing production costs. The heart of the 500 series was a low-cost receiver made from seamless drawn steel tubing, not more expensive forged steel.

In February 1939, Remington announced that the new **Model 510 Targetmaster** would be ready for delivery on March 15th. This rifle was advertised as a low-priced gun that was self-cocking upon opening of the bolt, a firing indicator which showed when the rifle was cocked and ready to fire, double locking lugs on the bolt, double extractors for positive extraction, and streamlined design. The rifle was available with a Weaver No.344 scope, mounted at the factory. Variations of the Model 510 include:

- **Model 510A Rifle**—This firearm was developed to replace the Model 33, and has these features: takedown; 25-inch round barrel; step-adjustable rear sight; white metal bead front sight; one-piece

Above: Remington Model 121 Slide Action Rifle.

American walnut pistol-grip stock with semi-beavertail fore-end; weight of 5lbs/12oz; and chambered for .22 Short, Long or Long Rifle ammunition. In 1948 the **Improved Rifle** featured a chrome-plated bolt, bolt handle and trigger. The Model 510A was discontinued in December 1962.

- **Model 510SB Rifle**—This is a smooth bore version of the single-shot M510A, and it retailed for the same price when introduced in 1939. The barrel is marked 22 CAL. SMOOTH BORE and it sported a white metal bead front sight and no rear sight.

- **Routledge Bored M510 Rifle**—Remington manufactured a limited number of Routledge bored M510 rifles in 1940, and these have 24-inch barrels intended for .22 caliber shot cartridges. The barrel is marked ROUTLEDGE BORE FOR .22 LONG RIFLE SHOT CARTRIDGE (in two lines).

- **Model 510 Skeetrap Rifle**—Concurrently, Remington marketed the Model 510 Skeetrap rifle which was also smooth bore with a white metal bead front sight and no rear sight. It had a 26-inch barrel which was bored to Loewi specifications with a muzzle piece. The barrel is marked .22 SKEETRAP. Like the Routledge bored rifle, this rifle was never offered in a Remington catalog.

- **Model 510P Rifle**—The company also made Model 510P rifles which were basically the same as the M510A, except for a Patridge-type front sight mounted on a ramp and a Remington adjustable rear peep sight with interchangeable discs. The M510P cost $6.70 when introduced in 1939. After World War II Remington offered this rifle with a Remington Point-crometer receiver-mounted peep sight. The Model 510P was discontinued in December 1960.

- **Model 510 Targetmaster Carbine**—Remington first marketed the Model 510 Targetmaster Carbine in 1961, and advertised it as the perfect single-shot 22 rifle for teen-age shooters.

In all, Remington made a total of 558,686 Model 510 rifles in the twenty-three year period between 1939 and 1962.

Remington Model 511 "Scoremaster" Bolt Action Rifles

At the same time that Remington introduced the single shot Model 510, the factory also brought out a box-magazine version, the Remington Model 511 repeating rifle. The rifle was also available with a Weaver No.344 scope, mounted at the factory. Three variations of this repeater were announced to the public in February 1939, stating that rifles would be ready for delivery on April 15th:

- **Model 511A**—This rifle shared the same characteristics as the single-shot Model 510, except it is a detachable, box-magazine repeating rifle. The magazine holds six rounds of 22 Short, Long or Long Rifle ammunition, and a 10-shot magazine was an optional accessory. It has a white metal bead blade-type front sight on ramp, and a sporting-type, step-adjustable rear sight. This repeater weighs 5lbs/12oz, and the barrel is marked: MODEL 511.

- **Model 511P**—This is the same as the M511A, except it has a Patridge-type front sight mounted on a non-glare ramp, and a Remington "Point-Crometer" pear peep sight, adjustable for windage and elevation, with two interchangeable discs. The barrel was initially marked MODEL 511-P, and later MODEL 511P.

- **Model 511SB**—This rifle is the same as the M511A except it is smooth bore, and has a white metal bead shotgun-style front sight and no rear sight. It was chambered only for .22 Long Rifle shot cartridges. The barrel was marked MODEL 511 and 22 CAL. SMOOTH BORE. It was last offered in the 1945 Remington Price List.

Remington Rifles and Carbines • 77

Above: Remington Model 511 Bolt Action Rifle with scope.

Above: Remington Model 513T Target Rifle.

- **Routledge Bored Model 511**—This special order rifle featured a 24-inch proprietary smoothbore barrel by Fred Routledge. The barrel was marked ROUTLEDGE BORE FOR 22 LONG RIFLE SHOT CARTRIDGE (in two lines).

The Model 511P was discontinued in December 1960, and the Model 511A was discontinued in 1963, although it was last advertised by Remington in 1962. In all, Remington made a total of 381,267 Model 511 rifles in the twenty-four year period between 1939 and 1963.

Remington Model 512 "Sportmaster" Tubular Magazine Rifles

One year after Remington introduced the Model 510, the company produced a bolt action, tubular magazine repeating rifle based on the same design, calling it "The New 1940 Sportmaster Remington Model 512". Three variations of this repeater was announced to the public in February 1940:

- **Model 512A**—This small-bore rifle shared the same characteristics as the Model 510A, except it is a tubular magazine repeater with a capacity of 22 Shorts, 17 Longs or 15 Long Rifle rimfire cartridges. It has a white metal bead blade-type front sight on ramp, and a sporting-type, step-adjustable rear sight. This rifle weighs 5lbs/12oz, and the barrel is marked: MODEL 512.
- **Model 512P**—This rifle is the same as the M512A except it has a Patridge type front sight mounted on a non-glare ramp, and a Remington "Point-Crometer" rear peep sight, adjustable for windage and elevation, with two interchangeable discs. The barrel was initially marked MODEL 512-P, and later MODEL 512 P. The Model 512P was discontinued in December 1959.
- **Model 512SB**—This rifle is the same as the M512A except it has a non-rifled smooth bore, and a white metal bead shotgun-type front sight and no rear sight. It was chambered only for .22 Long Rifle shot cartridges, and the tubular magazine held 15 cartridges. The barrel was marked MODEL 512 and 22 CAL. SMOOTH BORE. It was last offered in 1945.

A total of 393,665 M512 rifles were sold from 1940 through 1963, although they were last advertised in the 1962 Remington catalog.

Remington Model 513T "Matchmaster" Bolt-Action Target Rifle

After months of development, Remington announced a new small-bore, bolt-action target rifle—the **Remington Model 513T Matchmaster Target Rifle**, one of the Series 500 Family of Rifles. It was ready for delivery in May 1940, and featured a heavy 27-inch semi-floating target barrel, a full target-style pistol-grip stock with beavertail fore-end, an adjustable front sling swivel, Redfield globe front sight with 7-interchangeable discs, a new Redfield No.75 micrometer rear sight, adjustable trigger stop, short firing pin travel, 6-shot detachable box-magazine, and 9-pound weight. Remington also offered this target rifle as M513TX without sights.

In all, Remington sold a total of 123,625 M513T Target Rifles in the twenty-nine year period between 1939 and 1968.

Remington Model 513S Bolt-Action Sporting Rifle

Concurrently with the introduction of the M513T in 1939, Remington introduced the **Model 513S Sporter Grade Rifle** which featured the same components as the M513T, except for a tapered barrel, streamlined sporting-style stock with checkering, Patridge-type front sight mounted on ramp, step-adjustable rear sight on barrel, screw-eyes for sling swivels, and weighing 6lbs/12oz. Officially it was referred to as the Model 513SA rifle. Production was interrupted during WWII, but resumed in 1945, when another variation was offered—the **Remington Model 513SP Sporter Grade** which was the same as the M513SA, but with a Remington "Point-crometer" receiver peep sight. Serial numbers of the M513T were shared with the M513S. The M513SP was last offered in 1951, and the M513SA was last offered in 1956. In all, the factory sold 13,677 M513S rifles in the seventeen-year period between 1939 and 1956.

Remington Model 550 Autoloading Rifles

In July 1938, Remington began work on a new blow-back, autoloading rifle based on the Remington Model 500 Series "Family of Guns" to replace the Model 241. The **Remington Model 550 Autoloading Rifle** functioned with the "Remington power piston" was announced to the public in January 1941, stating that deliveries of these rifles would commence in April.

referred to as the Model 550-1. The Model 550A autoloader was last advertised in 1970, and guns were sold through December 1971. In all, Remington sold a total of 764,573 M550 autoloading rifles in the 32-year period going back to 1939.

Remington Model 610 Bolt-Action Rifles

In 1936, Remington decided to develop a series of small-bore, bolt-action rifles chambered with a new rimfire cartridge to compete against Winchester rifles chambered for .22 W.R.F. ammunition. The eventual result was a proprietary .267 rimfire cartridge with bolt-action rifles to shoot it. Frame and barrel assemblies of the 600 Series were based upon Remington's 500 Series of guns. The new bolt-action rifles shared the following characteristics: 25-inch round tapered barrels; white metal bead front sight and step-adjustable rear sight; and one-piece American walnut stock with pistol-grip and semi-beavertail fore-end.

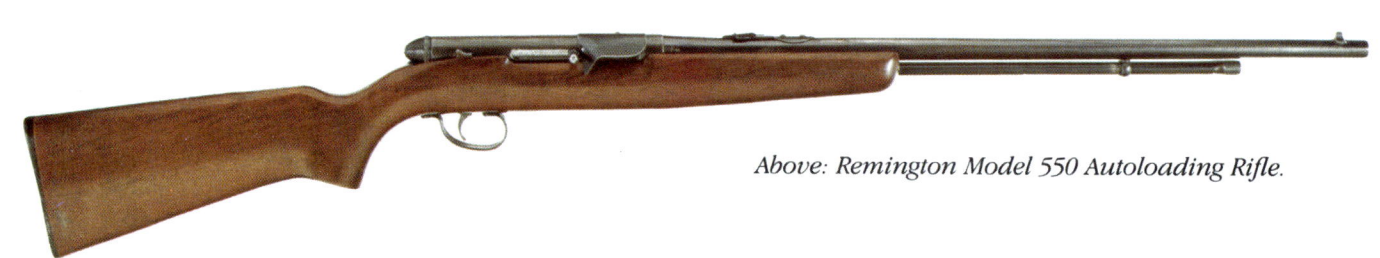

Above: Remington Model 550 Autoloading Rifle.

- **Model 550A autoloading rifle**—This basic model has these characteristics: 24-inch barrel; tubular magazine holds twenty-two Short, or seventeen Long or fifteen Long Rifle .22 caliber cartridges; Short, Long or Long Rifle ammunition can be loaded and fired interchangeably without adjustment; 6lbs/4oz weight; one-piece American walnut stock with pistol-grip and semi-beavertail fore-end; shotgun-style butt plate; and white metal bead front sight and step-adjustable rear sight. The M550A rifle was discontinued in December 1970, after 30 years of production.
- **Model 550P autoloading rifle**—This rifle differs from the M550A rifle in that it is equipped with a Patridge-type blade front sight on non-glare ramp, and a Remington "Point-crometer" rear peep sight with two interchangeable discs. It was discontinued in December 1951.
- **Model 550-2G Gallery Special rifle**—This gun was introduced in 1950, intended for use in shooting galleries, and was chambered only for .22 caliber Short rimfire cartridges. It was discontinued in December 1959.

The earliest M550 rifles were manufactured with two ejectors in the bolt head. However in late 1946, the gun was redesigned with only one ejector, and was thereafter

- **Model 610A Standard single-shot rifle**—Only 63 rifles were made between 1940 and 1945. This single-shot rifle weighs 5lbs/12oz. A **Model 610P Special single-shot rifle** was also produced which was identical to the M610A, except that it was fitted with a Patridge-type front sight on non-glare ramp, and a Remington "Point-crometer" rear peep sight.
- **Model 611A Standard box-magazine repeater**—This rifle was a 5-shot box-magazine repeating version of the M610 rifle. Only 29 rifles were made in 1940 and 1942. A **Model 611P Special box-magazine rifle** was also produced, fitted with a Patridge-type front sight on non-glare ramp, and a Remington "Point-crometer" rear peep sight.

- **Model 612A tubular-magazine repeater**—Little is known of these enigmatic rifles except that only 9 were made by Remington in 1940.
- **Model 613S Sporter box-magazine repeater**—Only 9 of these higher finish sporting rifles were made in 1940. Characteristics include: Patridge-type front sight; step-adjustable rear sight; and lacquer-finished stock with checkering on pistol-grip and fore-end.

Problems arose during development of these rifles, including occasional burst heads due to insufficient support of the cartridge rims, excessive leading in the bore after extensive shooting, and unacceptable and unsustained accuracy. Remington designers could not solve the accuracy problems with their 600 Series of .267 caliber rimfire rifles. Despite long hours and many failures, Remington could not determine whether the problem lay with the rifle, or with the ammunition, or both. M610/M611/M612/M613 rifles were not offered to the shooting public and were never a Remington catalog item.

Remington Model 720 Bolt-Action Rifles

As part of a DuPont inspired gun modernization program in the last half of the 1930s, Remington worked on a replacement for the Model 30 Express rifle, which was costly to manufacture. By 1940, the Remington Arms Company had completed tooling for a new bolt-action sporting rifle, the Remington **Model 720** high-power rifle, and production was scheduled to begin the following year. The new rifle utilized a modified M14/M1917-style receiver, somewhat different from the M30 receiver. Initially this hunting rifle was to be chambered for the .30-06, and later for the .270 Win and .257 Remington-Roberts chamberings. A wide array of model variations were planned and some were built, including the Model 720R with a 20-inch carbine-length barrel. No sooner had production commenced on the new rifle than the United States was thrust into an all-consuming World War, requiring Remington's full attention to the manufacture of military weapons. Consequently, only an initial run of 4,000 Model 720 subassemblies was completed when production was halted for the demanding military commitment.

At the beginning of the war the U.S. Navy contracted with Remington to acquire most of the initial production run of Model 720 rifles chambered for the .30-06 service cartridge, some with 24-inch barrels, but most with 22-inch barrels. The Navy acquired about 1,000 Remington rifles from the inventory in Ilion, and many others which had been shipped to jobbers and wholesalers. Factory records indicate that 427 of these rifles had been sold commercially in 1941, another 1,022 had gone to the Navy in 1942, 973 had been sold to parties unknown in 1943, and a final 5 had been sold in 1944. Evidently the 1,000 or so Navy Model 720 rifles were not issued to sailors or marines during the war, and remained in Naval inventory. Starting in 1964, the Navy began awarding new-in-the-box Model 720s as marksmanship trophies by the Navy and Marine Corps under the title of "Secretary of the Navy Trophy" or "Secretary of Defense Trophy."

U.S. Rifles, Caliber .30, Model 1903

In 1941, when the United States needed firearms it called upon Remington. The company stepped forward to provide both rifles and ammunition, eventually

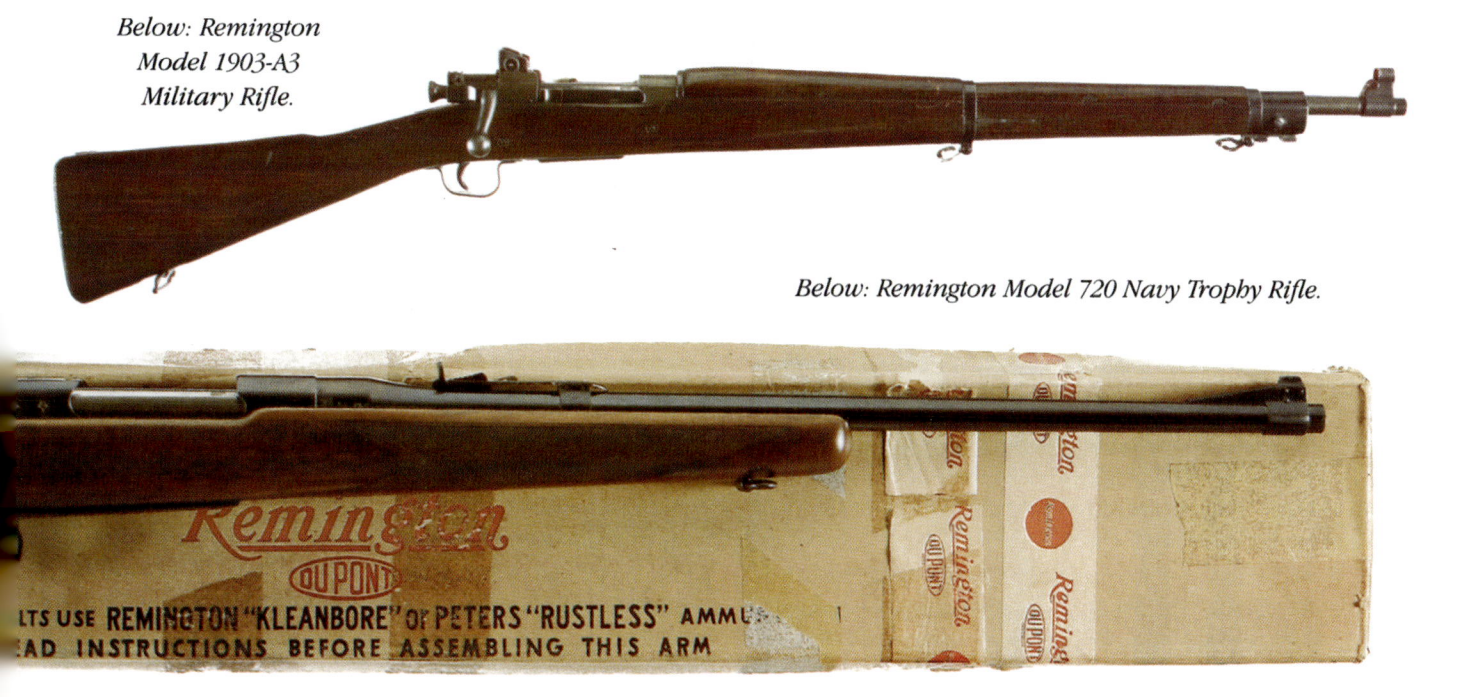

Below: Remington Model 1903-A3 Military Rifle.

Below: Remington Model 720 Navy Trophy Rifle.

increasing its workforce twenty-fold, and producing materiel with an aggregate value of over one billion dollars. On December 12, 1940, Great Britain asked Remington to produce Model 1903 Springfield rifles chambered for the .303 British service cartridge. On June 30, 1941, a contract was signed which called for 500,000 of these rifles. However, because of pressing U.S. needs this contract was canceled, and in its place came a cost-plus-fixed fee contract from the U.S. Government on September 11, 1941, to produce 134,000 **U.S. Rifles, Caliber .30, Model 1903**.

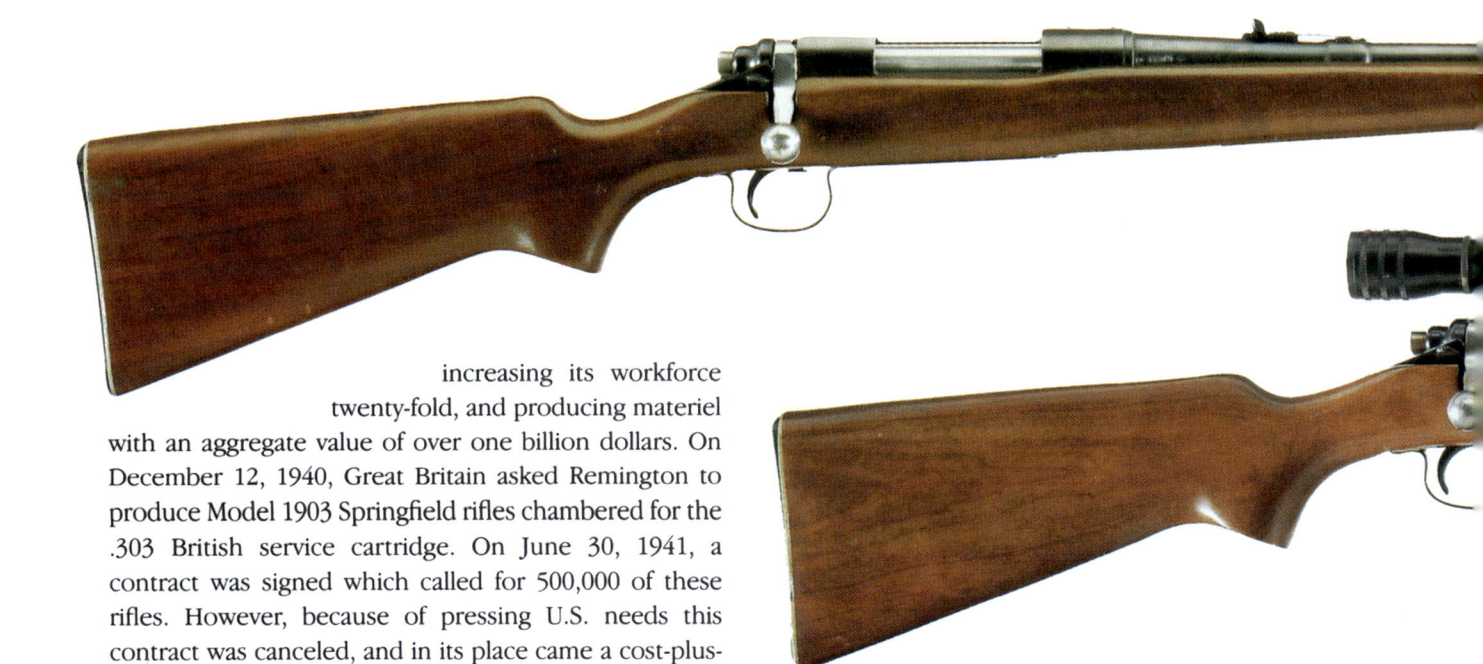

The Ordnance Department asked Remington to tool up to produce as many Springfield bolt-action service rifles as possible, in as short a time as possible. A second contract was sent to Remington on November 24th for an additional 74,000 rifles, and another on December 13th for 100,000 more. Rifle production commenced in October 1941, utilizing government-owned machinery, tools, jigs and fixtures which had been used at the Rock Island Arsenal and Springfield Armory during World War I. Deliveries on the first Model 1903 rifles commenced in November 1941, and continued through May 1942. During that seven-month period about 160,000 rifles were made in Ilion.

In April 1942, approval was given by the Ordnance Department for Remington to simplify production of the M1903 rifle, including the substitution of stamped instead of machined parts. The resulting weapon was called **U.S. Rifle, Caliber .30, Model 1903** (Modified) and Remington produced about 188,000 between June and December 1942.

On May 21, 1942, the U.S. Ordnance Commission ordered standardization of the bolt-action service rifle, to be called **U.S. Rifle, Caliber .30, Model 1903A3**. On June 8, Remington was authorized by the Ordnance Department to begin the production changeover to the new design, as soon as machinery and tooling were available. On July 20, 1942, an order was received to fabricate 720,000 of the new rifles. Deliveries commenced in January 1943, and continued for the next fifteen months. On December 7, 1943, Remington received a change-order from the Ordnance Department which called for cessation of production on February 29, 1944. A total of 707,629 Remington M1903A3 rifles had been delivered.

On January 18, 1943, Remington was issued a contract to "divert 20,000 M1903 rifles from production and convert them to sniping arms, as per specifications furnished." These were to be designated **U.S. Rifle, Caliber .30, Model 1903A4 (Sniper's)**. On June 20th, an additional 8,365 sniper rifles were ordered. Production commenced on these weapons in February 1943, and continued through June 1944, when the order was canceled. In all, Remington had produced 28,365 M1903A4 rifles, making them the first mass-produced sniper rifle manufactured in the United States. Each had been fitted with a civilian Weaver M330C rifle scope (later given the military designation of M73B1) with 2.5X optics fitted with cross-hair reticles.

Model 721 Bolt-Action Rifles

By 1944 Remington officials decided to replace this M14/Enfield 1917/Model 30 derivative with two new bolt-action, high-power guns—Remington Model 721 and Model 722 rifles. Remington introduced the Model 722 rifle concurrently with the Model 721, which were nearly identical except for different length receivers, and a slight difference in weight and overall length. The new Model 721 (long action) and Model 722 (short action) rifles allowed Remington to gain a competitive advantage over other manufacturers. The new models cost less to produce than the guns they replaced, and had more pleasing lines. Each rifle featured a shrouded bolt head, which provided additional support to the cartridge case, and a ring-type extractor. These features gave the new rifles exceptional strength.

The Model 721A Standard Grade rifle with plain stock was announced in January 1948, in .270 Win, .30-06 and .300 H & H Magnum calibers. It featured a longer

Above: Remington Model 721 Bolt Action Rifle.

Above: Remington Model 722 Bolt Action Rifle.

Above: Remington Model 514A Rifle.

1950), .222 Remington Magnum (introduced 1958), .243 Win (introduced 1959), .244 Remington (introduced 1956), and .308 Win (also introduced 1956) centerfire ammunition. In 1959, all grade variations except for the basic M722A were dropped. Remington discontinued the Model 722 in December 1961, after producing 117,751 rifles.

receiver than the Model 722. This rifle weighed 7lbs/4oz. and deliveries commenced in March 1948. Barrels measured 24 inches in length in all calibers except for those of .300 H & H Magnum, which were 26-inches long. By the following year M721AC, M721B Special Grade, D Peerless Grade, and F Premier Grade rifles were offered, all with checkered stocks.

In June 1949, Remington introduced an improved Model 721 for "big game hunters," chambered for the potent .300 H & H Magnum cartridge, complete with recoil pad. It weighed 8lbs/8oz in the M721A Standard Grade. In February 1955, the M721AC and M721B versions were dropped, but Remington introduced Model 721ADL and BDL versions. In January 1959, all grades except the basic M721A were dropped. In January 1960, the .280 Remington caliber was added to the line and in January 1961, the .264 Win Magnum was added. Remington discontinued the Model 721 rifle in December 1961, having produced 173,124 over a thirteen-year period.

Model 722 Bolt-Action Rifles

Introduced in January 1948, the Model 722 A Standard Grade rifle was initially chambered for the .257 Roberts and .300 Sav, and featured a receiver slightly shorter than the Model 721. The rifle weighed about 7 pounds, and had a 24-inch barrel. In 1949 this rifle was also offered as M722 AC (dropped in 1955), M722 B Special Grade (also dropped in 1955), D Peerless Grade and F Premier Grades, all with checkered stocks. Model 722 ADL and BDL versions were introduced in January 1955. Later calibers added included .222 Remington (introduced

Model 521TL "Junior Special" Target Rifles

In July 1947, Remington announced its latest .22 caliber target rifle, the Model 521 TL "Junior Special." This rifle was intended to be a low-cost rifle for young marksmen who didn't need or couldn't afford a new Model 513T, or the more expensive Model 37. The M521 TL had a 25-inch barrel, weighed about 7 pounds, and its stock resembled the one on the M513T Matchmaster. It featured a beavertail fore-end with adjustable front swivel, double locking lugs, Patridge-type blade front sight and Lyman No.57RS micrometer rear sight. It had a 6-shot, detachable box magazine, and came with a leather sling. The receiver was the same as used in the Model 511, the outgrowth of the 500-series of rifles, begun by Remington in the late 1930s. In January 1959, Remington officially changed the designation to Model 521T (Target). Remington discontinued the Model 521T in December 1968, after selling 66,338 rifles over this twenty-one year period.

Model 514 Bolt-Action Rifles

In April 1948, Remington announced the **Model 514A** single-shot, bolt-action. This 5lb/4oz rifle had a 24-inch round barrel with blade-type front sight and step-adjustable rear. In January 1949, Remington introduced the **Model 514P**, a peep sight version of the M514A. This model was only made for a few years, and was

Below: Remington Model 760 Scoped Slide Action Rifle.

deleted from the line in mid-1951. In January 1961, the **Model 514BC "Boy's Carbine"** was introduced with a 20-inch barrel (4 inches shorter than the original), and with a stock which is one-inch shorter than the original. It sold for $19.65, the same price as the full-sized M514A. In January 1962, the M514A barrel was reduced to 20 inches, the same as on the "Boy's Carbine." In January 1963, the barrel on the M514A was lengthened to 24 inches, and in January 1965, the designation of the Model 514BC was changed to **Model 514BR "Boy's Rifle."** Remington produced the Model 514 single-shot rifle through 1970, and in twenty-two years sold 757,624 rifles.

Remington Model 760 "Gamemaster" Slide-Action Rifles

In 1952, Remington introduced the Model 760 "Gamemaster" high-power rifle. This was the first Remington slide-action sporting rifle to be chambered for the .30-06 cartridge. Other chamberings soon followed. In 1954, Remington introduced a Model 760 ADL version, and a Model 760 BDL version. This powerful rifle had a 22-inch barrel, a 4-shot detachable box magazine, and weighed about 7lbs/8oz.

In 1966, the company sold 4,610 Remington 150th Anniversary models of this gun, all in .30-06 caliber. In 1976, approximately 3,800 American Bicentennial-edition Model 760 rifles were sold. Remington ceased manufacturing and advertising the Model 760 high-power rifle in December 1980, however, the gun sold well into the following year when it was replaced by the Remington Model 7600 pump-action rifle. In all, Remington sold 1,034,462 Model 760 rifles & carbines in this twenty-one year period.

Model 760C Carbines

The **Model 760C carbine** with an 18-inch barrel was announced in January 1960. It weighed only 6lbs/8oz.

Production of the Remington Model 760C carbine stopped in 1980. In a twenty-year period a total of 42,236 Model 760C carbines were sold.

Model 572 "Fieldmaster" Rifles

In December 1954, Remington announced the **Model 572A "Fieldmaster"**, a slide-action, .22 caliber rifle to replace the Model 121. The tubular magazine held 20 Short, 17 Long, or 15 Long Rifle rimfire cartridges. A Whelen-type, 1 inch" wide leather sling strap was an optional accessory. The **Model 572 SB "Smooth Bore"** (with choke bore) was introduced in 1962.

It was intended to shoot .22 Long Rifle shot loads. In 1966, Remington introduced the **M572 BDL "DeLuxe"** rifle to supplement the M572A and M572 SB. The BDL featured a ramp front sight, a barrel-mounted rear sight (adjustable for elevation and windage), and a checkered pistol-grip and fore-end. In 1966, Remington made 3,815 limited edition **M572 "150th Anniversary Edition" rifles**. The M572 SB was last offered in a Remington bolt action of this new rifle was based on the successful design of the Model 721-722. It had a rigid receiver with a large cylindrical bedding surface, adjustable trigger, and dual extractors. It also featured a Remington "Group Tightener" which allowed the shooter to adjust the directional force exerted on the barrel by the stock. Initial variations in 1955 included **Model 40X-S1** with standard barrel and Redfield Olympic target sights, and weighing

Above: Remington Model 760 Slide Action Rifle.

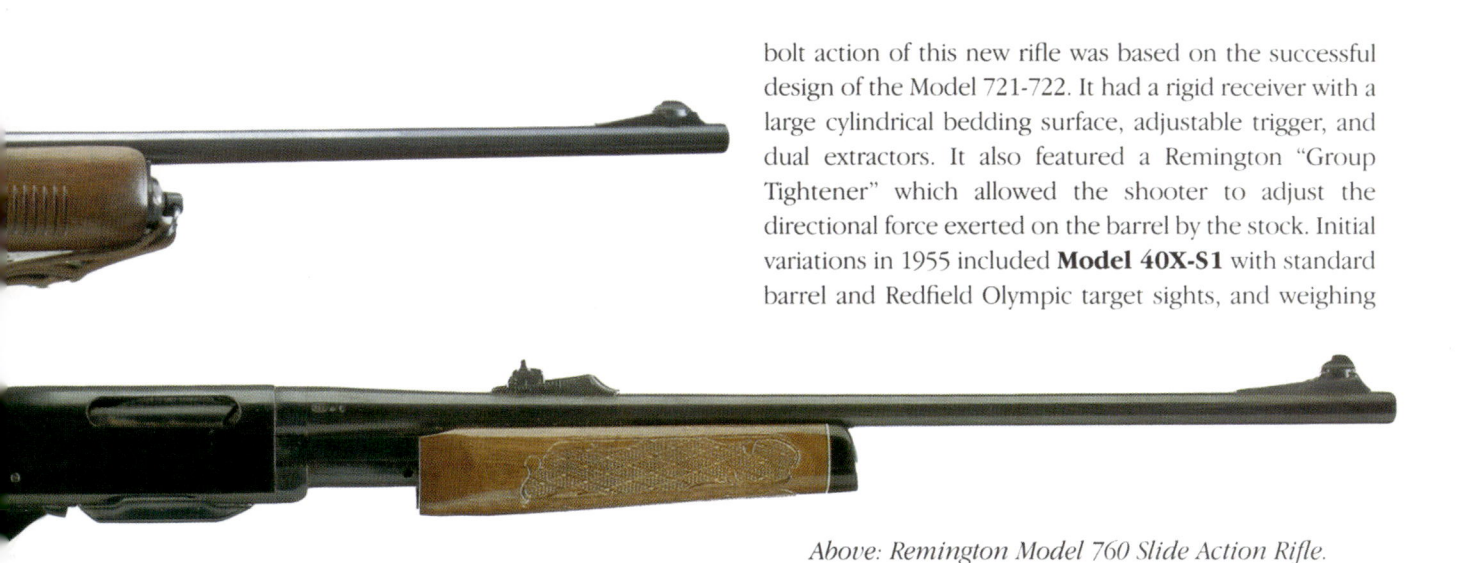

catalog in 1978, and the M572A was last offered in the Remington 1987 catalog, which left the M572 BDL as Remington's sole small-bore, slide-action rifle.

Remington Model 740 "Woodsmaster" Autoloading Rifles

In 1955, Remington introduced the Model 740 gas-operated, high-power autoloading rifle in .30-06 caliber. Initial versions of this rifle included a M740A Standard Grade, a M740 ADL Deluxe Grade, and two Custom Gun Shop versions: M740D Peerless Grade, and M740F Premier Grade. A M740 BDL "Deluxe Special" version was introduced in 1957. Model 740 "Woodsmaster" autoloaders featured a "Power-Matic" action, and weighed 7lbs/8oz. In only five years, Remington sold 251,398 Model 740 rifles. This autoloader was discontinued in December 1959.

Model 40X Bolt Action Rifles

In July 1955, Remington announced "an ultra precision .22 Long Rifle target rifle" to replace the expensive Model 37 target rifle—the **Model 40X "Rangemaster"** The

10lbs/12oz, **Model 40X-S2** with standard barrel and no sights, **Model 40X-H1** with heavy barrel and Redfield Olympic target sights, and weighing 12lbs/12oz, and **Model 40X-H2** with heavy barrel and no sights.

In 1959, Remington brought out two high-power versions of the popular Model 40X "Rangemaster" target rifle: **Model 40X-CF-S2** with standard barrel and Redfield Olympic sights and **Model 40X-CF-H2** with heavy barrel and no sights. The initial caliber offered was .308 Win "and others on special order." In 1960, the following additional high-power calibers were offered: .222 Remington, .222 Remington Magnum, .30-06 and .300 H & H Magnum.

At the request of the U.S. Army, Remington Design Team engineers began working with members of the U.S. Army Advanced Marksmanship Unit (AAMU) at Fort Benning, Georgia, to design a radically different target

Above: Remington Model 40X Bolt Action Target Rifle.

rifle. The result came in 1959, when Remington Arms Company introduced the **International Free Rifle** in .22 Long Rifle and centerfire calibers. This top-of-the-line target rifle featured a 40X type action, precision heavy barrel, rough-turned laminated wood stock (ready for individual finishing by the shooter), no sights, 15-pound weight, adjustable butt plate with interchangeable rubber pad or hook, adjustable palm rest, adjustable front sling swivel, and either 1-ounce or 2-ounce target trigger. The centerfire version was chambered for 7.62mm NATO and .30-06 ammunition ("and others on special order" including .222 Remington and .222 Remington Magnum). In 1962, a left-hand stock (not a left-hand action) was available at additional cost. Starting in 1969, finished stocks were offered instead of rough-turned stocks, and International-type or Olympic-type target sights were standard. A total of 123 rimfire International Free Rifles were sold between 1960 and 1973, and a total of 594 centerfire versions were sold from 1960 to 1976.

In 1965, the Model 40X designation was changed to **Model 40-XB**, and a Model 700-type action replaced the former Model 722-type action. Stainless steel barrels were made available at extra cost. For the first time in 1965, box-magazine repeating models intended for the National Match Course were offered to augment the Model 40-XB single-shot models. Calibers included .22-250 Remington, .222 Remington, .222 Remington Magnum, .223 Remington, 6mm Remington, 6mm International, 6mm-47, 6.5mm-55, 7mm Remington Magnum and 7.62mm NATO. The .22 Long Rifle version of the Model 40-XB remained a single-shot target rifle. In 1967, additional calibers were added, including .243 Remington and 6.5mm Remington. In 1970, .25-06 Remington was added, and in 1971, Remington added .300 Win Magnum. Model 40-XB rimfire and centerfire rifles were last sold in 1975, when they were replaced by the Model 40-XR series. The Model 40-XB was reintroduced around 1985. As of 1998, Model 40-XB rifles are current production items with walnut or Kevlar-reinforced synthetic stocks.

In 1998, the Remington Custom Gun Shop began offering the Model 40-XB with a thumb-hole laminated stock (in green, brown and desert coloring) and brown rubber butt pad, stainless steel receiver and barrel (without sights).

In 1970, Remington's Custom Shop introduced the **Model 40-XB Sporting Rifle**, a high-quality, clip-fed repeater which was chambered for .22 Long Rifle ammunition. It featured a select, hand-checkered American walnut stock with high cheek piece and Monte Carlo comb, and sling studs and swivels. Finish was DuPont RK-W or hand-rubbed oil. The barrel (offered with or without sights) and receiver were blued and highly polished, and the bolt was jeweled. Around 1986, Remington introduced the single-shot **Model 40-XR Custom Sporter Grade II**. In 1990, the Custom Gun Shop introduced the **Model 40-XR KS Rimfire Sporter** with Kevlar-reinforced stock. It had a 24-inch barrel. The clip-fed repeater was discontinued in the late 1970s.

In 1971, Remington introduced the single-shot **Model 40XB-BR (Bench Rest)**, a precision rifle in .222 Remington for bench rest shooters. It was designed to meet National Bench Rest Shooters Association rules for sporter and light varmint events, including a heavy 20-inch stainless steel barrel, and a wider, squared-off fore-end for resting on sand bags. For shooters competing in the heavy varmint class, a version with a 26-inch stainless steel barrel, and weighing 13lbs/8oz was also offered in 1971. In 1972, additional chamberings included .222 Rem Mag, .223 Rem, 6mm International, 6mm-47 and 7.62 NATO. In 1978, a .22 Rem-BR chambering was added, followed in 1979 by the 6mm Rem BR cartridge. As of 1998, Model 40-XB-BR rifles continue to be current production items. The rifle was also available as a **Model 40-XB-BR** Scope with a 20X target scope and mount.

The last year Remington offered this scope was 1974. **A Model 40-XB-BR KS** was first offered in 1998. It featured Kevlar-reinforced stock, hand-bedded action and stainless steel barrel.

Remington began offering a **Model 40-XR-BR** bench rest rimfire rifle in late 1993, chambered for .22 Long Rifle ammunition. It featured a 22-inch heavy target barrel, a green Kevlar-reinforced stock.

In 1974, Remington introduced the **Model 40-XR Rimfire Position Rifle**, designed for International Shooting Union requirements for a standard rifle. This single-shot .22 rifle featured a special target stock with an adjustable swivel block on a guide rail, 24-inch heavy target barrel, wide and adjustable target trigger, extra-long bolt with double extractors, two-way vertically adjustable butt plate, adjustable sling swivel/hand stop, and optional Redfield Olympic sights. It weighed 10lbs/2oz without sights. This model first appeared in the 1988 Remington catalog with Kevlar-reinforced stock and hand-bedded action and barrel. The Model 40-XR Rimfire Position Rifle was last advertised in the 1989 catalog with a walnut stock.

Remington introduced the **Model 40-XC National Match Course Rifle** in 1974, with a new stock configuration characterized by a deep fore-end and a pronounced pistol-grip. This precision target rifle was chambered for .308 Win ammunition, and the hand-bedded receiver was clip-slotted for five-shot clips which load from the top of the receiver. The free-floated stainless steel target-weight barrel was 23 inches in length. Other features included an adjustable trigger, adjustable sling swivel/hand stop and adjustable butt plate. This rifle met all International Shooting Union Army Rifle specifications. In 1989 this rifle was also offered with a birch stock.

In 1988, Remington introduced the **Model 40-XC-KS**, with Kevlar-reinforced stock, adjustable cheek piece and 24-inch, stainless steel, heavy barrel chambered for .308 Win.

In 1987, Remington's Custom Gun Shop introduced the **Model 40-XB Varmint Special**, which featured a black synthetic Kevlar-reinforced synthetic stock and a 27-inch stainless steel barrel. The rifle weighed 10 pounds, and was chambered for 14 calibers including the .220 Swift cartridge. This rifle could be ordered as a single-shot or, in certain calibers, as a repeater. The stock had a beavertail fore-end with flat bottom and a 1-inch thick recoil pad. The trigger pull was adjustable from 1 to 3 pounds pull, and a 2-ounce trigger was available on single-shot models.

Model 572 "Fieldmaster" Lightweight Rifles

In December 1957, Remington announced a special lightweight version of the popular Model 572, the Model 572 "Fieldmaster" Lightweight rifle. It weighed just 4 pounds (1 pound less than the standard Model 572A). The reduced weight was due to an anodized aluminum receiver, trigger guard, butt plate and jacket for the steel barrel liner.

This distinctive gun was available in three color schemes: **Model 572 CWB "Crow-Wing" Black**; **Model 572 BT "Buck-Skin" Tan**; and **Model 572 TWB "Teal-Wing" Blue**. The rifles each had a checkered, light-colored, "Sun-Grain" walnut stock and fore-end. The M572 TWB was discontinued in 1960, and the other two colors were last advertised in the Remington 1962 catalog, stating "subject to stock on hand." A total of 34,785 Model 572 "Fieldmaster" Lightweight rifles were sold over a four-year period, although the standard M572 "Fieldmaster" continues to be made to this very day.

Remington Model 552 "Speedmaster" Autoloading Rifles

In February 1957, Remington introduced an autoloading companion gun to the Model 572 slide-action rifle—the **Model 552A Standard Grade rifle**. Its tubular magazine held 20 Short, 17 Long, or 15 Long Rifle rimfire cartridges. The Model 552A was offered through 1987.

In 1958, Remington introduced the **Model 552GS "Gallery Special" Rifle** for shooting gallery use. It was chambered only for .22 Shorts, and featured a chain ring on the magazine tube, which would be utilized to secure the rifle to the gallery counter. This rifle was discontinued after 1977.

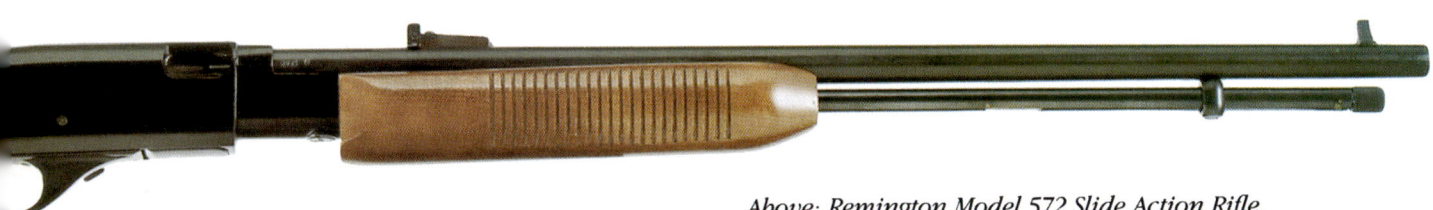

Above: Remington Model 572 Slide Action Rifle.

In 1961, Remington brought out the **Model 552C "Speedmaster" Carbine** with 21-inch barrel, but with the same tubular magazine capacity as the M552A rifle with its 25-inch barrel. The Model 552C was sold through 1977.

In 1966, Remington made 6,565 limited edition **M552 "150th Anniversary Edition" rifles**. It was in this year that **Model 552 BDL "DeLuxe" Rifles** were first offered. The BDL features a ramp front sight and barrel-mounted rear sight which is adjustable for elevation and windage, and checkered pistol-grip and fore-end. The Model 552 BDL remains extremely popular with small-bore shooters, and is still in the current line of Remington sporting rifles.

Remington Model 725 Bolt-Action Rifles

In 1958, Remington introduced a new high-power hunting rifle, the Model 725ADL "DeLuxe" Grade. The Model 725 rifle was designed by Wayne Leek and Charlie Campbell, a product-improved Model 721 to compete with Winchester's Model 70. This new rifle had a hinged floor-plate magazine with a 4-shot capacity. A 22-inch barrel was standard, except for rifles chambered for .222 Remington ammunition which had 24-inch barrels. The Monte Carlo-style stock facilitated scope use, but the rifle was also equipped with a hooded ramp front sight and a barrel-mounted rear sight which was adjustable for windage and elevation.

Above: Remington Model 725 Bolt Action Rifle.

In 1961 and '62, Remington's Custom Gun Shop produced 28 **Model 725 Kodiak rifles** in .375 H & H Magnum and 24 in .458 Win Magnum, all with 26-inch barrels. These "big game" rifles were fitted with built-in muzzle brakes and ventilated recoil pads and weighed 9 pounds complete with leather sling. Between 1958 and 1961, the Custom Gun Shop also produced a total of eight Grade D Peerless and Grade F Premier rifles.

In 1958, the initial chamberings for the Model 725 were .270 Win, .280 Remington and .30-06, and in the following year, .222 Remington and .244 Remington were offered. In January 1960, .243 Win was added. In 1961, .375 H & H Magnum and .458 Win Magnum calibers were offered only in the Custom Gun Shop's Model 725 Kodiak rifles. The Model 725 high-power rifle was discontinued in December 1961, after only four years of production. In that time, Remington had sold 16,635 Model 725 rifles.

Nylon 66 Autoloading Rifles

In January 1959, Remington introduced a new concept in firearms to the shooting fraternity—a small-bore .22 that used DuPont structural Zytel nylon. This was the Nylon 66 Autoloading Rifle. This lightweight, four-pound rifle featured a one-piece, nylon stock with molded checkering on the pistol-grip and fore-end. This unique autoloader had a steel bolt which recoiled in the plastic receiver, and a 19-inch barrel. The tubular magazine in the butt stock held 14 Long Rifle rimfire cartridges, and the ammunition was loaded through an opening in the butt plate. Variations of the Nylon 66 include:

- **Nylon 66SG "Seneca Green" Automatic Rifle**—Available only from March 1959 to 1962. Remington sold a total of 42,500 of these rifles in this 3-year period.
- **Nylon 66 MB "Mohawk Brown" Automatic Rifle**—Available from 1959 to 1987. This autoloader had a Mohawk Brown plastic stock, and blued receiver plates and barrel. The Nylon 66MB was also offered with a Universal MUA 4-power scope and mount from 1975 to 1983.
- **Nylon 66 GS "Gallery Special" Automatic Rifle**—Sold from April 1961 to 1981, and chambered for .22 caliber Shorts only. This rifle featured a 20-shot magazine, a spent shell deflector mounted on the right side of the receiver, a shooting gallery counter chain retainer, and a blued barrel and blued receiver plates. This gallery rifle had a Mohawk Brown plastic stock.
- **Model 66AB "Apache Black" Automatic Rifle**—Available from 1962 to 1983. This "presentation grade" rifle features an Apache Black nylon stock and a chrome plated barrel and receiver cover.
- **Nylon 66 BD "Black Diamond" Automatic Rifle**—Sold from 1978 to 1987. The Nylon 66BD was also offered with a 4-power scope from 1978 to 1983.
- **Nylon 66 Chrome Finish Automatic Rifle**—Total production, 220,564 rifles.
- **Nylon 66 "150th Anniversary" Automatic Rifle**—This Mohawk Brown rifle was available only in

1966 to commemorate Remington's 150th Anniversary. Remington sold 3,792 rifles. A commemorative oval was embossed in gold-tone paint on the left receiver plate.

- **Nylon 66 "Bicentennial" Automatic Rifle**—This rifle was produced in 1976, to commemorate America's 200th Anniversary. It featured an American Bicentennial stamping on the left receiver plate, and a 18-inch barrel. It was available only with a Mohawk Brown plastic stock with white diamond inlays in the fore-end and white line spacers. This rifle was available with a 4-power scope. A total of 10,279 Nylon 66 Bicentennial rifles were sold.

The Nylon 66 was last offered in 1985, and in that 24-year period Remington sold 987,949 rifles of all variations.

Nylon 76 "Trailrider" Lever-Action Rifles

Remington introduced a lever-action nylon .22 rifle in 1962, calling it the Nylon 76 "Trailrider." It was available in **Nylon 76AB "Apache Black"** and **Nylon 76MB "Mohawk Brown"**. This unique rifle featured a lever action with a short, 35E lever throw. It utilized the Nylon 66 bolt with a locked-breech, rack and pinion action. It featured a round barrel, 19-inches in length, and chrome-plated receiver plates and lever. The tubular magazine held 14 Long Rifle cartridges, loaded through a brass tube in the butt stock. The stock was either Mohawk Brown or Apache Black in color. The Nylon 76 was discontinued in December 1965, after Remington had sold 26,927 rifles.

Nylon 10 Bolt-Action Rifles

In 1962, Remington introduced a trio of bolt-action Nylon rifles: the Nylon 10 single-shot; the Nylon 11 box-magazine repeater; and the Nylon 12 tubular magazine repeater. All shared common parts including an injection molded Mohawk Brown nylon stock, with white diamond inlays in the fore-end and white line spacers on the butt plate, grip cap and fore-end. The rifles also shared a common bolt action with enclosed bolt head, dual extractors, two locking lugs and a chrome plated bolt handle, the same bolt design as Remington's 500-series.

Remington introduced the **Nylon 10** single-shot, bolt-action rifle in June 1962. This rifle chambered either .22 caliber Short, Long or Long Rifle rimfire ammunition, and weighed only 4lbs/2oz. Concurrently, Remington offered a smooth-bore version, the **Nylon 10-SB**, which was the same as the Nylon 10 except for a smooth-bored barrel intended for .22 caliber shot cartridges.

Remington discontinued the Nylon 10 and the Nylon 10-SB in December 1964, with diminished sales in 1965. In less than three years of production Remington sold 10,670 of these rifles.

Nylon 11 Bolt-Action Rifles

A box-magazine version of the Nylon 10 bolt-action rifle was actually introduced five months earlier than the Nylon 10. It was called the **Nylon 11**, and it had a detachable plastic magazine which held six .22 rimfire cartridges. A 10-round magazine was optional, and the

Above and below: Remington Model Nylon 66. Autoloading Rifle.

rifle weighed a scant 4lbs/4oz. The first repeaters were distributed on December 12, 1961. The Nylon 11 was eventually discontinued in December 1964, with diminished sales in 1965. During this period Remington had sold 22,423 rifles.

Nylon 12 Bolt-Action Rifles

Remington introduced a tubular repeater concurrently with the Nylon 11, calling it the **Nylon 12**. Its tubular magazine beneath the barrel held 21 Short, 16 Long, or 14 Long Rifle cartridges (interchangeably). This lightweight repeater weighed 4lbs/8oz. The Nylon 11 was discontinued in December 1964, with diminished sales in 1965. Remington had sold 27,551 rifles during this period.

Nylon 77 Autoloading Rifles

A spinoff from the Nylon 66 was the Nylon 77, introduced in 1970. This autoloading rifle featured a 5-shot box magazine (an optional 10-round plastic magazine was also available). The nylon stock was Apache Black or Mohawk Brown in color, with checkered pistol grip and fore-end with white diamond inlays, and white line spacers on the butt plate, grip cap and fore-end. The Nylon 77 was produced for only two years, and was last featured in the 1971 Remington catalog. During that period a total of 15,327 rifles were sold. The following year Remington brought out a variation of the Nylon 77, renamed the Mohawk 10-C.

Mohawk 10-C Autoloading Rifles

Remington introduced the Mohawk 10-C in 1972, as a promotional rifle offered to distributors in large quantities at special discount. This autoloading .22 caliber rifle was essentially a Nylon 77 with a 10-round box magazine as standard equipment. The Mohawk 10C had an injection molded DuPont Zytel structural nylon Mohawk Brown stock. It featured 3-point bedding, checkering molded onto the pistol-grip and fore-end, and with white diamond inlays in the fore-end. There was a black fore-end cap, a pistol-grip cap and a butt plate, all with white line spacers. Mohawk 10-C rifles were sold through 1978. A total of 128,358 were sold over this seven-year period even though the Mohawk 10-C was never listed in any Remington catalog.

Apache 77 Autoloading Rifles

The last of Remington's Nylon stocked rifles, a total of 54,781 of these rifles were made for and sold only by K-Mart in 1987. The stock was bright green. Some barrels had a bright, jet black finish, while others had a dull, sand-blasted black painted finish. This rifle fired only .22 caliber Long Rifle rimfire ammunition, and featured a 10-round box magazine.

Remington Model 742 "Woodsmaster" Autoloading Rifles

In January 1960, Remington introduced the **Model 742 "Woodsmaster" Autoloading Rifle**. This autoloader featured gas operated, Power-Matic action with dual action bars, a solid frame, a rotary breech block, and side ejection. Its inner parts were coated with friction-freeing DuPont Teflon S. The rifles had the same bolt design as on the Model 760 Slide Action Rifle. It had a free-floating, round barrel, 22 inches in length, a detachable 4-shot clip magazine, and weighed 7lbs/8oz. Initially the Model 742 was available in three high-power chamberings: .280 Remington, .30-06 and .308 Win. Remington added a 6mm cartridge in 1963, and added .243 Win in 1968. Variations of the Model 742 include:

- **Model 742A "Standard Grade" Rifles**—The A "Standard Grade" was introduced in January 1960 and was discontinued in December 1967.

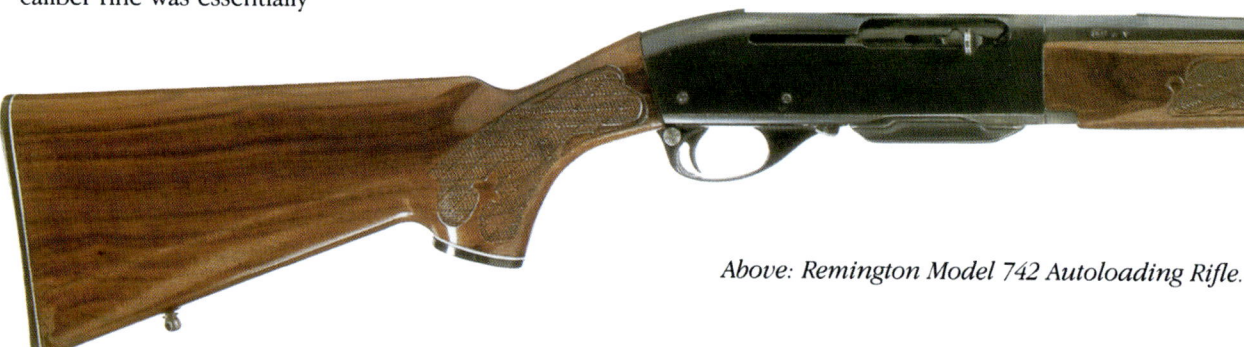

Above: Remington Model 742 Autoloading Rifle.

- **Model 742 ADL "DeLuxe" Rifles**—The ADL "Deluxe Grade" was also introduced in January 1960. It featured an inscribed receiver showing North American game scenes, and a flat faced, gold bead on ramp front sight. In January 1964, Remington changed the checkering pattern to a Fleur-de-lis pattern on the pistol-grip and fore-end.
- **Model 742 BDL "Custom Deluxe" Rifles**—This variation was introduced in 1966 with Monte Carlo stock, white-line spacers on the pistol-grip cap and fore-end tip, and basket-weave pattern checkering. A left-hand version was also introduced in 1966.
- **Model 742C "Standard Grade" Carbines**—This high-power carbine which was intended for use in brush was introduced by Remington in January 1961. The carbine was chambered for .280 Remington, .30-06 and .308 Win ammunition, and featured an 18-inch barrel, Remington "Power-Matic" action and weighed only 7 pounds.

commemorating Remington's 150th year of manufacturing firearms, all chambered for .30-06 centerfire ammunition.
- **Model 742 "Canadian Centennial" Rifles**—A total of 1,968 of these rifles were sold in 1966, commemorating Canada's 100th Anniversary, all chambered for .308 Win centerfire ammunition.
- **Model 742 "Bicentennial" Rifles**—In 1976, Remington sold 10,000 Bicentennial rifles celebrating the 200th Anniversary of the United States, all chambered for .30-06 ammunition.

Remington discontinued the Model 742 in 1980. However, the following year about 60,000 additional rifles were assembled from parts and specially priced to three distributors, including J. C. Penney, Maurice Sporting Goods and Jerry's Sports Center. In all, total sales of the Model 742 were 1,433,269 rifles and carbines between 1960 and 1981. This model was replaced by the Model 7400 and Remington's Model 4 autoloaders.

Above: Elmer Keith looks over a rack of rifles at Remington's Ilion plant with Mike Walker—circa 1960s.

Remington Model 700 Bolt-Action Rifles

Without a doubt, the Remington Model 700 is the most popular commercial high-power, bolt-action rifle in the world. The Model 700 is actually a product-improved Model 721 and Model 722 bolt-action rifle,

Above: Remington Model 700 BDL Scoped Bolt Action Rifle.

In August 1961, Remington began chambering the carbine for .280 Remington. The carbine was first offered with a plain, non-checkered stock and fore-end with serrations. However in January 1968, the checkering was changed to a different pattern on the pistol-grip and fore-end with white-line spacers.
- **M742CDL "Deluxe Grade" Carbines**—This version featured an inscribed receiver scene on both sides and press-checkered pistol-grip and fore-end wood. The CDL grade was discontinued in December 1967.
- **Model 742 D "Peerless"**, and **F "Premier Grade" Rifles**—Only four of these special rifles were ever made, all the product of craftsmen in Remington's Custom Gun Shop.
- **Model 742 "150th Year Anniversary" Rifles**—In 1966, Remington produced 11,412 rifles

the brain-child of Merle "Mike" Walker and his Remington design team in the 1940s. Remington introduced the Model 700 in January 1962, in ADL and BDL versions, both with a blind magazine and hinged floor plate. The ADL and BDL designations were originally acronyms for A "Deluxe Grade" and B "Deluxe Grade." Both grades come in short and long actions. While each year since 1962 brought cosmetic changes or new chamberings, it was 1969 when Remington made several significant changes. A jeweled finish was applied to the unblued portion of the bolt. The rear bolt shroud was extended to cover the area around the firing pin assembly. The stock was restyled and a new checkering pattern was introduced on regular production models. And the butt plate on standard chamberings was changed from anodized aluminum to a hard black plastic. Nearly every other part of the rifle went through some change.

Above: Remington Model 700 BSL.

Above: Remington Model 700 BDL.

Above: Remington Model 700 Varmint laminated stock.

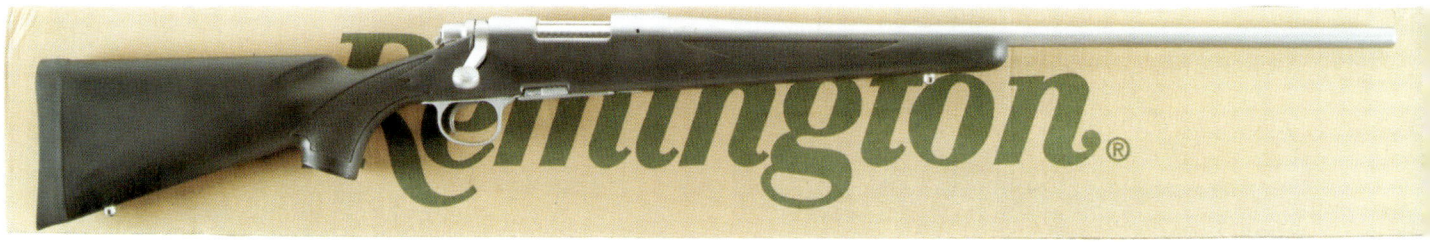

Above: Remington Model 700 BDL.

Above: Remington Model 700 ADL.

Above: Model 700 BDL Custom Deluxe.

The following is a listing of model variations and historical data on the 700:

- **Model 700 ADL "Deluxe Grade" Rifles** have blind magazines, hooded ramp sights, checkered, and Monte Carlo-style walnut stocks. In 1969, Remington redesigned the Model 700 with an improved butt plate and heavier barrel
- **Model 700 ADL Synthetic Rifles** were introduced in 1996, and featured a black matte-finish, checkered, fiberglass-reinforced synthetic stock with a straight comb and raised cheekpiece and a black rubber recoil pad.
- **Model 700 BDL "Custom Deluxe Grade" Rifles**, as introduced in 1962, have Fleur-de-lis style checkering, black fore-end and pistol-grip caps, white-line spacers, sling strap and detachable swivels. The BDL has a better metal finish than does the ADL version.
- **Model 700 BDL SS Rifles** (Stainless Synthetic) were introduced in 1992, and featured a satin-finished 24-inch barrel, receiver and bolt, a black synthetic stock and rubber butt pad, and no sights.
- **Model 700 BDL SS DM Rifles** (Stainless Synthetic, Detachable Magazine) were introduced in 1995, and featured a satin-finished 24-inch barrel, receiver and bolt, a black synthetic stock and rubber butt pad, and no sights.
- **Model 700 BDL SS DM RIFLES** (Stainless Synthetic Detachable Magazine) were introduced in 1995, and featured a satin-finished, stainless steel barrel and textured-finish, black synthetic stock and detachable box magazine. A variation added in 1996 was the **Model 700 BDL SS DM-B** (Muzzle Brake), available in 4 magnum calibers.
- In 1993 Remington introduced the **Model 700 BDL European**, which featured a hand-rubbed oil finish, Monte Carlo comb and raised cheek piece, skipline checkering, hinged floorplate, hooded ramp front sight and adjustable rear.
- **Model 700 BDL Varmint Special Rifles** were introduced in 1967. These were actually BDL guns with a heavy barrel and in varmint chamberings.
- **Model 700 VS** (Varmint Synthetic) was introduced in 1992, and the **Model 700 VS L-H** (Varmint Synthetic, Left-Hand) was introduced in 1998. Both featured a Kevlar fiberglass and graphite stock and a free-floating, heavy black matte-finish 26-inch barrel and receiver and bolt.
- **Model 700VS SF Rifles** (Varmint Synthetic, Stainless Fluted) were introduced in 1994, and featured a Kevlar fiberglass and graphite stock and a free-floating, fluted, stainless steel 26-inch barrel and receiver and bolt. In 1998 Remington introduced muzzle porting to dampen muzzle jump.

- **Model 700BDL VLS Rifles** (Varmint Laminated Stock) were introduced in 1995. They featured a blued, heavy 26-inch varmint barrel and blued receiver and bolt. The stock was two-tone, resin-impregnated laminated wood with checkered pistol-grip and beavertail fore-end.
- **Model 700 VLS Rifles** (Varmint Laminated Stock) were introduced in 1998. They featured a two-tone, resin-impregnated laminated wood stocks with Monte Carlo cheek piece and checkered pistol-grip and fore-end. They also had fluted, free-floating, stainless steel 26-inch barrels, receivers and bolts.
- Model 700 Custom Rifles include the **Model 700 D Peerless** and **F Premier Custom Grade Rifles** which were introduced in 1963, and Model 700 C Custom Grade Rifles which were available to customers the following year. The Model 700 C had hand-checkered wood, and they were made in the Custom Gun Shop.
- **Model 700 Custom Grades I, II, III** and **IV** were added to the product line in 1983, replacing the C, D and F Grade guns. All were Remington Custom Gun Shop guns.
- **Model 700 Safari Grade Rifles** were special order, Custom Gun Shop firearms, and were available as early as 1962, in .375 H & H Mag and .458 Win Mag calibers. The stocks on these rifles had hand-cut checkering, and no white-line spacers. The grip cap and fore-end tip were of a contrasting wood, usually rosewood. Safari Grade rifles differ from BDL rifles in that they have an extra reinforcing pin in the stock to help contain the recoil and prevent the stock from splitting. The pins are covered with contrasting inlays. The earlier barrels were 26 inches in length, and were equipped with muzzle brakes as standard features in 1962 and 1963. In 1983 the Safari rifle was first available with a Classic stock in .375 H & H Mag. Classic versions with 8mm Rem Mag and .458 Win Mag chamberings were introduced in 1986.
- **Model 700 Classic Rifles** were introduced in 1978, and featured a "classic style" walnut stocks (without Monte Carlo comb and cheek piece). They had a satin varnish finish and machine cut checkering on the pistol-grips and fore-ends, brown solid rubber butt pads (magnum calibers have a presentation-style recoil pad), and hinged magazine floor plates. Sights were discontinued after 1978. Model 700 Classic rifles were initially chambered for .22-250 Rem .243 Win, .270 Win, 6mm Rem, .30-06 and 7mm Rem Mag ammunition. However, in 1981 Remington started a tradition of offering a Limited Classic run of this rifle chambered for a new caliber each calendar year. Limited Classics have included: 7mm Mauser in 1981; .257 Roberts in 1982 and .300 H & H Mag in 1983; .250 Sav in 1984; .350 Rem Mag in 1985; .264 Win Mag

in 1986; .338 Win Mag in 1987; .35 Whelen in 1988; .300 Weatherby Mag in 1989; .25-06 Rem in 1990; 7mm Weatherby Mag in 1991; .220 Swift in 1992; .222 Rem in 1993; 6.5 x 55 Swedish in 1994; .300 Win Mag in 1995; .375 H & H Mag in 1996; .280 Rem in 1997; and 8mm Rem Mag in 1998.

- **Remington Sportsman '78 Rifles** were introduced in 1984, as lower-cost hunting rifles which were built on Model 700 barreled actions. The Sportsman '78 has not been available since the late 1980s.
- **Model 700 Mountain Rifles** were introduced in 1986, featuring lightweight, 22-inch barrels, hinged magazine floorplates, rubber butt pads, and either checkered American walnut or synthetic Kevlar stocks. The rifle weighs just 6lbs/12ozs. In 1988 this rifle was first offered in a short action version.
- **Model 700 Mountain Rifle Stainless Synthetic** This model was cataloged only in 1993.
- **Model 700 KS Mountain Rifles** (Kevlar Stock) were introduced in 1986, in both RH (right hand) and LH (left hand) versions. These rifles feature lightweight barrels and lightweight Kevlar stocks.
- **Model 700 APR Rifles (African Plains Rifles)** were introduced in 1994, and featured a blued magnum receiver, a blued 26-inch barrel, and a pressure laminated wood stock with raised cheek piece and checkered pistol-grip and fore-end.
- **Model 700 AWR Rifles (Alaskan Wilderness Rifles)** were also introduced in 1994, and featured a black-matte finished 26-inch barrel, receiver and bolt. The stock is a black composite synthetic reinforced with Kevlar.
- **Model 700 LSS Rifles** (Laminated Stock Stainless) were introduced in 1996, and featured a laminated wood stock layered with light and gray tones, Monte Carlo comb and cheek piece, hinged magazine floorplate, and a satin-finished stainless steel, 24-inch barrel without sights. In 1998 Remington introduced a left-hand version **Model 700 LSS L-H Rifle**. The left-hand version was available on a limited basis in 1997.
- **Model 700 Gun Kits** were introduced in 1987. These were barreled actions and unfinished wood stocks ready for the purchaser to finish. Model 700 Gun Kits last appeared in the 1988 Remington catalog.
- **Model 700 FS Rifles** (Fiberglass Stock) were introduced in 1987 in camo-colored or gray fiberglass stocks, with a blind box magazine. This model was produced for only a few years and was superseded by later generation synthetic models.
- **Model 700 RS Rifles** (Rynite Stock) were introduced in 1987 in camo-colored or gray synthetic stocks, and with a hinged floorplate. Following 1988, the Model 700 RS Rifle was superseded by lighter weight synthetic models.
- **Model 700 ML** (Muzzleloading) **and MLS** (Muzzleloading Stainless Steel) **Black Powder Rifles** were introduced in 1996 for black powder, muzzleloading sportsmen. This .50 caliber rifle featured a blued, satin-finish barrel, action and bolt, a black, fiberglass-reinforced synthetic stock with recoil

Above: Model 700 MLS Muzzleloading Rifle.

Below: Model 700 MLS with blue finish.

Below: Model 700 Sendero SF Rifle.

pad, ramp front and adjustable rear sights, and a ramrod recessed into the fore-end and secured by a barrel band. The rifle has a Model 700 short action, but the breech is closed by a stainless steel plug and nipple. In the modified bolt the firing pin is replaced with a cylindrical hammer. In this same year Remington also introduced Model 700 MLS Black Powder Rifles with satin-finished, stainless steel barrel, receiver and bolt.

- **Model 700 ML** and **MLS Camo Black Powder Rifles** were introduced in 1997, and featured synthetic stocks covered with Mossy Oak Break-Up camo pattern.
- **Model 700 ML and MLS Custom Black Powder Rifles** were introduced in 1998, and were fabricated in Remington's Custom Gun Shop. This rifle featured a two-tone gray laminated thumbhole stock with roll-over cheek piece.
- **Model 700 Sendero Rifles** were introduced on a limited basis in 1993, and cataloged beginning in 1994. The original barrel length was 24 inches and increased to 26 inches in 1994. These rifles featured heavy profile, free-floated, blued barrels, graphite composite synthetic stocks and rubber butt pads, and no sights.
- **Model 700 Sendero SF Rifles** (Stainless Fluted) were introduced in 1996, and featured a fluted, satin-finished 26-inch free-floated barrel, receiver and bolt, a black synthetic stock and rubber butt pad, and no sights.
- **Model 700 Police Rifles** were produced by Remington for law enforcement use, each with DuPont Kevlar reinforced stocks. These fiberglass stocks were laid up around an aircraft-grade aluminum bedding block that runs the full length of the receiver. Stock exteriors are textured black and non-reflective, and come with sling swivel studs. The **Model 700 Police Rifle** is chambered for .223 Rem ammunition, has a 26-inch barrel and weighs nine pounds. The **Model 700 Police D.M. Rifle** is chambered for .308 Win ammunition, has a 26-inch barrel, and also weighs nine pounds. The D.M. refers to the detachable box magazine. Remington also offers the **Model 700 T.W.S. D.M.**, a package that includes a Model 700 Police D.M. Rifle, a Leupold Vari-X III (3.4x10) scope with a Duplex reticle and flip-open lens covers, a Harris bipod, a Michaels 1-inch Quick-Adjust sling with swivels, and a Pelican hard case.
- **M40 Marine Corps Sniper Rifles** (officially known as Rifle, 7.62mm Sniper, M40 Remington, Model 700) were developed in early 1966 by the Remington Custom Shop. This weapon was entered into a design competition conducted by the U.S. Marine Corps, who were looking for a new bolt action sniper rifle. The initial Remington sniper rifles utilized M40-XB target actions. In April 1966, the Marine Corps gave Remington an order to fabricate 800 sniper rifles (550 with Redfield (3X-9X) telescopic scopes and 150 with a Redfield base only), and one-piece, smooth, oil-finished wood stocks. Over the next six years Remington made 995 M40 Sniper Rifles for the Marine Corps, all utilizing Model 700 actions. Many of these were used by Marines in Viet Nam.
- **Model 700 SWS Sniper Rifles** were developed in 1986, at the request of the U.S. Government for a new sniper rifle. Forty-five days later Remington submitted a sample which was accepted, resulting in a contract awarded in July 1987. Remington eventually produced 2,510 Model 700 SWS Sniper Rifles for the U.S. Army and 1,000 for Egyptian forces. Accuracy of these precision rifles meets or exceeds government requirements of 1.3 AMR (average mean radius) at 200 yards. SWS stands for "Sniper Weapon System." The rifle features a free-floating 24-inch stainless steel barrel chambered for 7.62 NATO ammunition, a Model 700 long action receiver, a Kevlar reinforced synthetic stock, bipod, and a Leupold-Stevens Ultra M3A 10X scope with range-finding reticle. The rifle, bipod and scope weighs 13lbs/13oz.

Model 510X, 511X & 512X Bolt Action Rifles

In 1964, Remington introduced replacements for the Model 510, M511 and M512 series of .22 caliber, bolt-action rifles. The new rifles shared common receiver parts, 24-inch barrels, non-checkered plain American walnut stocks, ramp front sights, and rear sights adjustable for windage and elevation.

- **Model 510X "Targetmaster"** single-shot, .22 caliber bolt-action rifle was available with rifled or smoothbore, and weighed a scant 4lbs/12oz. It was advertised as "a favorite first gun because of its safety features."
- **Model 511X "Scoremaster"** was a clip magazine repeater with a 6-round clip-magazine, but a 10-round magazine was also available. It weighed 5 pounds.
- **Model 512X** tubular magazine repeater was also a repeater, and the magazine held 21 Short, or 16 Long, or 14 Long Rifle cartridges. It weighed 5lbs/4oz.

Remington last advertised M510X, M511X and M512X rimfire rifles in the 1966 catalog. In all, Remington had sold 18,088 Model 510X rifles, 1,813 M510X Smoothbore rifles, 29,120 Model 511X rifles, and 30,683 Model 512X rifles. The series was replaced in 1967 by Remington's new M580, M581 and M582 rifles.

Model 600 and Model 600 Magnum Carbines

In 1964, Remington introduced a new high-power, bolt action sporting firearm—the **Model 600 Carbine**. This diminutive arm was a lethal hunting gun. Characteristics of this carbine included an 18-inch vent rib barrel, blade ramp front sight, U notch rear adjustable for windage and elevation, custom checkered, American walnut stock with Monte Carlo and fluted comb, fixed box magazine, and weighing only 5lbs/8oz. While many were sold in 1964, it did not appear in the Remington catalog until 1965. Remington dropped the Model 600 Carbine in December 1967, after 80,944 were sold in only a four-year period.

In 1964, the Billings Hardware Company petitioned Remington to fabricate one thousand special order Model 600 Carbines to commemorate the 75th Anniversary of Montana's Statehood, and the 100th Anniversary of Montana as a Territory. Remington agreed, and these limited edition guns were sold through the hardware companies' network. These carbines were all chambered for 6mm Remington ammunition, and a commemorative medallion was inletted into the stock and a special inscription was stamped on the receiver.

Remington brought out the **Model 600 Magnum Carbine** in 1965. This high-power hunting arm was distinguished by a laminated stock of American walnut and beech wood, Monte Carlo cheek piece, rubber recoil pad, quick-release swivels and strap, and 18-inch vent rib barrel. The M600 Magnum Carbine had a 4-shot fixed box magazine, and it weighed a scant 6lbs/8oz. Like the Model 600 Carbine, the M600 Magnum Carbine was also dropped in December 1997, after 13,142 were sold in only a three-year period.

Model 580, Model 581 and 582 Bolt Action Rifles

In January 1967, Remington introduced its latest "family of guns"—the Model 580, Model 581 and Model 582 series of bolt action, .22 caliber rifles, replacing the Model 510-M511-M512 series.

The three rifles shared common parts including 24-inch barrel, bead front sight, U notch lock-screw rear sight, dual extractors, receiver with bolt with 6 locking lugs, and Monte Carlo style stock with pistol-grip.

- The **Model 580** was a single-shot rifle that weighed an even 5 pounds, and cost $39.95 when introduced in the 1967 Remington catalog. Remington later advertised this as "the preferred .22 for beginners." The Model 580SB was identical to the M580, except it had a smooth bore and was intended for .22 caliber shot cartridges. It, too, cost $39.95.
- The **Model 581** was a box magazine repeater with a 5-shot clip magazine. It weighed 5lbs/4oz, and cost $44.95.
- The **Model 582** was a tubular magazine repeater, which held 20 Short, 15 Long or 14 Long Rifle cartridges. It weighed 5lbs/8oz, and cost $49.95 when introduced in 1967.

In October 1968, Remington announced the availability of the **Model 581-LH**, touted to be "the only left-hand, bolt action rimfire rifle ever manufactured in America." This box magazine repeater sold for $49.95. In 1971, the **Model 580-BR "Boys' Rifle"** was introduced "with all the features of the standard Model 580, but the stock is 1-inch shorter for the young shooter. The Model 580SB was deleted in December 1977, followed in December 1978 by the Model 580 and the Model 580-BR. In January 1979, Remington introduced the **Model 581-BR "Boys' Rifle,"** a box magazine repeater with shorter stock than the standard M581. Remington stopped advertising all variations of the Model 581 and Model 582 with the 1983 Remington catalog, however sales continued through dealers into 1985.

Model 788 Bolt Action Rifles

In January 1967, Remington introduced a new moderately priced, bolt action hunting rifle, the **Model 788**. This rifle was designed by Wayne Leek, manager of Remington's Firearms Research & Design Department. It featured a bolt with nine locking lugs, a detachable box magazine, 24-inch barrel, and a plain, straight-grain American walnut stock. This rifle boasted of an incredibly fast lock time—2.4 milliseconds. Remington also added a left-hard Model

Above: Remington Model 788 Bolt–Action Rifle.

Above: Remington Model 600 Magnum Carbine

788 rifle in 1969. In January 1974, Remington introduced a new promotion, a Model 788 rifle with 4-power Universal Model UA scope, rings and mount . In 1975, the company began offering the Model 788 rifle with 4-power scope as a catalog item. In 1980, in 1980, Remington re-sculptured the stock, adding a fluted comb, a thicker pistol-grip and wider fore-end. In December 1983, Remington dropped the economical Model 788 hunting rifle, as it was replaced by the Sportsman 78 bolt action rifle in 1984. Remington had sold a total of 564,108 Model 788 rifles in eighteen years of production.

Model 660 and Model 660 Magnum Carbines

Remington brought out a replacement for the **M600** and **M600 Magnum Carbines** in 1968, Model 660 and Model 660 Magnum Carbines. These were, ostensibly, redesigns of the guns they replaced, except the ventilated rib was eliminated, a black fore-end tip, black grip cap and white line spacers were added, and the barrel length was increased from 18 inches to 20 inches. The Model 660 Carbine was chambered for .222 Remington, 6mm Remington, .243 Win and .308 Win centerfire cartridges, and although they were never a catalog item, the factory fabricated 227 M660 Carbines in .223 Remington between 1968 and 1970. The American walnut stock was similar in design to that of the M660 Carbine. Both carbines were discontinued in December 1970. In only three years, Remington sold 45,332 M660 Carbines and 5,204 M660 Magnum Carbines.

Mohawk 600 Carbines

In 1971, Remington brought out **Mohawk 600 Carbines** as high-volume, non-catalog guns for its dealers. In 1972, the minimum order for these reduced-price carbines was 200 units, and reorder quantities of 50 units. The following year, the initial minimum order was reduced to 100 units, and reorders remained 50 units. The carbines were further discounted when ordered in 300 or more units.

Mohawk 600 Carbines are essentially the same design as the M660 Carbines, except they had no black fore-end tip, grip cap or white line spacers, the barrels were reduced to 18 inches. Remington sold a total of 48,573 Mohawk 600 Carbines in a nine-year period ending in 1979.

Model 591 and Model 592 Rimfire Magnum Rifles

In January 1969, Remington introduced two new rimfire, bolt action rifles. These were identical in design, except for the type of magazine and cartridge capacity. Common features included 24-inch barrel, 6 rear locking lugs on the bolt, dual extractors, and plain one-piece American walnut stock with Monte Carlo comb, pistol-grip and laquer finish. The **Model 591** weighed 4lbs/14oz, and featured a 4-shot clip magazine. The **Model 592** weighed an even 5 pounds, and had a 10-shot tubular magazine beneath the barrel. Soon after introduction Remington changed the stocks to "walnut-finished hardwood." Remington discontinued these 5mm rimfire longarms in December 1973, having sold 27,015 Model 591 rifles and 24,728 Model 592 rifles.

Model 540X Bolt Action Match Target Rifle

Remington introduced its newest .22 caliber, target rifle in January 1969. This single-shot rifle was designed as a moderately priced, small bore target rifle "for the intermediate and junior shooter." The receiver was from the Model 580 "series of rifles," featuring six locking lugs. This rifle also featured an adjustable trigger, a four-way adjustable butt plate, and a one-piece heavy walnut-finished hardwood stock had thumb cuts. The heavy target barrel was 26 inches in length, and the rifle weighed 8lbs/8oz with sights. This rifle featured a Redfield No.63 front sight and a Redfield No.75 micrometer rear sight. A sling strap with front swivel block assembly, an extra-cost item, could be installed at the factory. The Model 540X was dropped in December 1973, replaced by the Model 540-XR and Model 540XRJR Position Rifles. Some of these target rifles continued to be sold into 1975, and in all, 6,385 were sold in this seven-year period.

Model 541-S "Custom" Sporting Rifle

Remington introduced the .22 caliber **Model 541-S "Custom" Sporting Rifle** in January 1972. It featured a tapered 24-inch barrel, a one-piece cut-checkered American walnut stock with plastic (simulated rosewood) butt plate, fore-end tip and grip cap with white spacers, a 5-shot box magazine, a scroll-engraved receiver drilled and tapped for aperture or scope mounts, dual extractors, and an adjustable trigger. This sporter weighed 5lbs/8oz, and came without sights. The Model 541-S Custom Sporting Rifle was discontinued in December 1983, after twelve-years production, and was replaced by the Model 541-T. During that period Remington sold 31,045 Model 541-S rifles.

Model 540-XR and Model 540-XRJR Position Rifles

In January 1974, Remington introduced two replacements for the Model 540X target rifle, the **Model 540-XR** and **Model 540-XRJR Position Rifles**. They both featured a new Monte Carlo stock design with greater fore-end depth and a newly designed pistol-grip that more readily allowed the shooter to pull the rifle into the shoulder. A 4-way adjustable butt plate, a redesigned bolt, and a fully adjustable target trigger were all new features. They were single-shot, and fired .22 caliber Long Rifle rimfire ammunition, and had a Redfield

Above: Remington 541-S Custom Bolt Action Rifle.

Below: Remington Model 7600 Slide Action Carbine.

No.63 front sight and Redfield No.75 micrometer rear target sight. The barrel measured 26 inches in length, and the Model 540-XR rifle weighed 9lbs/6oz with sights. The **Model 540-XRJR Position Rifle** was identical, but had a 1 inch shorter stock for the "junior shooter's physique." Either rifle retailed for $124.95 (without sights) when introduced in 1974. Installed front and rear target sights cost $29.95 additional. A sling strap with front swivel block assembly cost an additional $6.95, installed at the factory. In January 1979, the rear sight was changed to a Williams #FPTX. Both rifles were discontinued in December 1983, although they continued to be sold into the following year. In this eleven-year period Remington sold 5,088 Model 540-XR rifles and 1,723 Model 540-XRJR rifles.

Model Four Autoloading Rifles

In 1981, Remington brought out a new semi-automatic, the **Model Four**, which sported a 22-inch barrel. This gas-operated hunting rifle featured a gloss-finished, checkered American walnut pistol-grip, Monte Carlo–style stock and checkered, flared fore-end. Ramp front and adjustable open rear sights were standard, and the receiver was tapped for scope mounts. A detachable box magazine made reloading easy in this 7lb/8oz rifle. A distinctive touch is that a facsimile of the cartridge head is inlaid into the underside of the receiver. Concurrently, Remington's Custom Shop offered the Model Four in D "Peerless Grade" and F "Premier Grade." The Model Four was discontinued in December 1987.

Model 7400 Autoloading Rifles

Remington also introduced the Model 7400 autoloader in 1981. This rifle is basically the same as the Model Four, differing only in the shape of the stock and fore-end, and receiver and barrel markings. The Model 7400 featured impressed-checkered pistol-grip and fore-end in a fleur-de-lis pattern, and straight comb stock. The barrel length was 22 inches from the start, however in 1988, a 18 -inch carbine-length barrel with a .30-06 chambering was offered. In this same year .35 Whelen was added. In 1991, Remington introduced the 175th Anniversary Edition Model 7400, and it featured a Monte Carlo–style stock, cut-checkering, and anniversary scroll on the receiver. It was offered only in this commemorative year. Also in 1991, Remington upgraded Model 7400 rifles by offering them with a Monte Carlo–style stock in satin or gloss finish, and cut-checkering. In 1993, Remington introduced the **Model 7400 SP "Special Purpose,"** which featured a non-reflective finish on the wood and metalwork, sling and sling swivels, and two chamberings: .270 Win and .30-06. This variation was short-lived, as it was discontinued in December 1994. For 1997 only, Remington brought out a limited edition **Buckmasters® American Deer Foundation Model 7400 Rifle** chambered for .30-06, and featuring fine-line and decorated receivers. In 1998, Remington introduced the **Model 7400 Synthetic**, which has a Monte Carlo–style, black fiberglass reinforced stock and fore-end. All exposed metal parts have a matte-black, non-reflective finish, and it is available in the following calibers: .243 Win, .270 Win, .280 Remington, .30-06, .308 Win, and a carbine version with 18-inch barrel in .30-06.

Model Six Pump-Action Rifles

In 1981, Remington also introduced a new pump-action hunting rifle, the **Model Six**, which, except for the action, shared many of the same characteristics as the Model Four, including the wood and metal finish. The Model Six was chambered for 6mm Remington, .243 Win, .270 Win, .30-06 and .308 Win centerfire calibers. The Model Six was discontinued in December 1987.

Model 7600 Autoloading Rifles

Remington also introduced the **Model 7600** pump-action rifle in 1981. This rifle is basically the same as the Model Six, differing only in the shape of the stock and fore-end, and receiver and barrel markings. The Model 7600 featured impressed-checkered pistol-grip and fore-end in a fleur-de-lis pattern, and straight comb stock. The barrel length was 22-inches from the start, however in 1988, a 18-inch carbine-length barrel with a .30-06 chambering was offered. In this same year .35 Whelen was added. In 1991, Remington upgraded Model 7600 rifles by offering them with a Monte Carlo–style stock in satin or gloss finish, and cut-checkering. In 1993, Remington introduced the **Model 7600 SP "Special Purpose,"** which featured a non-reflective finish on the wood and metalwork, sling and sling swivels, and two chamberings: .270 Win and .30-06. This variation was short-lived, as it was discontinued in December 1994. For 1997 only, Remington brought out a limited edition **Buckmasters American Deer Foundation Model 7600 Rifle** chambered for .30-06, and featuring fine-line and decorated receivers. In 1998, Remington introduced the **Model 7600 Synthetic**, which has a Monte Carlo–style, black fiberglass reinforced stock and fore-end. All exposed metal parts have a matte-black, non-reflective finish, and it is available in the following calibers: .243 Win, .270 Win, .280 Remington, .30-06, .308 Win, and a carbine version with 18-inch barrel in .30-06.

Model Seven Bolt Action Rifles

In January 1983, Remington introduced a new, lightweight and compact, bolt action hunting rifle, the **Model Seven**, in five short-action calibers: .222 Remington, .243 Win, 7mm-08 Remington, 6mm Remington and .308 Win. This rifle had a 18-inch free-floated barrel, and weighed a scant 6lbs/4oz. Other features included a hinged floor plate, a fully enclosed bolt head and extractor, ramp front and fully adjustable rear sights, checkered American walnut stock, and sling swivels. The clip magazine was 4-shot in all calibers except .222 Remington, which was 5-shot. .223 Remington was added in late 1984, and in 1985, the .222 Remington was dropped. Remington introduced the **Model Seven FS** in 1987, which featured a Kevlar-reinforced fiberglass one-piece stock in two color schemes, gray or gray camo, a solid rubber butt plate, and sling swivels. This 4-shot, 5lb/4oz rifle was available in .243 Win, 7mm-08 Remington and .308 Win calibers. The Model Seven FS was available only through 1989.

In 1987, Remington's Custom Gun Shop first offered the **Model Seven Custom KS Rifle**, which featured a camo-pattern Kevlar stock with straight comb, cheek piece, European knob pistol grip, and 1-inch black Old English recoil pad. It was initially available with iron sights in .35 Remington or .350 Remington Magnum calibers. Later .223 Remington, .260 Remington, .308 Win and 7mm-08 Remington chamberings were added, all in rifles without sights. This custom rifle weighed 5lbs/12oz. In 1993, the Custom Shop introduced the **Model Seven MS**, a Mannlicher-style full-length stocked rifle with 20-inch barrel. The laminated stock features a straight comb with raised cheek piece, fitted to a rubber recoil pad. Remington offered this custom gun in eleven calibers. Also new for 1993 was a new caliber for the Model Seven, the .17 Remington centerfire, and a new version of the

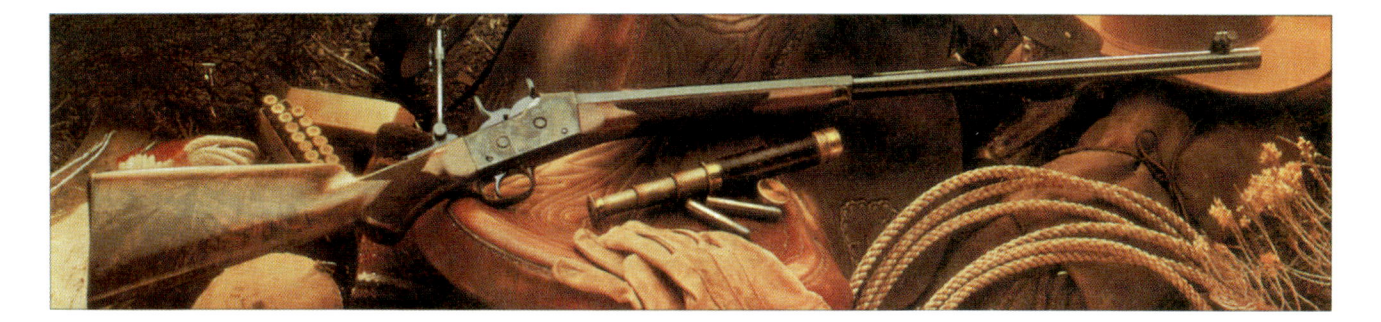

Above: Remington No. 1 Rolling Block Creedmoor.

rifle, the **Model Seven Youth**, featuring a one-inch shorter hardwood stock than the standard Model Seven rifle. It was initially chambered for 6mm Remington, .243 Win and 7mm-08 Remington, and .260 Remington was added in 1998. In 1994, Remington brought out the **Model Seven SS "Stainless Synthetic"** with 20-inch stainless steel barrel and receiver with a black textured synthetic stock. It weighed 6lbs/4oz, was offered in .243 Win, 7mm-08 Remington and .308 Win calibers. The 6mm Remington and the .17 Remington were dropped in December 1995. In 1997, Remington added .260 Remington. As of 1998, the Model Seven, Youth and Stainless Synthetic remain in current production.

Sportsman 74 Auto Rifles

This autoloading hunting rifle features a plain, straight-combed stock and fore-end, iron sights on a 22-inch barrel, drilled & tapped receiver, 4-round box magazine, 7lb/8oz weight, and chambered for the .30-06 cartridge. This rifle was discontinued in December 1987.

Sportsman 76 Pump Rifles

This pump-action hunting rifle features a plain, straight-combed stock and fore-end, iron sights on a 22-inch barrel, drilled & tapped receiver, 4-round box magazine, 7lb/8oz weight, and chambered for the .30-06 cartridge. This rifle was discontinued in December 1987.

Sportsman® 78 Bolt Action Rifles

This bolt action hunting rifle features a plain, straight-combed stock, iron sights on a 22-inch barrel, drilled & tapped receiver, 4-round box magazine, 7 pound weight, and chambered for the following ammunition: .270 Win and .30-06. In 1985, Remington added .243 Win and .308 Win calibers. In 1986, Remington added .223 Remington. This rifle was discontinued in December 1989.

Model 541-X Bolt Action Target Rifles

In 1984, '85 and '86 Remington manufactured 9,077 **Model 541-X** small-bore, nine-pound target rifles for the U.S. military. The military designation of these rifles is M13. They were inexpensively built, to assure being low bidder on the military contract, although Remington quality came through in such features as wood-to-metal fit, a crowned muzzle, a metal balance block within the stock, and quality sling swivels and mounts. These rifles have a 27-inch heavy barrel with a Redfield No.68 target globe front sight and Williams "Foolproof" micrometer rear sight, and 5-shot plastic box magazine. The plain, one-piece, oil-finished hardwood stock has no checkering, and it has a full pistol-grip and beavertail fore-arm. U.S. is stamped over the serial number. These rifles were only sold to the U.S. military, and were never advertised in any Remington catalog or sporting arms brochure.

Model 541-S Bolt Action Rimfire Sporting Rifle

In 1986, Remington introduced the Model 541-S rifle. Characteristics of this high-grade sporter included a 24-inch barrel and premium wood and finish. By 1998, it was still in current production.

Remington Sportsman 581-S Rifles

In 1987, the **Sportsman 581-S Rimfire Rifle** was introduced in the Remington catalog, which stated that it was "called back by popular demand" and is "the ideal beginner's gun with a single-shot adapter." Similar to its predecessor, this bolt action .22 featured a plain, but full size Monte Carlo–style stock with pistol-grip, 24-inch barrel, bead and post front sight, rear sight adjustable for windage and elevation, and 5-shot clip.

Model 522 Viper

In 1993, Remington introduced the **Model 522 Viper**, a new .22 caliber autoloading rifle with a black, injection-molded one-piece stock of Rynite synthetic resin. The receiver is also constructed of a lightweight, tough engineered synthetic, and was permanently affixed to the blued steel 20-inch barrel. New features on this rifle include a red indicator which shows when the gun is cocked, a disconnector which disables the trigger when the 10-round magazine is removed, an ejection port shield molded into the receiver, and a last-shot bolt hold-open feature which lets the shooter know when the gun is empty. The rifle had a ramp-mounted bead front sight and open rear sight, adjustable for windage and elevation. This lightweight rifle weighed 4lbs/10oz. Remington discontinued the Model 522 Viper in December 1997.

Remington 1816 Commemorative Flintlock Rifle

In 1995, Remington introduced a flintlock long rifle to commemorate the first rifle of Eliphalet Remington II— the **Remington 1816 Commemorative Flintlock Rifle**—said to be "an authentic replica—lock, stock and barrel—of the first Remington rifle ever built." These special-order rifles were crafted for Remington by an outside gunsmith, and featured a 39-inch, .50 caliber octagonal barrel and full-length, one-piece curly-maple stock with brass furniture and patchbox. This black powder rifle was offered only in 1995.

Model 597 Rifles

In October 1996, Remington announced a new "family of rifles," innovative new small-bore autoloading rifles known as the Model 597. The development of this firearm is credited to Mike Keeney and his team of engineers. To start off, the stock dimensions are the same on all three variations, complete with a large-sized pistol-grip and beavertail fore-end. The alloy receiver features a unique bolt guidance system of twin rails, and the 20-inch barrels are free-floated for accuracy. Receivers are grooved for standard tip-off mounts, and they are drilled & tapped for scope mounts. Open, adjustable sights are standard. The rifles have a staggered clip magazine with a quick drop-out release feature. Variations of this rifle include:

- **M597** is chambered for .22 Long Rifle ammunition, and exterior metal parts have a non-reflective, matte-black finish. The one-piece stock is dark gray synthetic, the rifle weighs 5lbs/8oz.
- **M597 LSS "Laminated Stock Synthetic"** is also chambered for .22 Long Rifle ammunition, and has a satin-finish stainless steel barrel and matching, gray-toned alloy receiver. The stock is laminated wood of contrasting light and dark brown shades. This rifle weighs 5lbs/8oz.
- **M597 Magnum** is nearly identical to the **M597**, except it is chambered for the more potent .22 Win Magnum rimfire ammunition. The bolt is heavier than .22 Long Rifle version, so the rifle weighs more, 6 pounds.
- **M597 Sporter** was introduced in 1996, and features a one-piece hardwood stock and a blued barrel and receiver.
- **M597 SS "Stainless Synthetic"** was also introduced in 1996, and features a dark gray synthetic stock and a stainless steel barrel and gray-toned receiver.
- **M597 Magnum LS "Laminated Stock"** was also introduced in 1996, and features an impregnated laminated wood stock and a blued barrel and receiver. It is chambered for .22 Win Magnum rimfire ammunition.
- **M597 Custom Target** was introduced as a Custom Gun Shop rifle in 1998. Available in .22 Long Rifle or .22 Win Magnum calibers, it features an ergonomically shaped, resin-impregnated wood stock with Monte Carlo–style profile and beavertail fore-end. The laminated wood is green and wood-tone in color. The stainless steel barrel is 20-inches long and has no sights. The receiver is a matching gray-tone, with scope mounting grooves.

No.1 Mid-Range Creedmoor Rolling Block Rifles

In 1997, Remington's Custom Gun Shop reintroduced a single-shot rifle that the company last produced in 1887, the **No.1 Mid-Range Creedmoor Rolling Block Rifle**. This precision target rifle is available only in 1997, and was a near-identical twin to the rifle which won numerous mid-range matches at the National Rifle Association's range on Long Island, known as Creedmoor. This rifle was reintroduced for black powder shooters and for collectors, and has these features: chambered for .45-70 black powder cartridges; a 30-inches part-round/part-octagonal blued barrel with bubble-balance globe front sight; a mid-range vernier rear sight mounted on the top tang; a case-hardened receiver; single-set trigger; figured and cut-checkered pistol-grip stock and fore-end; case-hardened steel snaubel and butt plate; weight of 9lbs/14oz; and protected by a key-locked hard case.

No.1 Rolling Block Sporting Rifles

In 1998, Remington's Custom Gun Shop reintroduced a single-shot sporting rifle that the company last produced in the 1870s and '80s, the **No.1 Rolling Block Sporting Rifle**. Available only for 1998, this rifle is quite similar to the single-shot hunting rifle that was used by General George Armstrong Custer and by many buffalo hunters on the frontier and elsewhere. This rifle is available in three chamberings: .45-70, .30-30 Win, and .444 Marlin. It is intended primarily for black powder shooters, and has these features: a blued 30-inch round barrel with post front sight with white bead; an open Buckhorn rear sight adjustable for windage; a blued receiver; figured and cut-checkered pistol-grip stock and fore-end; black plastic butt plate; and weight of 8lbs/12oz. Options for this rifle include a part-round/part-octagonal barrel; a tang-mounted rear sight, a globe front sight, a single-set trigger, semi-fancy American walnut stock and fore-end, steel snaubel fore-end tip, steel butt plate, and case-colored receiver.

CHAPTER 4

Remington Shotguns

Remington Single-Barrel, Muzzleloading Shotguns

In mid-1866, the company took barrels, stocks and other parts from surplus Civil War rifle muskets and began fabricating inexpensive, single-barrel, muzzleloading, percussion shotguns. More than 10,000 of these **Remington Single-Barrel, Muzzleloading Shotguns** were made and sold through 1878. These 20 gauge percussion shotguns are not marked.

Remington Double-Barrel Outside Hammer Shotguns

E. Remington & Sons encouraged inventors to come to Ilion to perfect their gun designs. Andrew E. Whitmore was one such entrepreneur. Wishing to offer the sporting public a quality shotgun, Remington acquired rights to manufacture Whitmore's guns, and production commenced in 1873:

- The first double-guns made by E. Remington & Sons were **Remington-Whitmore, Hammer-Lifter, Model 1873 Shotguns**, and about 5,000 10 gauge and 12 gauge shotguns were made over the next five years. When the top lever is lifted, a sliding plate between the bolsters is drawn back, which brings the exposed hammers into safety notches, or half-cock position. These exposed-hammer sporting guns were

Above: Remington Whitmore Double Barrel Shotgun.

Above: Wells Fargo Remington Hammer Shotgun.

Above: Remington Model 1889 Double Barrel Shotgun.

Above: Remington Double Barrel Model 1889 with shortened barrels.

Above: Remington Model 1894. Double Barrel Shotgun.

offered in three grades, each more fancy than the next. In 1875, the gun was offered with one shotgun barrel and one rifle barrel.
- In 1875, Remington introduced an improved double-gun—**Remington-Whitmore, Model 1875, Lifter Shotguns**—which featured Lewis L. Hepburn's patented rebounding locks. The improved gun also eliminated a recurring problem with the M1873 shotgun—insufficiently strong hammer shoulders, which tended to crack off after prolonged use. More than 3,350 of these 10 gauge and 12 gauge, exposed-hammer double-guns were made over a short, three-year period, and the gun was also offered as a combination shotgun/rifle and as a double-rifle.

- **Remington Model 1876, Lifter Shotguns**—this gun is essentially the same as the M1875 shotgun, except for a different profile hammer. Over 2,500 were made over a seven-year period.
- **Remington Model 1878, 10 Gauge Heavy Duck Guns**—this massive exposed-hammer gun was intended for wetlands hunting, and over a five-year period an estimated 2,400 of these were made.
- **Remington Model 1879 Lifter Shotguns**—produced in 12 gauge, this gun has a lighter frame than the M1878 Heavy Duck Gun. Available in four grades, this was the first Remington double-gun made with the patented Deeley & Edge fore-end latch. Less than 100 of these guns were made over a four-year period.
- **Remington Model 1882 Shotguns**—this was Remington's first shotgun made without the Whitmore-Latch, as it featured a recognizable, rotating top-lever to open the action. Made in both 10 gauge and 12 gauge, each had a different frame size. This shotgun was offered initially in five grades, and later another was added. It was the first double-gun which was offered with Remington's Auxiliary Rifle Barrel, a rifled chamber/tube which was inserted into one of the shotgun barrels. The M1882 double-gun proved to be a popular seller for the Remingtons, as more than 16,000 were made over the six-year period until the company was placed in receivership in 1886.
- **Remington Model 1883 Shotguns**—this double-gun shared the same characteristics as the M1882 gun, except for a change in hammer style. Less than 100 of these guns, in either 10 gauge or 12 gauge, were made by E. Remington & Sons over a two-year period.
- **Remington Model 1885 and 1887 Shotguns**—the mid-1880s were difficult years for the once-proud factory in Ilion. Despite severe economic conditions, Remington re-designed their M1882 double-gun, and offered it in 10 and 12 gauge, and for the first time—16 gauge—each made in a different frame size. The new model gun also differs from its predecessor in the shape of the exposed hammers. It too was a popular-selling gun, as about 7,000 of these shotguns were made over the next four turbulent years.
- The first new firearm designed and manufactured by the Remington Arms Company was the **Remington**

Below: Remington Model 1894/1900 Double Barrel Hammerless Shotgun.

Model 1889 Double Barrel Shotgun, which was essentially a redesign of E. Remington & Sons' M1887 double gun. Factory records indicate that 38 Model 1889 shotguns were shipped in late 1888, with full production achieved by 1889, when an additional 2,237 guns were shipped. Both 10 gauge and 12 gauge guns were available, and the first shotguns sold for $40^{00} to $100^{00}, depending on finish and type of barrels ordered. The Remington Arms Company eventually shipped 134,200 Model 1889

Above: The shotgun final assembly room at Remington Arms Company—circa 1906.

REMINGTON SHOTGUNS • 103

Below: Remington Model 1900 K.

Above: Remington Model 11 Autoloading Shotgun.

Above: US Martial Remington Model 10 Riot Shotgun.

Above: Remington Model 17 Slide Action Shotgun.

Remington Model 1894 Hammerless Double-Barrel Shotgun

The **Remington Model 1894 Hammerless Double-Barrel Shotgun** was Remington's first hammerless, side-by-side shotgun, and was available with or without automatic shell ejectors, and in 10 and 12 gauges. In 1897, 16 gauge guns were added. Double-barrels were initially Damascus twist, but ordnance steel barrels were available in 1896. These were quality guns, manufactured in five grades: A, B, C, D and E, each finer quality than the outside-hammer, double guns in a twenty-year period of manufacture between 1888 and 1908.

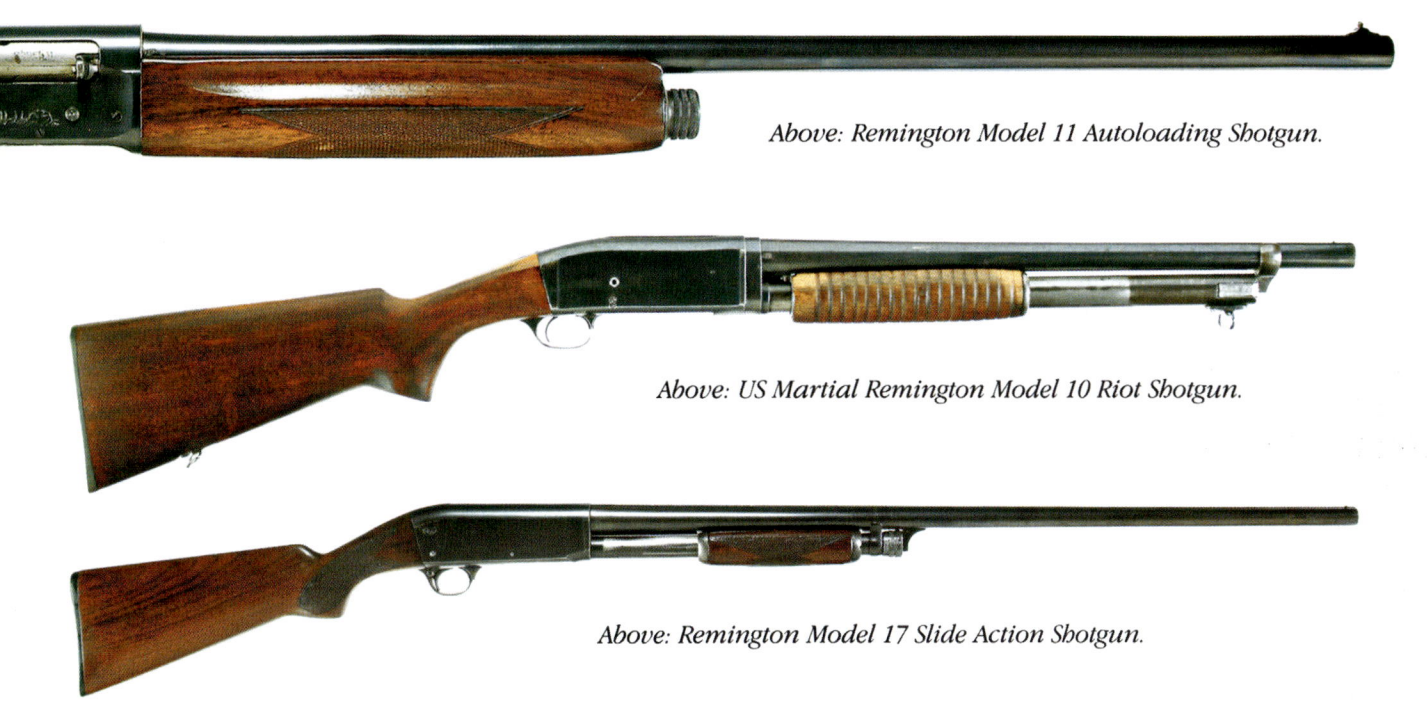

Remington Model 1893, No.3 Single-Barrel Shotgun

On September 1, 1893, Remington Arms Company introduced an inexpensive, single-barrel shotgun to take the place of their Remington No.1 and No.2 rolling block shotguns. The new gun was a break-open design, activated by a top-lever, and had a cocking lever on the left side of the case-hardened receiver. This **Remington Model 1893, No.3 Single-Barrel Shotgun** was initially offered in 12 gauge with blued 30-, 32- or 34-inch choke-bored barrel, and cost only $10⁰⁰. The gun was utilitarian in style, with two-piece, non-checkered pistol-grip stock and fore-end. In 1894, 16 and 20 gauges were added, and in 1898, the company added 10, 24 and 28 gauges—making this Remington's first shotgun to be offered in six different gauges. This proved to be a very popular selling shotgun, as Remington Arms Company produced 86,801 of these guns through 1903.

last. When offered in 1894, prices ranged from $67.50 to $247.50. Remington Arms Company manufactured a total of 41,194 M1894 shotguns through 1910.

In 1902, Remington Arms Company announced the ultimate in side by side shotguns—the **Model 1894 Remington Special, Double-Barrel Shotgun**. Remington catalog advertising stated: "This gun was made in 12 gauge, with any length barrel, and was priced at an astonishing $750⁰⁰, more than the Parker A-1 Special". It is not surprising that only about a dozen Model 1894 Remington Special Shotguns were made between 1902 and 1910.

Remington Model 1900 Hammerless Double-Barrel Shotgun

In 1900, Remington Arms Company brought out the **Remington Model 1900 Double Barrel Shotgun** "to offer the sportsman a fine double at a lesser price to broaden the sales market." It did not replace any shotgun in their inventory, and was sold concurrently with the higher priced Model 1894 double gun. The Model 1900 shotgun was available in 12 and 16 gauges, with blued steel barrels (without automatic ejectors) for $35⁰⁰, and with Damascus barrels (with automatic ejectors) for $45⁰⁰. This economy-priced gun was sold from 1900 to 1910, with 98,508 shotguns made.

Remington No.9 Single-Barrel Shotgun

In 1902, Remington announced the **Remington No.9 Single-Barrel Shotgun** to replace their highly successful No.3 single-barrel gun. Eventually this versatile, low-priced, $10⁰⁰ shotgun was offered in 10, 12, 16, 20, 24 and 28 gauges. Like the gun it replaced, it featured a plain, non-checkered, pistol-grip stock and fore-end, and a break-open design activated by a top-lever, and had a cocking lever on the left side of the case-hardened receiver. A total of 65,698 Remington No.9 shotguns were made between 1902 to 1910.

Remington Model 11 Autoloading Shotguns

Browning's shotguns were initially advertised as the **Remington Autoloading Gun**, and the 1906 Remington Arms Company catalog listed the following variations: No.1 Standard Grade for $40⁰⁰, No.2 Special Grade for $50⁰⁰, No.3 Trap Grade for $50⁰⁰, No.4 Tournament Grade for $70⁰⁰, No.5 Expert Grade for $100⁰⁰, No.6 Premier Grade for $150⁰⁰, and No.0 Riot Grade for $40⁰⁰. This gun would be renamed the **Remington Model 11 Autoloading Shotgun** in 1911. This sporting shotgun was produced in 12 gauge exclusively for many years; 20 gauge was added in 1931 and 16 gauge was added the following year. In only its first six years of production, Remington Arms Company sold a phenomenal 277,722 Browning shotguns, making this the most successful firearm yet manufactured by the 94-year old company. Eventually, Remington would manufacture over 850,000 Model 11 autoloaders through 1948.

Remington Model 10 Pump-Action Shotguns

Under John D. Pedersen's direction, Remington announced their first pump-action shotgun in 1908. It would not be until 1911 that this gun became the **Remington Model 10 Pump-Action Shotgun**. In 1909, these solid-breech, 12 gauge, hammerless, bottom-ejection guns were available in No.1 Standard Grade or Field Grade for $27⁰⁰, No.2 Special Grade or No.3 Trap Grade for $47⁰⁰, No.4 Grade for $60⁰⁰, No.5 Grade for $90⁰⁰, and No.6 Grade for $140⁰⁰. In 1910, Remington Arms Company offered a No.10 Riot Grade gun for $27⁰⁰. Remington offered the Model 10 in eight grades, including: No.1 Standard Grade for $27⁰⁰; No.2 Special Grade for $47⁰⁰; No.3 Trap Grade for $47⁰⁰; No.3 Trap Special Grade for $45⁰⁰; No.4 Tournament Grade for $60⁰⁰; No.5 Expert Grade for $90⁰⁰; No.6 Premier Grade for $140⁰⁰; and No.0 Riot Grade for $27⁰⁰. These guns were available in 1919 in eight different grades with retail prices ranging from $44.60 for the basic Model 10A Standard Grade shotgun or the M10R Riot Grade shotgun, to $194.75 for the Model 10F Premier Grade shotgun. Other variations included the Model 10B Special Grade, 10C Trap Grade, 10D Tournament Grade, and 10E Expert Grade. In November 1921, Remington introduced a quality Model 10T Target Grade Pump Gun with a ventilated rib, intended for trap shooting, selling for $143.10. Concurrently, higher grades were offered including the Model 10TD Tournament Grade, the Model 10TE Expert Grade, and the Model 10TF Premier Grade (selling for $375.10). Initially, the bottom loading and bottom ejecting Model 10 shotgun was chambered only for 12 gauge shotshells. Remington produced 12 gauge Model 10 shotguns from 1905 to 1928, and in that 23-year period the factory sold 275,524 shotguns.

During the First World War, Remington manufactured 3,500 **Remington Model 10 Pump-Action Shotguns** with 23-inch barrels and fitted with bayonet attachments, and 1,150 standard Model 10R Shotguns with 20-inch barrels without bayonet attachments. The government used these guns primarily for guard purposes.

Remington Model 17 Pump-Action Shotguns

John M. Browning began developmental work on a new pump-action shotgun in 1913, and he granted manu-

Above: Remington Model 31-TC Pump Action Shotgun.

Above: Remington Model 31 Pump Action Shotgun.

facturing rights to Remington. It would be another six years until the company was ready to produce and market their first 20 gauge, pump shotgun—the **Remington Model 17**. Another famous Remington inventor, John D. Pedersen, in 1919, made refinements to Browning's basic Model 17 design.

The Model 17 is a pump-action, hammerless, underloading, tubular-magazine, bottom-ejecting, take-down shotgun which chambers both 2½-inch and 2¾-inch 20 gauge shotshells. Remington's Model 17A Standard Grade shotgun was announced on January 3, 1921. The shotgun weighed just 5lbs/12oz. Four other grades were offered in 1923, including the M17B Special Grade, the M17D Tournament Grade, the Model 17E Expert Grade, and the M17F Premier Grade. The M17R Riot Grade shotgun with a 20-inch choke-bored barrel was introduced in 1926, selling for $46.95. In all, Remington sold a total of 72,644 Model 17 shotguns between 1921 and 1941, although production had been halted in 1933.

Above: "The scarecrow" original painting by Ryder used in Remington Kleanbore 22 advertisement—1933.

Remington Model 29, Pump-Action Shotguns

Remington began working on a replacement for the Model 10 pump shotgun in 1926, and the factory announced in January 1929 that a new shotgun would be available by March. The result was the Remington Model 29, a pump-action, hammerless, tubular-magazine, bottom-ejecting, take-down shotgun which chambers 2-inch 12 gauge shotshells. Remington offered eight grades, including: Model 29A Standard Grade shotgun; the Model 29B Special Grade, the Model 29C Trap Grade, the Model 29S Special Trap Grade, the M29D Tournament Grade, the Model 29E Expert Grade, the Model 29F Premier Grade and the Model 29R Riot Grade shotgun. Concurrently, Remington offered several variations of Model 29T Special Trap Guns, including: the M29T Target Grade; M29TD Tournament Grade; M29TE Expert Grade; and the M29TF Premier Grade. Remington's Model 29 shotguns were produced only for five years, and Remington sold a total of 37,933 Model 29 shotguns during that time.

Remington Model 31 Pump-Action Shotguns

In early 1930, Remington began working on a pump-action shotgun to replace both the Remington Model 17 and Model 29. A new 12 gauge shotgun was introduced in August 1931, selling for $48.95. This was Remington's first side-ejecting, single-loading, repeating shotgun. Remington began offering Model 31 shotguns in 16 and 20 gauge in 1933. During World War II, Remington supplied 8,992 Model 31 shotguns to the U.S. Armed Forces, primarily for aerial gunnery training.

Remington produced the Model 31 shotgun in thirty-five variations and grades, including: the Model 31A Standard Grade (1931); Model 31AC and Model 31AP (both 1937, replacing the Model 31A); Model 31B Special Grade (1932); Model 31D Tournament Grade (1932); Model 31E Expert Grade (1932); M31F Premier Grade (1932); M31H Hunter's Special; Model 31 Police Gun with 18-inch barrel (1931); Model 31R Riot Gun with 20-inch barrel (1932); Model 31 Skeet Gun (1935); Model 31D Skeet Tournament; Model 31E Skeet Expert; Model 31F Skeet Premier; Model 31 Trap Special Grade (1932); Model 31S-D Trap Tournament; Model 31S-E Trap Expert; Model 31 S-F Trap Premier; Model 31 TC Trap (or Target) Grade (1932); Model 31 T-D Target Tournament; Model 31 T-E Target Expert; and the Model 31T-F Target Premier.

In 1941, Remington expanded their Model 31 shotgun line by also offering: New Improved standard weight guns—the Model 31 New Improved Skeet Gun (in 12, 16 and 20 gauges); M31 New Improved TC Target Grade (in 12 gauge only); M31 New Improved Police Special (in 12 gauge only); and the Model 31R New Improved Riot Gun (in 12, 16 and 20 gauges); New Improved Lightweight 12 gauge shotguns with aluminum receivers—Model 31 New Improved Lightweights: Model 31LA Standard Grade; Model 31LB Lightweight Special Grade; Model 31LD Tournament Grade; Model 31LE Expert Grade; Model 31LF Premier Grade; Model 31L Skeet Gun; and the M31LR Riot Grade; and Long Range guns: the Model 31 XA Standard Grade; New Improved Model 31 XA Standard Grade; New Improved Model 31 XS Trap Special Grade; New Improved Model 31 XH Hunter's Special Grade; and the New Improved Model 31 XTC Trap Grade shotguns.

Remington Model 31 shotguns were popular selling sporting arms for the company and were manufactured from 1931 to 1949. In those eighteen years a grand total of 189,243 Model 31 shotguns were made, including 117, 739 in 12 gauge, 40,312 in 16 gauge, and 31,192 in 20 gauge.

Remington Sportsman Shotguns

In 1931, Remington brought out a three-shot variation of the five-shot Model 11 autoloading shotgun, and called it **The Sportsman**. This streamlined shotgun was offered in 12, 16 and 20 gauges. In 1932, Remington offered The Sportsman in A Standard Grade, B Special Grade, C Trap Grade (discontinued in December 1937), D Tournament Grade, E Expert Grade, and F Premier Grade. In May 1935, Remington introduced The Sportsman Skeet Gun in 12, 16 and 20 gauges with special skeet bored barrels. Remington also offered The Sportsman Skeet Gun in grades A, B, D, E and F, with increasing quality of engraving and wood. In all, Remington sold 45,155 Sportsman 12 gauge shotguns, 49,176 Sportsman 16 gauge shotguns, and 44,155 Sportsman 20 gauge shotguns in the seventeen-year period between 1931 and 1948.

Above: Remington Model 3200 Over & Under Shotgun.

Above: Remington Model 32 Over & Under Shotgun.

Remington Model 32 Over & Under Shotguns

In the early 1930s, Remington developed the company's first over & under shotgun, and in March 1932, the first Remington Model 32 Shotguns were ready for delivery. The break-open Model 32 was made only in 12 gauge, and had automatic ejectors. The earliest guns had two triggers, but a single-selective trigger became available in 1934, and standard by 1938. This gun features a roll-engraved receiver, and a high-grade wood stock and fore-end. From the start the Model 32 was a quality-made gun, expensive to produce and expensive for the depression-era shooting public.

In the mid 1930s two additional variations were offered: the Model 32S Trap Special Grade with raised solid rib barrel and Hawkins recoil pad; and the Model 32TC Target Grade with raised ventilated rib and Hawkins recoil pad. In 1933, the Model 32 was also available in M32D Tournament Grade, M32E Expert Grade, and M32F Premier Grade. In 1934, Remington brought out the Model 32 Skeet Grade gun with skeet-bored barrels, both improved cylinder, and with single selective trigger. The Model 32S Trap Special Grade gun was last offered in 1937. Remington manufactured Model 32 Over & Under Shotguns through 1941, when most civilian production ceased because of the war effort. Guns in inventory continued to be sold in 1946 and 1947. In a most difficult decade of economic strife and world war, Remington managed to sell only 5,053 Model 32 shotguns.

Parker Double-Barrel Shotguns

On June 1, 1934, Remington Arms Company Inc. acquired the Charles Parker Company of Meriden, Connecticut. This included the Parker name, outstanding inventory of guns and parts, and tooling. The Parker Brothers had suffered through the Depression, and only about 300 Parker guns were made in 1932 and 1933. This acquisition cost Remington $100,000, and came about because Remington wanted to add a quality side-by-side double gun to its sporting shotgun line. Manufacturing was permitted to remain in Meriden, and this new entity of Remington became known as the Parker Gun Works.

Remington took steps to keep the well-deserved Parker reputation in place. Remington improved the quality of the wood that went into the new Parker guns, improved the already-good wood-to-metal fit, and Remington designers licked ejector problems that had plagued the Parker gun for many years. Remington did not embark upon an aggressive marketing effort for the Parker gun. The Parker 1936 Price List offered a number of side-by-side double guns and single-barrel guns: A.1. Special Grade; A.A.H.E. Grade; A.H.E. Grade; B.H.E. Grade; C.H.E. Grade; D.H.E. Grade; G.H.E. Grade; V.H.E. Grade; and their lower-priced Trojan Grade. Parker also offered a variety of Parker Double-Barrel Skeet Guns and Trap Guns, and five grades of Parker Single Barrel Trap Guns.

In January 1938, Remington closed Parker's Meridien Works and moved the gunmakers and machinery, tools, gauges, stock and other gunmaking equipment to Ilion, where the operation continued to be called The Parker Gun Works. Manufacturing of Parker guns was interrupted when the U.S. entered World War II, and when America returned to a peacetime economy, production and marketing studies at Remington showed that there was little market for an expensive, domestically produced double gun.

Model 11-'48 and Sportsman '48 Autoloading Shotguns

The first new shotguns to be introduced by Remington after World War II were the 5-shot **Model 11-'48 Autoloading Shotgun** and the 3-shot **Sportsman '48**.

Above: "Ol' Mike" advertising die-cut for Remington shotshells - 1927.

They retained the same recoiling barrel-action as the Model 11, but they had a self-compensating friction brake to eliminate the need for readjustment for light or heavy loads. These new shotguns were introduced to the trade in January 1949, in 12, 16 and 20 gauges. Initial variations included: the M11-'48A or Sportsman '48A Standard Grade; the M11-'48R Riot Gauge with 20-inch barrel; M11-'48B or Sportsman '48B Special Grade; the M11-'48D or Sportsman '48D Tournament Grade; and the M11-'48F or Sportsman '48F Premier Grade. Sportsman '48 Skeet guns include the Sportsman '48 Skeet Grade, as well as the Special, Tournament and Premier Grade guns.

A 28 gauge version of the increasingly popular Model 11–'48 shotgun was introduced in 1952—the first autoloading shotgun in this gauge ever made on a production basis. In January 1954, Remington introduced a .410 version of this gun. In 1959, the Model 11–'48 RSS "Rifled Slug Special" was introduced for hunters, and it featured a blade-type front sight and step-adjustable rear. Remington ceased production of the Sportsman '48 in 1958, and the Model 11-'48 was last offered in the 1968 Remington Sporting Firearms catalog, although these shotguns sold well into the following year. In all, Remington sold 455,535 Model 11-'48 autoloading shotguns and 275,198 Sportsman '48 between 1949 and 1969.

Remington Model 870 "Wingmaster®" Shotguns

In early 1947, Remington decided to replace the tried-and-true Model 31 pump-action shotgun. Utilizing common parts from the sleek, new Model 11-'48 autoloader, Remington developed the soon-to-be-famous Model 870 shotgun. In January 1950 Remington announced its new Model 870 Wingmaster shotgun, which has become the best selling pump action shotgun in the world. Like the M11-'48, the new M870 shotgun breech locked securely in a hardened barrel extension, and a new locking block and slide was devised for a smooth and effective operation. The introduction chronology of this versatile shotgun is as follows:

1950 Remington introduced fifteen versions of the Model 870 shotgun including: M870 AP Standard Grade shotgun), the M870 BC Special Grade, the M870 ADL Deluxe Grade shotgun, the Model 870 BDL Deluxe Special Grade shotgun, M870D Tournament Grade, M870F Premier Grade, M870TC Trap Grade, M870TD Trap Tournament Grade, M870TF Trap Premier Grade, M870S Trap Special Grade, M870SA Skeet Grade, M870SB Skeet Special Grade, M870SD Skeet Tournament Grade, M870SF Skeet Premier Grade and the M870R Riot Grade shotgun.

1954 M870 Magnum-AP Standard Grade shotgun and the M870 Magnum-ADL Deluxe Grade shotgun.

1959 M870 RSS Rifled Slug Special

1960 M870 ADX

1961 M870 AP "Brushmaster" shotgun

1963 Remington produced the Model 870 in a new Deluxe grade for all field models with custom checkering and improved wood finish.

1966 M870 150th Anniversary Edition Shotgun

1969 Remington introduced M870 field models in 28 gauge and .410, which were issued with scaled-down receivers, and lightweight mahogany stocks and fore-ends. Remington also introduced M870 "Matched Pair" 20 gauge and .410 Skeet guns.

1970 28 gauge and .410 shotguns were offered

REMINGTON SHOTGUNS • *109*

Above: Model 870 Slug Shotgun.

Above: Model 870 Mag Shotgun.

Above: Model 870 Express Shotgun.

Above: Model 870 Magnum Special Purpose Shotgun.

Above: Model 870 Shotgun.

Below: Model 870 Magnum Special Purpose Shotgun.

Above: Model 870 with Choke barrel.

Above: Model 870 Competition Shotgun.

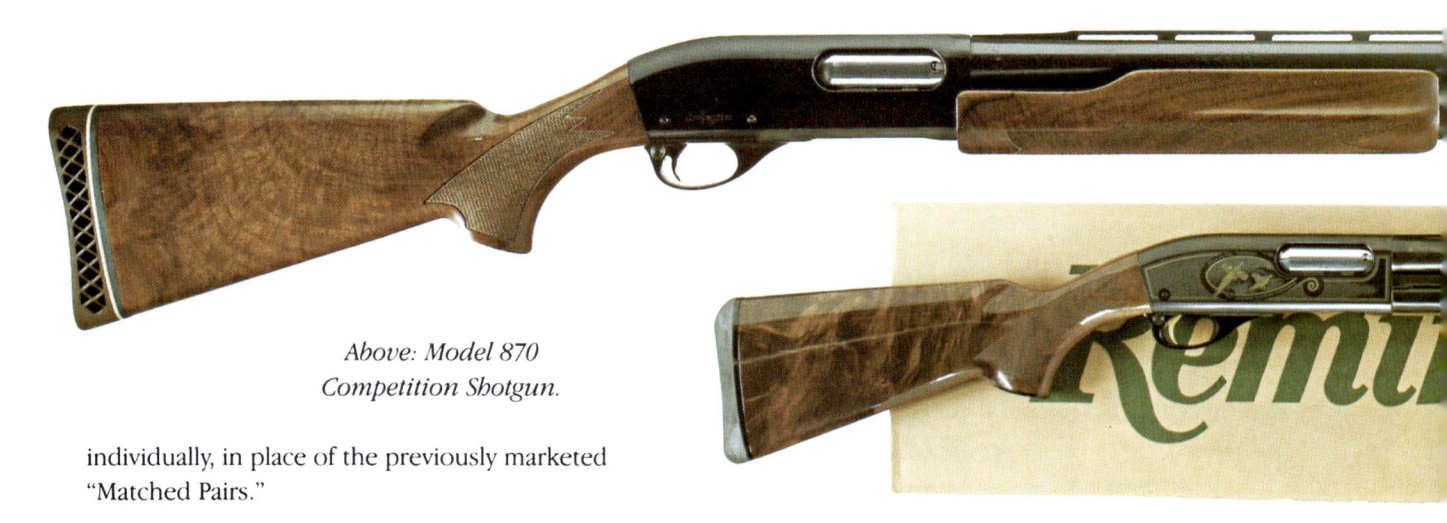

individually, in place of the previously marketed "Matched Pairs."

1971 Left-handed versions of the M870 were offered in Field, Magnum and Trap grades, in 12 gauge and 20 gauge guns.

1972 M870 "All American" Special Trap Gun and the 20 gauge Lightweight M870.

1973 In October, Remington announced making their two-millionth Model 870 shotgun!

1974 M870 DU (Ducks Unlimited) shotguns

1976 Bicentennial Commemorative M870 SA Skeet Grade, M870 TB Trap Grade and M870 TBMCS Trap shotguns

1978 M870 LW-20 Lightweight Deer Gun. In May Remington announced the production of their three-millionth Model 870 shotgun.

1981 Model 870 "Competition" Trap gun. Model 870 20 gauge Lightweight Limited.

1983 Ducks Unlimited Commemorative M870 Mississippi Magnum shotguns

1984 M870 "Special Field" Remington also changed the name "Lightweight Limited" to 20 gauge Lightweight "Youth Gun".

Below: Final assembly department for Model 12 slide-action 22 rifles—Remington factory, Ilion, New York—circa 1914.

Below: Model 870 special edition 'Wildlife for Tomorrow'.

1985 M870 SP Special Purpose Magnum gun

1986 M870 SP Special Purpose Deer Gun

1987 Model 870 Express

1988 M870 Express Combo shotgun

1991 Model 870 Express Turkey, Model 870 Express Cantilever Scope Mount Deer Gun, Model 870 Express Rifle Sighted Deer Gun, Model 870 Express Small Gauge, Model 870 Express Youth Gun, Model 870 SP Cantilever Scope Mount Deer Gun, Model 870 SPS Special Purpose Synthetic, Model 870 SPS-T Special Purpose Synthetic-Turkey Gun.

1992 M870 Marine Magnum. Remington introduced a fully camouflaged version of the Model 870 SP-CAMO shotgun in Mossy Oak Bottomland camo.

1993 M870 SPS BG-Camo gun, M870 SPS-Deer

1994 M870 Wingmaster in 12 and 20 gauges. M870 SPS. Model 870 Express Small Gauge shotgun. M870 Express Youth Gun.

1995 Model 870 Express HD (Home defense)

1996 Remington re-introduced the M870 TC Trap gun

continues page 114

Above: Model 870 Express Turkey Shotgun.

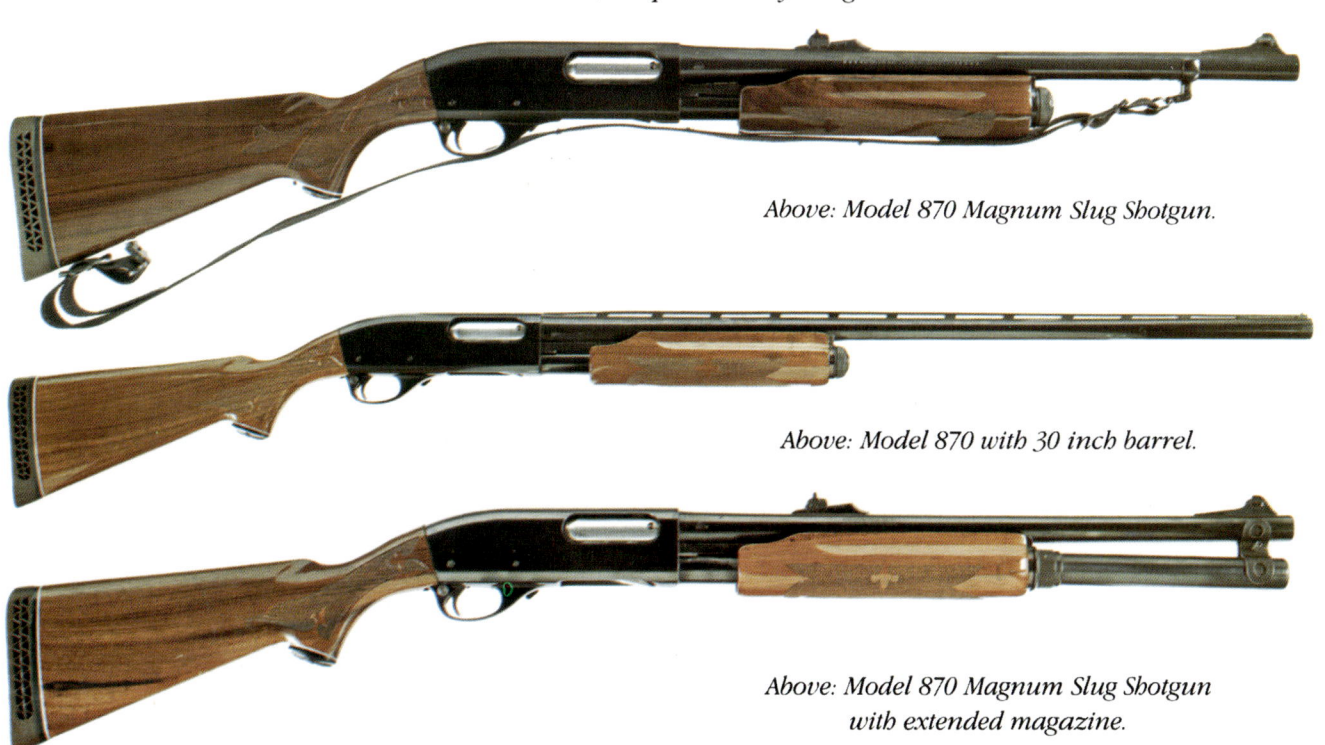

Above: Model 870 Magnum Slug Shotgun.

Above: Model 870 with 30 inch barrel.

Above: Model 870 Magnum Slug Shotgun with extended magazine.

Hunting: The Remington Tradition

The name REMINGTON is synonymous with hunting. Since its inception in 1816, Remington has made the finest rifles and shotguns in America. Following a long-standing tradition for perfection first espoused by Eliphalet Remington, hunting firearms made today by Remington in Ilion, New York and Mayfield, Kentucky *"shoot where ya aim em."*

Above: This unidentified hunter is armed with a Remington No.3 Hepburn sporting rifle.

When America was still quite young, Eliphalet Remington's rifle barrels were sold to gunsmiths throughout the settled United States from Maine to New Orleans, and from Pittsburgh to Georgia. Tens, possibly hundreds of thousands of flintlock and percussion rifles made by countless American gunsmiths were made with barrels fabricated at Remington's forge in upstate New York. By the early 1850s, Remington was selling more than 10,000 gun barrels a year. One can only imagine the number of rabbits, squirrels, deer and bear that were brought down by muzzle loading and percussion rifles sporting Remington's accurate gun barrels.

The earliest sporting rifles made in their entirety by E. Remington & Sons Armory, included percussion revolving rifles, Beals' patent single-shot rimfire rifles, and split-breech sporting rifles in the immediate post Civil War years. These were followed in 1868 by the soon-to-be-famous Remington "rolling block" sporting rifle in rimfire and centerfire versions, which were popular through the late 1880s. The short-lived Remington-Keene bolt-action, tubular magazine rifle followed in 1879, and the more popular single-shot, falling block Remington Hepburn rifle was introduced in 1880. When smokeless powder ammunition became popular in the 1890s, Remington offered the Hepburn rifle and Remington-Lee Model 1899 sporting rifle.

Remington entered the sporting shotgun field in 1873, with the introduction of the Remington-Whitmore, hammer-lifter, double gun. This was followed by a succession of exposed hammer guns through the Model 1889. Taking heed of the hammerless demand, the company offered the Model 1894 and later less-expensive Model 1900 guns.

Probably the most innovative autoloading shotgun ever devised, was the Remington Model 11 shotgun, designed by John Browning and first offered to American sportsmen in 1904. This design was modified numerous times in the decades that followed, resulting in the *"Sportsman"*, the Model 11-'48 and the Model 11-'58. Contemporary pump-action shotguns included the J.D. Pedersen inspired Model 10 (introduced in 1908), the Browning-inspired Model 17 (1921), the Model 29 (1929) and later the Model 31 (1931).

John Browning also invented Remington's first autoloading, high-power rifle, the Model 8, first offered in 1906, which was improved into the Model 81 in 1938. Answering the call for high-power, slide-action hunting rifles, Remington offered the Pedersen-designed Model 14 and Model 14½ in 1912, and the medium-powered, slide-action Model 25 rifle in 1923. Later slide-action high-power rifles included the Model 141 in 1935.

Remington small-bore .22 rifles, popular with hunters of varmints and light game in the early part of the 20th century, included the venerable Model 12 (introduced in 1909), the autoloading Model 16 (1915), the autoloading Model 24 (1922), the single-shot Model 33 in (1931), the tubular magazine repeating Model 34 in (1932), the Model 241 autoloader (1935), the single-shot Model 41 rifle in (1936), Model 341 bolt-action, tubular-magazine repeaters (1936), and the Model 121 slide-action (1936). In the late 1930s, Remington's first *"family of guns"* (utilizing common parts) began as the bolt-action Model 500 series. These included the Model 510 single-shot (1939), the Model 511

Above: Original painting "Lunch Time" by Frank Leyendecker, used in a variety of Remington advertisements - circa 1919.

box-magazine (1939), and the Model 512 tubular-magazine 22s (1940). Successive hunting 22s included the Model 513S (1945), and the "Carbine", the Williams inspired Model 550 autoloader (1941).

Following World War I, Remington entered the high-power bolt-action market with the Model 30 (introduced in 1921), followed by the Model 30 Express rifle (1926) and the Model 30S (1930). As these proved to be overly expensive to produce, Remington came out with the Model 720 bolt-action rifle in 1939, but the war soon interrupted production.

Remington introduced their first over & under shotgun, the Model 32, in 1932. It was later replaced by other over & under guns including the Model 3200 (1973), the "Peerless" in 1993, the Model 396 in 1996, the Model 300 "Ideal" in 2000, and the Model 332 in 2002. Many hunters prefer the feel of an over & under for wing shooting.

The years immediately following World War II, Remington introduced millions of returning GIs to the pleasures of high-power hunting by offering the Mike Walker designed bolt-action Model 721 and Model 722 rifles in 1948. Returning GIs requesting repeating shotguns were offered Remington autoloading Model 11-48 shotguns in 1948.

The most popular pump-action shotgun ever designed – the Remington Model 870 shotgun – was first offered in 1950. In the 55 years since its introduction, the Remington Company has sold more than 8,000,000 of these shotguns to sportsmen throughout the world. The company continued to offer more shotgun innovations in the years that followed, including the autoloading Sportsman 58 in 1956, the Model 878 autoloader in 1959, the Wayne Leek designed Model 1100 autoloader in 1963, the Mohawk '48 autoloader in 1970, the Sportsman 12 pump-action shotgun in 1984, the Sportsman 12 autoloading shotgun in 1985, the Model 11-87 autoloader in 1987, the SP-10 magnum autoloading shotgun in 1989, the single-barrel Model 90-T trap gun in 1991, and the Model 11-96 *"Euro Lightweight"* in 1997. The Remington Company seems to come out with improved models of their entire shotgun line every year for today's hunters.

Believed to be the best bolt-action, high-power rifle ever made, Remington first offered the Mike Walker designed Model 700 in 1962. Millions have been made and the Model 700 is a mainstay firearm in Remington's stable of 21st Century hunting rifles. In 1964, Remington introduced the Model 600 bolt-action hunting carbine, followed in 1965 by the Model 600 Magnum carbine, and in 1968 by the Model 660 carbine and the Model 660 Magnum carbine. The Mohawk 600 carbine was brought out briefly in 1972. In 1967, Remington introduced the highly accurate, but moderately priced Model 788 rifle. In 1983, the company introduced the Model Seven bolt-action lightweight rifle. In 1984, Remington introduced the Sportsman Series of moderately priced centerfire rifles, including the Sportsman 74 autoloader, the Sportsman 76 slide-action, and the Sportsman 78 bolt-action rifle. In 2000 the company announced "Etronx" an electronic ignition system for Model 700 rifles utilizing an electronic primer. In 2001, Remington brought out the moderately priced Model 710 rifle and scope. Remington introduced the Model 673 rifle in 2003, essentially a reissue of the legendary Model 600.

In 1963, Remington introduced their first pistol since 1926, the XP-100, popular in various hunting venues. This pistol was made in numerous configurations until it was discontinued several years later.

Commemorative hunting rifles introduced by Remington include the 1816 Eliphalet Remington flintlock rifle in 1995, and the No.1 "rolling block" mid-range rifle in 1997. The following year the company brought out a lower-priced variation of this "rolling block" rifle for sportsmen seeking the thrill of hunting with a *"weapon from the past."*

The Remington Company continues to make fine rifles and shotguns for today's hunters, maintaining its nearly 190-year history of quality, accuracy and dependability.

114 • The History of Remington Firearms

and re-introduced the M870 Express Small Gauge gun in 20 gauge, 28 gauge and .410 bore.

1997 New Mossy Oak Break-Up Pattern on the M870 Magnum SPS gun, and M870 Turkey Gun in new Realtree X-Tra Brown camo. Introduced two new M870 Express Combo shotguns.

1998 Model 870 Express Super Magnum shotguns. Synthetic Super Magnum. Synthetic Turkey Camo gun.

Above: Remington 870 Pump Action Shotgun.

Below: Model 870 LW Magnum Shotgun.

Above: Model 870 Shotgun with extended magazine.

Above: Model 870 Police Riot Shotgun.

1999 Remington added 28 gauge and .410-bore versions to the Model 870 Wingmaster line. Introduced the Model 870 SPS "Super Magnum" Camo Shotgun, the Model 870 SPS-T "Super Magnum" Camo Shotgun and the Model 870 SPS "Super Slug" Deer Gun.

2000 Remington introduced the 50th Anniversary Model 870 Classic Trap Gun as a tribute to the world's best-selling pump shotgun. Also introduced the Model 870 Wingmaster Super Magnum, the Model 870 SPS-T RS/TG Shotgun and the Model 870 SPS-T Super Magnum Camo CL/RD Shotgun.

2001 Model 870 SPS-T Super Magnum Camo CL/RC Shotgun, the Model 870 SPS Super Magnum Camo Shotgun the Model 870 Classic Trap Shotgun, and Remington Model 870 SPS-T Youth RS/TG Synthetic Turkey Camo Shotgun

2002 Remington reintroduced the 16 gauge shotgun in four variations of the Model 870, including the Model 870 Wingmaster, the Model 870 Express, the Model 870 Express Synthetic and the Model 870 Express Synthetic Youth Shotguns. Also the Model 870 Express Shotgun in 28 gauge and .410 bore.

2003 Model 870 SPS-T

Sportsman-58 Autoloading Shotguns

In February 1956, Remington introduced the **Sportsman-58 autoloading shotgun**, the company's first autoloading shotgun that did not have a recoiling barrel action. This new autoloader featured a unique "Dial-A-Matic" load control. The shooter could dial in his gun for L, light, low-base shells, or H, heavy, high-base loads. Initially, Remington made only a 12 gauge gas-operated gun, but in the following year, 16 and 20 gauge versions were introduced. The Sportsman-58 featured a receiver inscribed with a decorative game scene, and a checkered or a gloss-finished walnut stock and fore-end.

Below: Remington 870 Express Turkey Shotgun.

Variations of the Sportsman-58 included the following, which were introduced in February 1956: ADL Deluxe Grade with plain barrel and with vent barrel), BDL Deluxe Special Grade with plain barrel and with ventilated rib barrel, D Tournament Grade with vent barrel, F Premier Grade with vent barrel, SA Skeet Grade with vent barrel, SC Skeet Target Grade with vent barrel, SD Skeet Tournament Grade with vent barrel, SF Skeet Premier Grade with vent barrel, and TB Trap Special Grade (introduced June 1956. In January 1959, Remington introduced two 12 gauge magnum versions of the Sportsman-58, which chambered 3-inch magnum length shells: an ADL version with plain barrel, and an ADL version with ventilated rib barrel. Both versions were fitted with a rubber recoil pad as standard equipment.

Between 1959 and 1962, Remington sold 819 Sportsman-58 shotguns in 12, 16 and 20 gauges, with light-colored "Sun-Grain" maple stocks and fore-ends, including the **Sportsman-58TX** and **Sportsman-58SX**. Also in 1959, Remington introduced the **Sportsman-58RSS**, intended for hunters who desired a shotgun which fired rifled slugs. It had a 26-inch improved cylinder, 12 gauge barrel with a flat-faced gold bead front sight and step adjustable rear sight with windage adjustment. Remington manufactured the Sportsman-58 through 1962, and last advertised this autoloader in the 1963 catalog. There were some run-off sales for several years thereafter. In all, Remington manufactured 270,760 Sportsman-58 shotguns, including 192,026 in 12 gauge, 40,253 in 16 gauge, and 38,481 in 20 gauge.

Remington Model 878 "Automaster" Autoloading Shotguns

On January 5, 1959, Remington announced a new, lightweight, gas-operated autoloading 12 gauge shotgun, with either plain or ventilated rib barrels. This shotgun featured a self-adjusting Remington "Power-Piston," a device which sensed the pressure rise between low base and high powered magnum shotshells, and provided a variable cut-off of the gas flow to operate the mechanism. This eliminated the need for manual adjustment of power level, and internalized all of the mechanism within the magazine tube. The Model 878 has a two-shot magazine capacity. The basic field shotgun was the Model 878A Grade, which had a plain receiver and plain walnut stock and fore-end, and sold at a substantially lower price than the Remington Sportsman '58. Deluxe versions were added in 1961, including the Model 878 ADL field

Above: Advertising die-cut "A New Thoroughbred" featuring Remington Nitro Express Kleanbore shotshells.

stock and roll-engraved receiver) and the high grade D, E and F grade and SD skeet gun, and the SF skeet grade guns. Model 878 shotguns were produced only for a few years, as they were superceded by the new Remington Model 1100. Model 878s were last advertised in the 1963 catalog, and sold through 1965, with run-off sales of left-over stock through 1969. In all, Remington sold 63,478 Model 878 shotguns.

MODEL 1100 AUTOLOADING SHOTGUNS

As far as autoloading shotguns are concerned, the **Remington Model 1100 Autoloading Shotgun** was one of the most successful sporting shotguns ever conceived. The following is the chronology of introduction of various models:

1963 Remington introduced the Model 1100 autoloading shotgun, the result of a three-year development program. The initial guns were 12

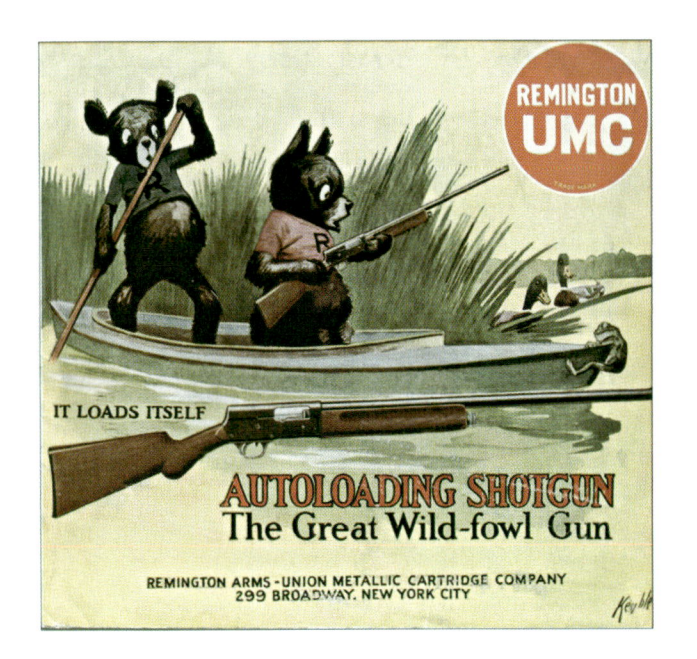

Above: Cover page announcing John Browning's new autoloading shotgun, later to be named the Remington Model 11 autoloader—circa 1904.

gun (roll-engraved receiver and checkered stock and fore-end), the ADX field gun, the BDL field gun, the SA skeet gun (with ventilated rib barrel, roll-engraved receiver, and checkered butt stock and fore-end), the SX skeet gun (with Sun-Grain stock and fore-end), the SC skeet gun (with checkered and figured American walnut gauge Field Grade (plain barrel and vent rib), Magnum Duck Guns (chambered for 3-inch magnum shells, with plain barrel and vent rib, SA Skeet Grade, SC Skeet Grade and TB Trap Grade models. High grade Model 1100 shotguns included the D Tournament Grade and the F Premier Grade.

1964 Remington introduced 16 and 20 gauge versions of the Model 1100 to the Field, Magnum and Skeet Model 1100 shotguns. Concurrently, the company introduced 16 gauge Field and 20 gauge Field, Magnum and Skeet versions.

1966 Remington introduced a new Model 1100 Lightweight 20 Gauge Shotgun with standard 20 gauge frame, but with a lightweight, checkered mahogany stock and fore-end, in Field and Skeet models. The plain barrel version—the ventilated rib version—and the M1100 SA Skeet version with vent rib barrel. In 1966, Remington also introduced the Model 1100 Deer Gun, a 12 gauge gun with 22-inch plain barrel choked for rifled slugs and buckshot loads, and ramp front sight and adjustable rifle-type rear sight. It also featured a checkered American walnut stock and fore-end, and a rubber recoil pad with white line spacer. In 1966 Remington Arms Company celebrated its 150th Anniversary by introducing two commemorative versions of the

Above and both below: Three examples of the Remington Model 1100 Autoloading shotgun.

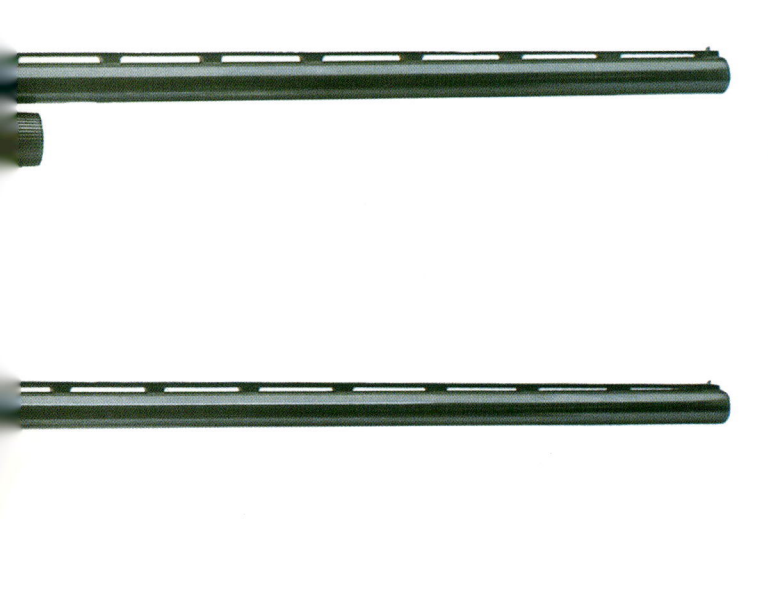

Model 1100, in Trap and Skeet configurations. A total of 2,929 were sold in 1966 and early 1967.

1969 Beginning this year, Remington began making .410 and 28 gauge versions. Initially they were only available as Model 1100 Matched Pairs—a .410 shotgun and a 28 gauge shotgun in Field and Skeet versions. Both plain and vent rib barrels were available. The Field gun came with mahogany stock and fore-end, and Skeet guns came in American walnut. The .410 and 28 gauge guns were offered only as a matched pair with matching serial numbers gilded in gold, and protected in a hard carrying case. A total of 5,067 Matched Pairs were sold in 1969 and 1970. Later in the year, Remington began offering the Model 1100 in .410 with full choke and in 28 gauge with modified choke. Stocks and fore-ends were made of lightweight mahogany, and either gauge was available with plain or vent rib barrel. In 1969, Remington also introduced a 20 gauge Model 1100 Deer Gun, which had a 22-inch long improved cylinder barrel equipped with rifle sights.

1970 Remington introduced a Model 1100 20 gauge Lightweight Field Gun which was built on a smaller 28 gauge frame, and had a lightweight checkered mahogany stock and fore-end. This gun was available with plain barrel or vent rib barrel, in full or modified chokes 28 inches in length, or improved cylinder barrels 26 inches in length. Also in this year, Remington began marketing Model 1100 SA Skeet guns in .410 and 28 gauge individually as standard models. These were available with 25-inch skeet choke barrels.

1971 In this year Remington added a Model 1100 20 gauge Lightweight in 3-inch magnum gun, weighing 6lbs/12oz. Plain 28-inch, with full choke barrels.

1972 In January of this year, Remington Arms Company proudly advertised producing the one-millionth Model 1100 autoloading shotgun. In only nine years of production the Model 1100 exceeded that of the venerable Model 11 autoloading shotgun, which was in production for more than 45 years. That shotgun is serial numbered L509235M. Also in January, Remington introduced a reversed, mirror-image, Left-Hand version of the Model 1100 in 12 and 20 gauge guns in Field Grade 12 gauge (with 30-inch full choke, 28-inch modified, and 26-inch improved cylinder vent rib barrels), and 20 gauge (with 28-inch full and modified, and 26-inch improved cylinder vent rib barrels), Magnum Grade 12 gauge only (with 3-inch chamber and 30-inch full choke, vent rib barrel), SA Skeet Grade 12 and 20 gauge (with 26-inch vent rib skeet barrel), and Trap Grade 12 gauge only (available with regular trap for, or Monte Carlo–style stock, and 30-inch full choke, vent rib trap barrel variations.

1973 Remington introduced a special limited edition Model 1100 Ducks Unlimited Commemorative

Shotgun, dedicated to the Ducks Unlimited organization. The right side of the receiver was roll-stamped with a simple gold-colored scroll pattern. Centered on the left side of the receiver panel is a multi-colored bronze medallion depicting a canvasback duck, the Ducks Unlimited mallard head logo, flanked by decorative scroll work. Six hundred of these guns were sold directly to DU Chapters for fund-raising dinners in 1973, and 10,000 sold conventionally.

1974 Remington introduced the Model 1100 TBMC Trap Gun, in 12 gauge with 30-inch, vent rib barrel in full or modified trap chokes. This gun featured a figured and checkered stock and fore-end, and had a rubber recoil pad. A Monte Carlo–style stock was optional. A left-hand version of this gun was also available. Due to a shortage of American walnut, in mid-year Remington began fitting some Model 1100 and Model 870 Field Grade shotguns with lightweight mahogany stocks and fore-ends.

1976 In January, Remington introduced a 12 gauge Model 1100 TB Trap Gun in right and left-hand versions, with select American walnut in regular Trap or Monte Carlo–style stock, rubber recoil pad, and ventilated rib. Advertising stated that this gun gives the shooter "the All-Events competitive edge." To honor America's Bicentennial Remington brought out four commemorative 12 gauge variations of the Model 1100: Model 1100 (28-inch plain barrel with modified choke); M1100 SA Skeet Bicentennial (26-inch vent rib with skeet choke; M1100 TB Trap Bicentennial (30-inch vent rib with full choke with standard stock or Monte Carlo–stock); and M1100 TBMCS Trap Bicentennial (with 30-inch vent rib with full choke and Monte Carlo–stock). Centered on the left side of the receiver panel is a gold-colored roll-engraved Bicentennial American Eagle and Shield with the dates 1776 and 1976 and scroll pattern. About 5,000 Bicentennial Model 1100 shotguns were sold.

1977 In March Remington Arms Company proudly announced the manufacture of the two-millionth Model 1100 shotgun. Also in 1977, Remington introduced a new, redesigned Model 1100 20 gauge Lightweight (called LT-20) in Field Grade, Magnum and Skeet versions. These guns are visually distinguishable from previous 20 gauge models by the contoured ejection port (long barrel extension).

1978 The Model 1100 LT-20 becomes standard 20 gauge Model 1100 in all Field Grade versions. Formerly, this gun was built on a larger 12 gauge

Above: Bottom Model 1100 Shotgun Set.

Left: Model 1100 LW.

frame. Concurrently, the Model 1100 20 gauge left-hand version was dropped, and was not available in LT-20 versions. The new Model 1100 LT-20 Deer gun replaced the older, large receiver 20 gauge Deer gun. The new gun had a 20-inch, improved cylinder barrel with rifle sights. Stocks on all Model 1100 LT-20 Field guns now were made of walnut instead of mahogany.

1979 In this year, Remington introduced a new stock checkering pattern and receiver scroll markings on all standard Model 1100 Field, Magnum, Skeet and Trap models. Model 1100 12 gauge 3-inch Mag shotguns were adapted to function with extra barrels chambered for 2-inch shells. Also in 1979, Remington introduced Model 1100 Tournament Grade Trap guns with 30-inch full or modified Trap barrels; and new Model 1100 Tournament Skeet guns in 12, LT-10, 28 and .410 gauge versions. New guns featured select walnut stocks with a new cut-checkered pattern. Remington also introduced Model 1100 TA Trap guns with regular grade stocks, as distinguished from Tournament Grade Trap guns, are introduced in both left and right-hand versions. Model 1100 TB Trap guns were discontinued in this year.

1980 Remington introduced the Model 1100 LT-20 "Limited," a 20 gauge lightweight Model 1100 Field gun with stock 1 inch shorter than standard, and 23-inch barrel for youthful, beginner shooters of smaller stature. This year Remington also introduced special Skeet weight-equalizer kits for Model 1100 .410, 28 gauge and LT 20 Skeet guns. The weight-equalizer kits were intended to give the three smaller gauge Model 1100s nearly identical balance and "point-ability" of the larger and heavier 12 gauge version. In September 1980, Remington announced the Model 1100 Limited Edition "One of Three Thousand." This was a high grade gun with positive cut-checkered fancy American walnut wood with a fitted rosewood grip cap and thin brown butt pad. It is 14K gold trimmed and etched with a hunting scene on the receiver. All metal parts including the receiver, barrel, bolt and magazine cap have a high-luster finish. This limited edition gun was available only in 1980, and was produced only in 12 gauge with a 28-inch, modified choke, vent rib barrel.

1981 Remington introduced the first of two Model 1100 Ducks Unlimited Commemorative guns in limited editions of 2,400 each, sequentially serial numbered with special markings. These guns were called "dinner guns" and were intended to be sold or auctioned-off only by Ducks Unlimited. Guns in this DU series were all "Atlantic Editions" which commemorated each of the country's flyways. The first was "The Chesapeake," a 12 gauge magnum with full choke, vent rib 30-inch barrel. It featured select, high-grade and checkered wood, gold-colored trigger, ivory bead front sight, and supplied with a foam-lined hard cover carrying case. The second Ducks Unlimited gun this year was called the "Ducks Unlimited Special," a Model 1100 LT-20, a lightweight 20 gauge with a 26-inch improved cylinder, vent rib barrel and 2-inch chamber. The right side of the receiver has the Ducks Unlimited mallard head logo flanked by decorative scrollwork. The left side of the receiver is stamped DUCKS UNLIMITED SPECIAL. The right side of the butt stock was laser-etched with a reproduction of the DU crest. Remington also announced a limited production run of Model 1100 12 gauge Magnum guns with 26-inch full choke, vent rib barrels and 3-inch chambers.

1982 Remington introduced a left-hand, 12 gauge Model 1100 Deer gun. Also added to the line was a 28-inch modified barrel for the Model 1100 LT-20 (20 gauge Lightweight) Magnum produced in 12 gauge Skeet version. Remington also introduced a Ducks Unlimited Commemorative Model 1100 this year which was available to all shooters through the standard dealer network. It was a 12 gauge magnum chambered for 3-inch shells with full choke, vent rib

32-inch barrel. This shotgun was available only in 1982, and was titled "The Atlantic," dedicated to the Atlantic Flyway.

1983 Remington announced that the company had manufactured its three-millionth Model 1100 autoloading shotgun. Also in 1983, Remington introduced the new Model 1100 "Special Field" shotgun in 12 and 20 gauges with a checkered straight-grip, English-style stock and 21-inch vent rib barrels in three field chokes.

1984 The Model 1100 LT-20 "Limited" name was changed to Model 1100 LT-20 Youth Gun.

1985 Remington introduced the new Model 1100 SP "Special Purpose" Magnum Shotgun with a low luster finish to the hardwood stock and fore-end and a sandblasted, dull blued finish on all exposed metal parts. This gun has a 3-inch chamber and a 26-inch, full choke vent rib barrel or 30-inch full choke barrel. A standard feature was a camouflaged nylon sling and sling swivels.

1986 Remington introduced the new Rem Choke system which thereafter will be fitted on all Model 1100 and Model 870 shotguns with 21-inch, 26-inch and 28-inch barrels. It was not available on 30-inch barrels, deer guns, target guns or as a retrofit. This patented device allows the shooter to use a wrench to change the shotgun to full, modified or improved cylinder chokes.

1989 Remington advertised that all Model 1100 autoloading shotguns featured stocks and fore-ends carved from American walnut and satin-finished and custom checkered. All vent rib barrels featured an ivory bead front and metal bead mid-sight. Also, every 20 gauge Model 1100 came equipped with Rem Choke tubes (except Deer guns which have a fixed choke).

1991 This year marked Remington's 175th year in the gun making field. Remington changed the Model 1100 LT-20 Youth Gun designation to Model 1100 Youth Gun. This was a 20 gauge gun "designed specifically for younger and small-framed shooters." A 21-inch barrel with Rem Choke tubes was standard.

1994 Remington introduced a 20 gauge Model 1100 with fully rifled cantilever deer barrel, intended for "long range deer hunting." This shotgun featured a 21-inch, fully rifled slug barrel. The Model 1100 "Special Field" shotgun now featured a 23-inch ventilated rib barrel with Rem Choke, a slimmed and shortened fore-end.

1996 Remington reintroduced the Model 1100 LT-20 Skeet Gun. This 20 gauge shotgun featured a satin-finished American walnut stock with sharp-line checkering, and a 26-inch vent rib barrel with Rem Choke. The Model 1100 Synthetic was first offered with a synthetic stock and fore-end in 1996, in both 12 gauge (with 28-inch barrel) and 20 gauge (26-inch barrel) versions. A ventilated rib barrel with Rem Choke was standard. Remington also introduced the Model 1100 Sporting 28, a 28 gauge shotgun for Sporting Clays competition. It featured a checkered American walnut, tournament-grade stock and fore-end, rubber recoil pad and 25-inch vent rib barrel with four Rem Choke tubes.

1997 Remington introduced the Model 1100 LT-20 Synthetic FR RS, a 20 gauge, rifle-sighted deer gun with a 21-inch fully rifled barrel. Concurrently, Remington introduced the Model 1100 Synthetic FR CL, a 12 gauge, fully rifled, cantilever deer gun.

1998 Remington introduced a Model 1100 Sporting 20, intended for shooters who prefer a lightweight, low-recoil 20 gauge autoloader in 12 gauge skeet events. This gun sports a gloss-finish, checkered, tournament grade American walnut stock and fore-end, recoil pad, and a 28-inch vent rib barrel with Rem Choke tubes.

Montgomery Ward Model ERI 600A "Western Field" Shotguns

In 1967, Remington manufactured a modified version of the discontinued Model 878 shotgun for Montgomery Ward, and it was called the **Ward Model ERI 600A "Western Field" Automatic Shotgun**. These private brand shotguns were made only in 12 gauge, with either plain or ventilated rib barrels. They featured a lacquered Wards-pattern skip-line checkered pistol-grip and fore-end, a Firestone-produced rubber recoil pad, and a 2-shot magazine. Within the factory Remington referred to these guns as Model 879 autoloading shotguns, and they were never offered in any Remington catalog or price list. Nor were these shotguns marked Remington in any manner. The first shipment of these guns were sent to Wards in June 1967. In all, Remington manufactured a total of 9,291 "Western Field" shotguns during a three-year period ending 1969, with run-off sales into the following year.

Model 310 Shotguns

In the early-1960s, Remington designers collaborated on the design of a .310 caliber, single-barrel, break-open shotgun with engineers at Remington's factory in Brazil,

Above: Original advertising die-cut featuring the Remington Model 8 autoloading rifle—circa 1914.

Companhia Brasileira de Cartuchos SA, more commonly known as C.B.C. Remington intended this gun to be part of a "Shooting Game Project," a skeet shooting package including gun, targets, ammunition, self-releasing target ejector, and coin-operated shooting booth. These units were test marketed at golf and shooting ranges, as well as at local carnivals and fairs. The study indicated that the guns would sell better in Europe and in other countries outside of the United States, so it was decided that these shotguns would be fabricated only in the Brazil plant, not in Ilion. The resulting gun was known as the Model 310 Shotgun.

Mohawk '48 Autoloading Shotguns

In 1970, Remington introduced the Mohawk '48 autoloading shotgun in both 12 and 20 gauges, as a re-introduction of the Model 11-'48 which was discontinued in 1968. The Mohawk '48 was never listed in Remington catalogs, and was produced only for five years, with diminished sales into 1975. In all, 55,610 Mohawk '48 shotguns were sold during this period.

Model 812 Shotguns

In 1971, Remington introduced another break-open shotgun made in C.B.C., the **Model 812**. Like the Model 310, this gun was a single-barrel gun, however it was chambered for 12, 16, and 20 gauge shotshells. It, too, was intended for sale outside the United States, and, reportedly, 74,300 shotguns were made in Brazil between 1971 and 1975. The Model 812 shotgun was never listed in any Remington catalog.

Remington 3200 Over & Under Shotgun

In January 1973, Remington reintroduced an over & under shotgun, the first since the Model 32 was discontinued in 1941. The new shotgun had these features: 12 gauge for 2-inch chambers; barrel selector; wide single trigger; automatic ejectors; ventilated rib barrels; ivory bead front sight and metal rear on trap and skeet grade guns; black-finish on exposed metal parts; simple roll-stamped figure of a Pointer on right side of receiver; and 20-line checkered American walnut stock and beavertail-style fore-end, with DuPont RK-W finish. Remington advertised the advantages of "separated barrels" whereby the heat of one did not adversely affect the aim of the other. Five major variations of the 3200 were available:

- **Remington 3200 Field Guns** have 26-inch, 28-inch, and 30-inch ventilated rib barrel lengths and various chokes.
- **Remington 3200 Skeet Guns**
- **Remington 3200 Trap Guns** have 30-inch ventilated rib barrels in Full-Full, or Imp. Mod-Full chokes, and standard or Monte Carlo–style stocks with rubber recoil pads. In 1975, 32-inch barrels were offered.
- **Remington 3200 "Special Trap" Guns** also have 30-inch ventilated rib barrels, come with a select grade of standard-style or Monte Carlo–style stocks with rubber recoil pads.
- **Remington 3200 "One Of 1,000" Trap Guns** were intended to be sold only in 1973, to commemorate Remington's re-entry into the over & under shotgun field. Only 1,000 of these elaborately engraved guns were made. They have a gold grip inlay cap, 30-inch ventilated rib barrels, and come with select standard or Monte Carlo–style stocks, complete with luggage-type carrying case.
- **Remington 3200 "One Of 1,000" Skeet Guns** were first offered in 1974, to commemorate Remington's re-entry into the over & under shotgun field. They carried the same embellishments as the previous year's "One Of 1,000" Trap Guns. A total of

Above: Model 11–87 Autoloading Shotgun.

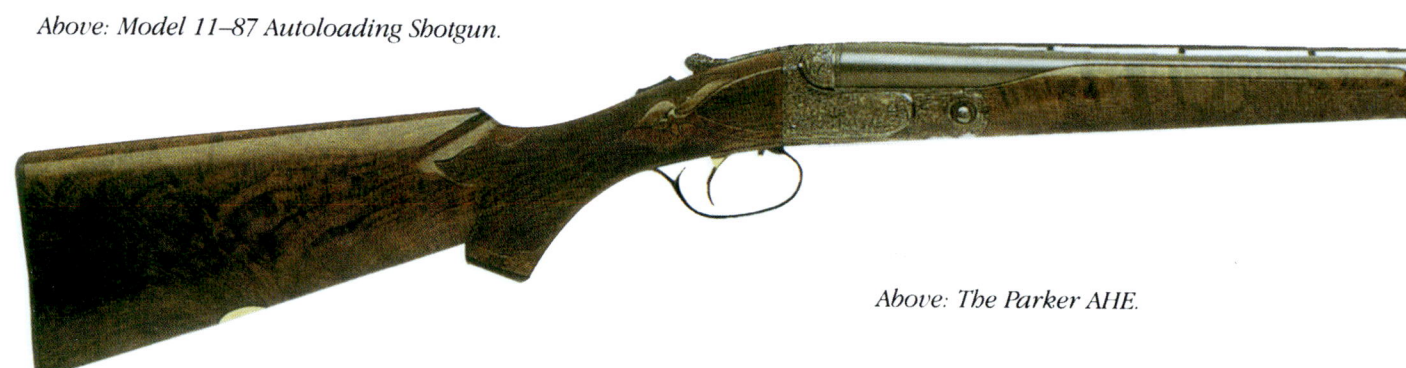

Above: The Parker AHE.

951 of these guns were sold between 1974 and 1979.
- **Remington 3200 Magnum Guns** were first introduced in January 1975, and featured 3-inch chambers for magnum shotshells and 30-inch barrels. Otherwise, they were the same as Remington 3200 Field Guns.
- **Remington 3200 "One Of 500" International Guns** were an international version of the "One of 1,000" guns manufactured for the domestic market. They were manufactured in Ilion, but sold in Europe in 1976, for approximately $1,200.00. They featured 30-inch vent rib barrels, standard or Monte Carlo–style stocks. Remington Arms GmbH in Germany had 116 of these guns engraved, and some decorated with gold inlays by Fissette in Belgium. These specialty guns sold for $1,500.00 to $2,100.00.
- **Remington 3200 Competition Trap Guns** were introduced in 1976, and featured 30-inch or 32-inch barrels, select wood with satin or high-gloss finish, standard or Monte Carlo–style stocks and rubber butt pads.
- **Remington 3200 Competition Skeet Guns** were introduced in 1976, and featured 26-inch or 28-inch skeet-bored barrels, select wood with satin or high-gloss finish and rubber butt pads.
- **Remington 3200 Matched Skeet Sets** were introduced in 1980 as a limited edition offering, and included a 12 gauge Remington 3200 Competition Skeet Gun and 20 gauge, 28 gauge and .410 additional barrels, all housed in a deluxe hard carrying case. Remington advertising referred to this set as "Four Part Harmony." A total of 636 sets were sold in 1979, '80 and '81.

Remington's Custom Gun Shop fabricated 104 Remington 3200 custom guns in 1991, 1992 and 1993, although the company had discontinued advertising all versions of the 3200 in December 1982. A total of 41,769 Remington 3200 shotguns of all types and varieties had been sold in ten years of production, and another 104 in the '90s.

Sportsman 12 Auto Shotguns

This autoloader was introduced in 1985, and featured an impressed-checkered, straight-combed stock, 28-inch or 30-inch vent rib barrel, 5-round magazine, 7lb/12oz weight, and chambered for 12 gauge 2-inch shells. In 1986, Remington added a 28-inch Rem Choke barrel. This economical shotgun was discontinued in December 1986.

Sportsman 12 Pump Shotguns

This pump-action shotgun features an impressed-checkered, straight-combed stock, 30-inch vent rib barrel, 5-round magazine, 7lbs/8oz weight, and chambered for 12 gauge 3-inch shells. In 1986, Remington added a 28-inch RemChoke barrel. Remington discontinued this gun in December 1986.

Model 11-87 Autoloading Shotguns

Remington introduced a new autoloading shotgun in 1987, the Model 11-87. This gun featured a new Pressure Compensating Gas System, which required no manual adjustment for any power shotshells, from 2-inch light load shells to 3-inch magnums. Vent rib barrels were standard on all except Deer Guns. Variations include:

- **Model 11-87 Premier Autoloading Shotguns** in

standard grade were introduced in 1987. A left-hand version was also offered.

- **Model 11-87 Premier Skeet Shotguns** were also introduced in 1987.
- **Model 11-87 Premier Trap Shotguns** were also introduced in 1987.
- **Model 11-87 Premier Trap—Monte Carlo–Stock Shotguns** were also introduced in 1987.

- **Model 11-87 SP "Special Purpose" 12 Gauge Guns** featured vent rib barrels with RemChoke system, a nonreflective Parkerized finish, hardwood stock and fore-end, recoil pad, and a detachable, padded camouflage sling. In 1989, American walnut stocks replaced the hardwood stocks. These guns were discontinued in December 1990.
- **Model 11-87 SP Special Purpose Magnum Deer Guns** featured rifle sights and 21-inch barrels. In 1995, this gun was available with checkered American walnut stock and fore-end, and rifled and RemChoke tubes.
- **Model 11-87 Cantilever Scope Mount Deer Guns** were introduced in 1989, and featured a new cantilever scope mounting system, and no rifle sights. In 1994, Remington improved the scope mount, offered fully rifled barrels, a rubber recoil pad and a nylon sling.
- **Model 11-87 175th Anniversary Edition Guns** were introduced in 1991, to commemorate the 175th year of Remington firearms. It featured screw-in RemChokes, and checkered American walnut stock and fore-end, and a roll-engraved receiver with Remington's 1816–1991 emblems.
- **Model 11-87 Premier Sporting Clays** were introduced in 1992, and featured a target-grade, cut-checkered American walnut competition stock, butt pad, matte-finished metal parts, vent rib barrel, and 2-inch barrel.
- **Model 11-87 Premier LC "Light Contour" Guns** were introduced in 1993, and featured 3-inch chambers, light contour RemChoke barrels, and a left-hand action gun.
- **Model 11-87 SPS Camo Guns** were also introduced in 1993, and featured 12 gauge, vent rib barrels. All exterior portions of this hunting gun were covered with a Mossy Oak Bottomland camouflage pattern.
- **Model 11-87 SPS-BG "Big Game" Camo Guns** were also introduced in 1993, and featured 21-inch rifle sighted barrels, and a Mossy Oak Bottomland camouflage pattern. The National Wild Turkey Federation's "Gun of the Year" was this gun with a brown Trebark finish on all exposed parts.
- **Model 11-87 SPS-T Camo Guns** were also introduced in 1993, and featured vent rib barrels, and a Mossy Oak Greenleaf camouflage pattern.
- **Model 11-87 SPS Guns** were also introduced in 1993, and featured a black matte-finish on all metal parts and on the synthetic stocks and fore-ends. These guns were 12 gauge and were available with vent rib barrels.
- **Model 11-87 SPS-Deer Guns** were also introduced in 1993, and featured a black matte-finish on all metal parts and on the synthetic stocks and fore-ends. These guns were 12 gauge and had 21-inch rifle sighted barrels. In 1994, Remington also offered this gun with a RemChoke smooth-bore barrel, rifle sights and Monte Carlo–style stock.
- **Model 11-87 SPS-T Guns** were also introduced in 1993, and featured a black matte-finish on all metal parts and on the synthetic stocks and fore-ends. These guns were 12 gauge and had vent rib barrels. In 1997, this turkey gun was available in a RealTree X-tra Brown camouflage pattern on all exposed parts.
- **Model 11-87 Sporting 28 Guns** were introduced in 1997, as a 28 gauge shotgun for sporting clays competition. It featured a checkered American walnut stock and fore-end with high-gloss finish, a sporting recoil pad, a vent rib barrel with RemChoke tubes.
- **Model 11-87 Premier SC NP Guns** (Sporting Clays Nickel Plated) were also introduced in 1997, and featured a nickel-plated receiver decorated with fine-line engraving, vent rib barrel with 2-inch chamber, satin-finished, checkered American walnut stock.
- **Model 11-87 Sporting 20 Guns** were introduced in 1998, as a 20 gauge shotgun for skeet competition. It featured a tournament grade, checkered American walnut stock and fore-end with gloss finish, a sporting recoil pad, a 28-inch vent rib barrel with RemChoke tubes.

The Parker AHE Shotgun

The legendary Parker shotgun was reintroduced by Remington in 1988, and like the original guns, were hand-crafted to exacting specifications. The **Parker AHE** Grade 20 gauge side-by-side was fabricated in The Parker Gun Works Division, a department within Remington's Custom Gun Shop. This gun featured 28-inch, rust-blued, vent rib barrels, ivory bead front and mid-sights, a rubber recoil pad or skeleton steel butt plate, and a completely new single selective trigger, which offered exceptionally fast lock time. The case-hardened receiver and most metal parts are exquisitely scroll engraved. Remington last advertised this Parker shotgun in the 1991 catalog.

SP-10 Magnum Shotguns

In 1989, Remington introduced the **SP-10 "Special Purpose" Magnum Shotgun**, touting it as "the only gas-operated, semi-automatic 10 gauge made today." And "it's one shotgun that's totally crafted to give waterfowlers a better shot at bagging their limit." This gun was engineered to shoot steel shot, and it came with 26-inch or 30-inch RemChoke vent rib barrels. It featured a low-luster, checkered American walnut stock and fore-end, and matte-finished metal parts. The 26-inch barrel gun weighed 10lbs/12oz, and the 30-inch barrel gun weighed 11 pounds.

In 1991, the **SP-10 "Turkey Combo" Shotgun** was introduced. It featured 26-inch or 30-inch RemChoke vent rib barrel, plus an extra 22-inch rifle sighted barrel for turkey hunting. It retailed for $1,363.00. In 1993, Remington introduced the **SP-10 Magnum Camo Shotgun**, which featured a Mossy Oak Bottomland camouflage pattern to exposed parts, and 23-inch RemChoke vent rib barrel. In 1998, Remington introduced the **SP-10 Turkey Camo NWTF Shotgun**, a National Wild Turkey Federation gun which featured a Mossy Oak Bottomland camouflage pattern to exposed parts, and the new TRUGLO light-gathering fiber-optic sights, and a 23-inch RemChoke vent rib barrel. The left face of the receiver had the NWTF 25th Anniversary logo.

Model 90-T Single Barrel Trap Gun

In 1991, Remington introduced a radically different 12 gauge trap shotgun, the **Model 90-T**. It was a hammerless, break-open gun with internal full-width horizontal bolt lockup, and had removable side plates and a drop-out trigger mechanism. This gun had a distinctive full choke, vent rib barrel in 32-inch and 34-inch lengths. Receiver, barrel and other metal parts have a deep black finish. The wood is finely finished, figured, deep-cut checkered American walnut, with a high cheek piece Monte Carlo–stock with rubber butt plate and beavertail fore-end. This 8lbs/12oz trap gun was fabricated for Remington by the Competition Arms Company.

In 1994, introduced an adjustable high-rib version of this gun "for shooters who prefer a more open target picture and higher head position." **The Model 90-T HPAR High-Post Adjustable Rib** also had an adjustable comb stock. Both versions of this trap gun were discontinued in December 1997.

Remington Peerless

In 1993, Remington introduced a new 12 gauge over & under sporting shotgun for the field, the Remington Peerless. The gun featured a pair of light contour 26-inch, 28-inch or 30-inch barrels which were joined at the muzzle, vent rib with target-grade front sight and stainless mid-bead, RemChokes, and a single selective trigger. The gun featured a 3-inch chamber. The cut-checkered American walnut stock and fore-end are Imron finished in a high gloss. A vented recoil pad is added to the stock. A gold-plated trigger contrasts to the deep black finish on all other metal parts.

Model 396 Sporting Over & Under Shotgun

In 1996, Remington introduced a new over & under shotgun which was designed for sporting clays competition, the **Model 396 Sporting Over & Under Shotgun**. This gun featured blued 28-inch or 30-inch RemChoke barrels which were factory ported and topped with a non-stepped vent rib. The receiver, side plates, trigger guard, top lever and fore-end trim are a contrasting gray nitride coloring. The trigger is a gold-tone color. The pistol-grip stock and wide fore-end are satin-finished, figured and checkered American walnut. A rubber butt pad is fitted to the stock. The receiver is fine-line engraved. Concurrently, Remington introduced the **Model 396 Skeet**, similar to the Sporting, without porting on the barrels. There are engraved renderings of a pointer and a setter on the receiver panels.

Model 11-96 Euro Lightweight Shotguns

In 1997, *Shooting Industry Magazine's* Academy of Excellence awarded its "Shotgun Of The Year Award" to Remington's newest autoloader, the **Model 11-96 Euro Lightweight**, stating that "its lightning-fast pointability and great balance make it the wingshooter's choice!" Features of this 12 gauge autoloader include a 26-inch or 28-inch light-contour vent rib barrel with RemChokes, a Claro walnut stock and fore-end with cut-checkering, and fine-line engraving on the receiver. This gun utilizes a lightened Model 11-87 receiver, and the 26-inch shotgun weighed 6lbs/14oz, and the 28-inch version weighed an even 7 pounds.

Remington Bullet Knives

Remington waited for the cessation of hostilities in Europe in 1918 to launch their Cutlery Works, Inc. The company recruited skilled staff from the factories of war torn Europe, Solingen in Germany and Sheffield in England.

The new division was formed in 1919 and the first product catalog was issued in 1920, crammed with pocket knives for a ready audience. It featured Boy Scout Knives, small penknives, manicure knives, ballet knives (so named as they resembled the shape of a dancer's leg), physician's knives and pruning knives.

The most successful product turned out to be the Bullet Knife. This was named after the cartridge shaped shield on the handle—based on the famous Model 1903 cartridge with a roundnose bullet.

At least 26 variations were released between 1920 and 1941 when World War II ended the run. In 1982 the company relaunched the series to promote two new rifles—Models Four and Six.

The first reproduction was that of Bullet Knife R1123 Trapper and it followed the original in every respect except for the blade which was improved by use of stainless-steel (No.440) and a DuPont Delrin handle. Sales were encouraging and the company decided to issue a new example every year going forward. The replicas have established a collectors following in their own right and the original price of $39.95 in 1982 has increased tenfold for examples in good condition.

Above: Bullet Knives ranging from 1990 to 1996.

Above: Knife number 1123 a reissue for 1982.

Above: Knives are more valuable in their original cases.

Index

African Plains rifles 92
air rifles 70
Alaskan Wilderness rifles 92
Albany 8
Alger, Charles C. 47
American Boy Scouts 62
American Deer
  Foundation 97
Ames, N.P. & Co. 43, 49
ammunition 15
Apache autoloading rifles 88
Argentina 52–3
Army Ordnance
  Department 27, 28, 29
Army revolvers 26–9
Austria 50
autoloading pistols 38–40
autoloading rifles 64, 65, 70, 73–4, 78, 83, 85–7, 88–9, 96–7
autoloading shotguns 104, 107–8, 114–20, 121, 122–3
"Automaster" autoloading shotguns 115–16

Baldwin Locomotive Works 66
Ballard & Marlin 63
Barnes, Charles H. 65
bayonets 45
Beals, Fordyce 22–3, 26–7, 28, 43, 48
Belgium 51, 122
Berthier military rifles 66
"Bicentennial" rifles 82, 87, 89
Billings Hardware Company 94
Birmingham 22
Birmingham Small Arms 67
Bishop, J. Leander 10
black powder rifles 92–3
Bolivia 54
bolt-action rifles 69–73, 74, 75–9, 80–2, 83–5, 86, 87–8, 89–96, 97–8
box-magazine rifles 78, 79
Boy Scouts 62, 125

Brazil 54
Bridgeport, Connecticut 18, 68, 69
Britain 66, 80, 125
Browning, John M. 15, 64, 68, 70, 104, 105
Browning machine guns 18, 68
Buckmasters American Deer Foundation rifle 97
Buffalo 8
Bullet Knife 125

cadet rifles 62
Campbell, Charlie 86
Canada 89
cane guns 44–5
carbines 11, 82, 88–9
  Light Baby carbines 61
  Magnum carbines 94, 95
  Mohawk carbines 95
  Navy carbines 43
  Remington-Keene carbines 56
  split-breech carbines 46–8
Carl Gustafs Stads Gevarsfaktori 50
cartridge revolvers 32–3
cartridges, smokeless powder 62
"cast steel" barrels 42
Central America 54
Chicago World's Fair (1893) 15
Chile 52, 54
China 60
"chipless" metal-working techniques 18–20
Cincinnati 42
Civil War 12–13, 27–9, 46, 48, 100
Classic rifles 91–2
Collins & Co. 45
Colt's Patent Fire Arms Company 18, 20, 25, 29, 38–9, 68
Columbia 54
Commemorative Flintlock rifle 99

Companhia Brasileira de Cartuchos SA (C.B.C.) 121
Cooper & Pond 27
Coxford, Wilhelm. F. 54–5
Creedmoor 99
Crozier, General William 68
crucible steel 42
Cuba 51–2, 60
Custer, General George Armstrong 99
Custom Grade rifles 91
Custom Gun Shop 40, 41, 59, 63, 84, 85, 86, 91, 93, 97, 99, 122
"Custom" sporting rifles 96
Cutlery Works, Inc. 125

Deeley & Edge 101
Denmark 50
derringers 30–2
Dildine, Andrew J. 23
Dominican Republic 54
double-action pocket revolvers 23–4
double-barrel shotguns 103–4, 107
double derringers 30–2
duck guns 101
Ducks Unlimited 117–18, 119–20
DuPont 40, 79, 86
Dyer 49

Ecuador 54
Eddystone, Pennsylvania 18, 66, 67
Egypt 35, 50–1, 52, 93
El Salvador 54
Elizabethtown, Kentucky 21
Elliot, Dr. William H. 15, 25–6, 27–8, 29, 30–2
Enfield rifles 16–18, 49, 66, 69
Erie Canal 8
Euro Lightweight shotguns 124

falling block rifles 63
farm implements 13
Fieldmaster rifles 74–5, 82–3, 85
Fissette 122
flintlock rifles 99
Fort Benning, Georgia 83
France 49, 51, 52, 65–6
Franco-Prussian War (1870–71) 49, 51, 52
Francotte 51
Frankford Arsenal 43–4
Franz Joseph, Emperor of Austria 50
Frazier, J.R. 54–5

gallery guns 74, 78, 85, 86
Gamemaster rifles 73, 82
Geiger, Leonard 46–7
General Motors 20
Germany 52, 65, 122, 125
Goodsal, Major P.T. 67
Greece 52
Griffiths, John 42
Guatemala 54

Hagner, Major 43
Hall, John 12
hammerless double-barrel shotguns 103–4
Harper's Ferry 12, 45–6
Hartford, Connecticut 29
Hartley, Marcellus 15
Hartley & Graham 31, 37
Hartley Dodge, M. 63, 66
Hepburn, Lewis L. 57, 101
Hepburn rifles 57–9, 63–4
Honduras 54, 72
Howland, Rufus 26
hunting 112–13
Husqvarna Vapenfabriks 50

IBM 20
Ilion, New York 10, 12, 18, 28, 47, 50, 51, 67
"inside contracting" system 10, 21
International Free Rifle 83–4

Index

International Shooting Union 85
Iroquois revolvers 35
Ismail, Khedive of Egypt 50, 51

Japan 52
Jenks, William 42–3
Jenks carbines 11
Jerry's Sports Center 89
Jones, T.J. 13
"Junior Special" target rifles 81

Kanzler, General Ermanno 51
Keene, John W. 56–7
Keeney, Mike 99
Kerensky, Alexander 66
Kittredge, B. & Company 33
knives 125
Kodak 20
Kodiak rifles 86

Lamberson, D.H. & Co. 56
large-frame revolvers 26–30
Lebel "rolling block" rifles 18
Lee, James P. 15, 59
Lee Arms Company 59–61
Leek, Wayne 86, 94
lever-action rifles 87
Light Baby carbines 61
lightweight rifles 85
Lincoln, Abraham 26
Loomis, Crawford C. 15, 65
Luxembourg 51

machine guns 68
magazine pistols 34
magazine rifles 66
Magnum carbines 94, 95
Magnum shotguns 124
Marine Corps sniper rifles 93
Martin, John D. 23
Matchmaster rifles 77, 81

Maurice Sporting Goods 89
Maynard, Dr. Edward 42, 43
Maynard tape-priming locks 43–4
medals 15
metal injection molding 20
Mexican War (1846–48) 11
Mexico 35, 53–4, 62
Michigan National Guard 60
Mississippi rifles 42–3, 45
Mohawk '48 autoloading shotguns 121
Mohawk carbines 95
Mohawk River Valley 8
Monaco 51
Montana 94
Montgomery Ward 120
Mosin-Nagant rifles 18, 66
Mountain rifles 92
muskets 43–4, 46, 49, 100
muzzleloading rifles 92–3
muzzleloading shotguns 100

Nagant, Emile and Leon 51
National Match Course 84, 85
National Rifle Association 58, 99
National Wild Turkey Federation 124
Navy Bureau of Ordnance 37, 48–9
Navy carbines 43
Navy revolvers 26–9
Netherlands 51
New Model revolvers 29–30, 34, 37–8
New York City 8
New York State 45, 49–50
Nicaragua 54, 73
Nicholas II, Czar 66
Norris, Samuel 47, 48, 52
North's 42
Norway 50
Nylon rifles 86–8

Ordnance Trial Board 42
outside hammer shotguns 100–3
over & under shotguns 107, 121–2, 124
Oviedo Arsenal 52
Ozagon, General Pedro 53

Palmer & Batchelders 27
Panama 54
Papal States 51
Paraguay 54
Paris Exposition (1867) 15, 50
Parker AHE shotgun 123
Parker Gun Works 107, 123
parlor pistols 24
patents 15
Pedersen, John D. 15, 39, 64, 65, 68–9, 104, 105
Pedersen Devices 18, 68–9
Penney, J.C. 89
percussion revolvers 22, 32–3
Peru 52, 54
pistols see individual types of pistol
"Plinker" pistols 37
pocket knives 125
pocket revolvers 22–4, 25, 30
police rifles 93
Position rifles 96
Poultney & Trimble 49
powder metallurgy 19–20
Puerto Rico 52, 54
pump-action rifles 97, 98
pump-action shotguns 104–6, 122

R & D technology center 21
Ramsay, Brigadier-General George D. 47
Rangemaster rifles 83–5
Rem-UMC 31, 39, 66, 67, 68
Remington, Eliphalet, Sr. 8–12, 22, 26, 42, 44, 45

Remington, Eliphalet III 27, 54
Remington, Philo 26–7, 54
Remington, Samuel 26–7, 28, 42, 54
Remington Agricultural Works 13
Remington Peerless 124
Remington-Rand 13
repeating air rifles 70
repeating rifles 64, 71, 74, 78, 79
revolvers see individual types of revolver
revolving breech rifles 48
Rider, Dildine, Martin & Company 23, 24
Rider, Joseph 15, 23–5, 34, 35–6, 46–7, 48, 51
rifles see individual types of rifle
rimfire rifles 95, 98
Ring-Trigger pistols 25–6
Ripley, Colonel James W. 26
Ritter y Bock 52
Robbins & Lawrence 42
Rock Island Arsenal 80
rolling block pistols 35–6, 38
rolling block rifles and carbines 48–55, 61–3, 65, 99
Rome 51
Routledge 74, 76
Russia 66

Safari Grade rifles 91
Savage, Arthur 15
Savage Revolving Fire Arms Company 12, 47, 48
Schuetzen target rifles 63–4
Schuyler, Hartley & Graham 15, 27, 52, 54, 55
Scoremaster rifles 76–7, 94
Sendero rifles 93
sewing machines 13

Sharps Rifle Company 59
Sheffield 125
Sholes, Christopher Latham 13
Shooting Industry Magazine 124
shotguns see individual types of shotgun
signal guns 39
Singer Sewing Machine Company 13
single-barrel shotguns 100, 103, 104
single-shot derringer 32
single-shot rifles 48, 78
Skeetrap rifles 76
slide-action rifles 65, 70, 74–5, 82
Smith & Wesson 20, 32–3, 38
smokeless powder cartridges 62
Smoot, William S. 15, 33–4
Snap-on-Tool 20
sniper rifles 80, 93
Solingen 125
South America 54
South Carolina National Guard 49
Spain 51–2

Speedmaster rifles 73–4, 85–6
Sperry-Rand 13
Spiros-Milios 52
split-breech carbines 46–8
sporting rifles 55–6, 57, 60, 61, 63, 96
Sportmaster rifles 74, 77
Sportsman rifles 92, 98
Sportsman shotguns 106, 114–15
Springfield Armory 49, 69, 80
Springfield rifles 18, 46, 67, 69, 80
Starr's Armory 54–5
Steel Materials Corporation 75, 76
Stevens (J.C.) Arms & Tool Company 62
Sweden 50

Talcott, George 42
target pistols 38, 40
target rifles 55, 63–4, 71–2, 77, 81, 83–4, 95–6, 98
Targetmaster rifles 75, 94
Thomas, John F. 44
Trailrider rifles 87
trap shotguns 124

tubular magazine rifles 77, 79
Tyler Davidson & Co. 27
typewriters 13

Union Metallic Cartridge Company 15
Unisys 13
Uruguay 51
U.S. Army Advanced Marksmanship Unit (AAMU) 83
U.S. Cavalry 35
U.S. Centennial Exposition (1876) 15
U.S. Marine Corps 93
U.S. Ordnance Commission 27, 28, 80
U.S. Rifle Works 12
Utica, New York State 8, 10, 12, 28, 29, 47
Utica Screw Manufacturing Company 28

vest pocket pistols 24–5
vest pocket, split-breech pistols 30
Viper 98–9

Walker, Louis N. 63

Walker, Merle "Mike" 15, 89
Washington Arsenal 42
"Western Field" shotguns 120
Westinghouse 68
Westley Richards 51
White, Rollin 32–3
Whitmore, Andrew E. 100–1
Whitney's 42
Whitneyville Armory 22
Winchester 71, 78, 86
Winchester, Ridabeck & Company 62
Wingmaster shotguns 108–14
Woodsmaster rifles 73, 83, 88–9
World War I 15, 16, 39, 65–6, 68–9
World War II 15, 18, 73, 79–80, 107, 125

Xerox 20

"Zig-Zag" pocket revolvers 25–6
"Zouave" rifles 45–6

Acknowledgements and Picture Credits

The author and the publishers gratefully acknowledge the invaluable assistance given by various management and support personnel and numerous individual collectors:
Remington Arms Company, Inc. Jay Bunting. Art Wheaton (retired). Paul Cahan. Al Russo. Fred Supry. Dennis Sanita (retired). Tim McCormack. Tom Goldin. Jennifer Bullins. Norma O'Steen. Jim Hennings (deceased). Sam Alvis (deceased). Rock Island Auction Company. Remington Society of America. Leon Wier, Jr.. Bob Creamer. Jay Huber. Edward Hull. Gene Myszkowski. John Gyde. Herkimer County Historical Society, New York. Sue Perkins, Executive Director, Ilion Free Public Library, Ilion, New York. Smithsonian Institution, Washington, D.C. Custer Battlefield National Monument, Montana. Gordon Fosburg, Lake, Michigan. Ron Willoughby, Jay Huber, Ft. Lauderdale, Florida. Tom Rowe, Rochester, New York. Vance Haynes, Tucson, Arizona.

The publisher gratefully acknowledges the invaluable assistance by various organizations and individual collectors with photographs appearing in this book:
Rock Island Auction Company, Moline, Illinois. Remington Arms Company, Inc., Madison, North Carolina. Gordon Fosburg, Lake, Michigan. Ron Willoughby. Jay Huber, Ft. Lauderdale, Florida. Tom Rowe, Rochester, New York. Vance Haynes, Tucson, Arizona. Gene Myszkowski, Stuyvestant Falls, New York. Roy Marcot, Tucson, Arizona. Herkimer County Historical Society, New York. Ilion Free Public Library, Ilion, New York. Smithsonian Institution, Washington, D.C. Custer Battlefield National Monument, Montana.